HELLBOY™
IN HELL

THE DEATH CARD

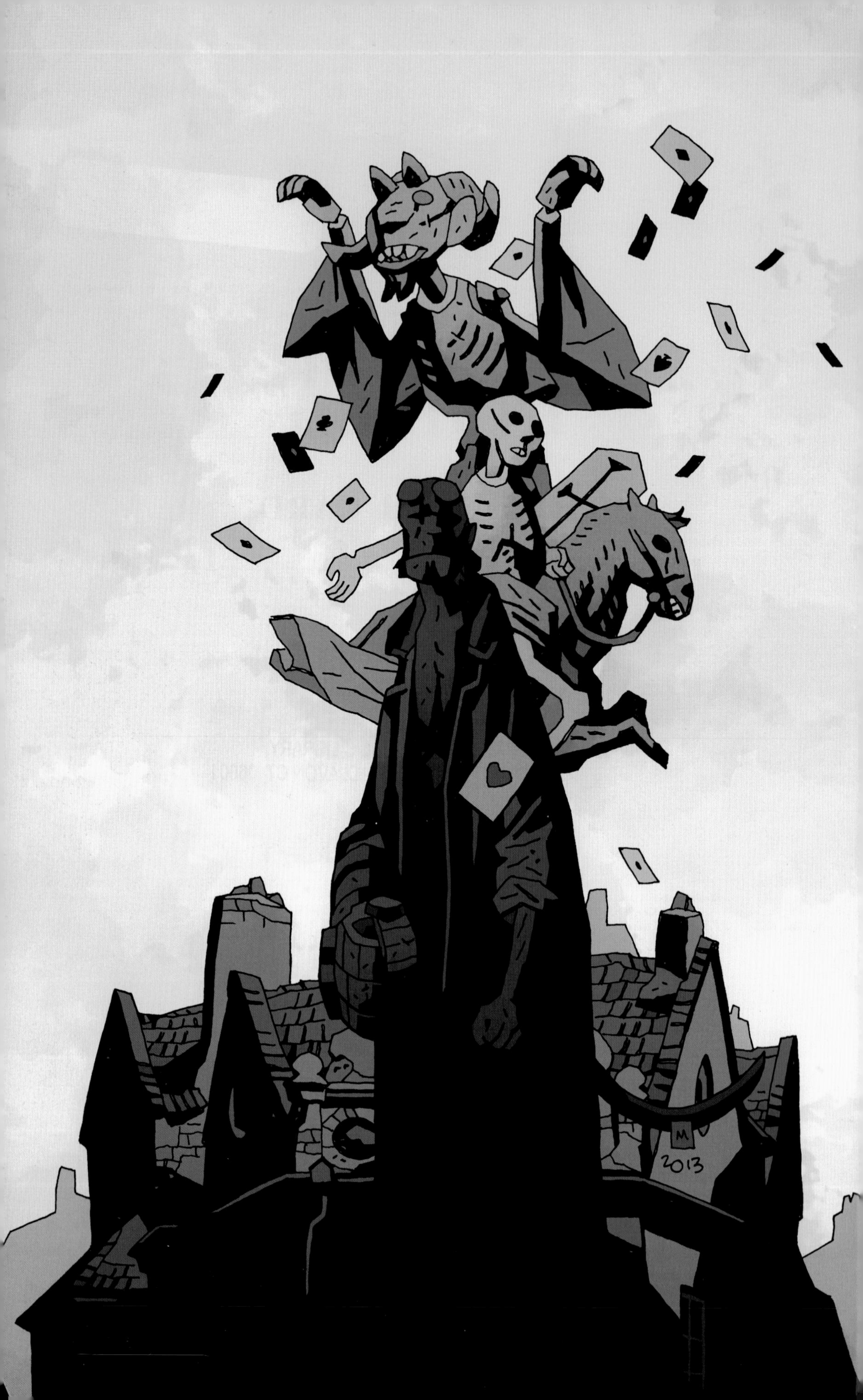
M
2013

HELLBOY™ IN HELL

THE DEATH CARD

Story and art by
MIKE MIGNOLA

Colored by
DAVE STEWART

Lettered by
CLEM ROBINS

✠

Cover art by
MIKE MIGNOLA & DAVE STEWART

Publisher
MIKE RICHARDSON

Editor
SCOTT ALLIE

Associate Editor
SHANTEL LaROCQUE

Assistant Editor
KATII O'BRIEN

Collection designed by
MIKE MIGNOLA & CARY GRAZZINI

Digital Art Technician
CHRISTINA McKENZIE

DARK HORSE BOOKS

Published by Dark Horse Books
A division of Dark Horse Comics, Inc.
10956 SE Main Street
Milwaukie, OR 97222

DarkHorse.com
Facebook.com/DarkHorseComics
Twitter.com/DarkHorseComics

Advertising Sales: (503) 905-2237
International Licensing: 503-905-2377

To find a comics shop in your area, call the
Comic Shop Locator Service toll-free at (888) 266-4226.

First edition: October 2016
ISBN 978-1-50670-113-4

HELLBOY IN HELL VOLUME 2: THE DEATH CARD

This volume collects *Hellboy in Hell* #6–#10 and "Hellboy: The Exorcist of Vorsk" from *Dark Horse Presents* Volume 3 #16, all originally published by Dark Horse Comics.

Library of Congress Cataloging-in-Publication Data

Names: Mignola, Michael, author, illustrator. | Stewart, Dave, illustrator. | Robins, Clem, 1955- illustrator.
Title: Hellboy in hell. Volume 2, Death card / story and art by Mike Mignola; colored by Dave Stewart ; lettered by Clem Robins ; cover art by Mike Mignola & Dave Stewart.
Other titles: Death card
Description: First edition. | Milwaukie, OR : Dark Horse Books, 2016. | "This volume collects Hellboy in Hell #6-#10 and Hellboy: The Exorcist of Vorsk from Dark Horse Presents Volume 3 #16, all originally published by Dark Horse Comics."
Identifiers: LCCN 2016015900 | ISBN 9781506701134 (paperback)
Subjects: LCSH: Comic books, strips, etc. | BISAC: COMICS & GRAPHIC NOVELS / Horror.
Classification: LCC PN6727.M53 H454 2016 | DDC 741.5/973--dc23
LC record available at https://lccn.loc.gov/2016015900

1 3 5 7 9 10 8 6 4 2

Printed in China

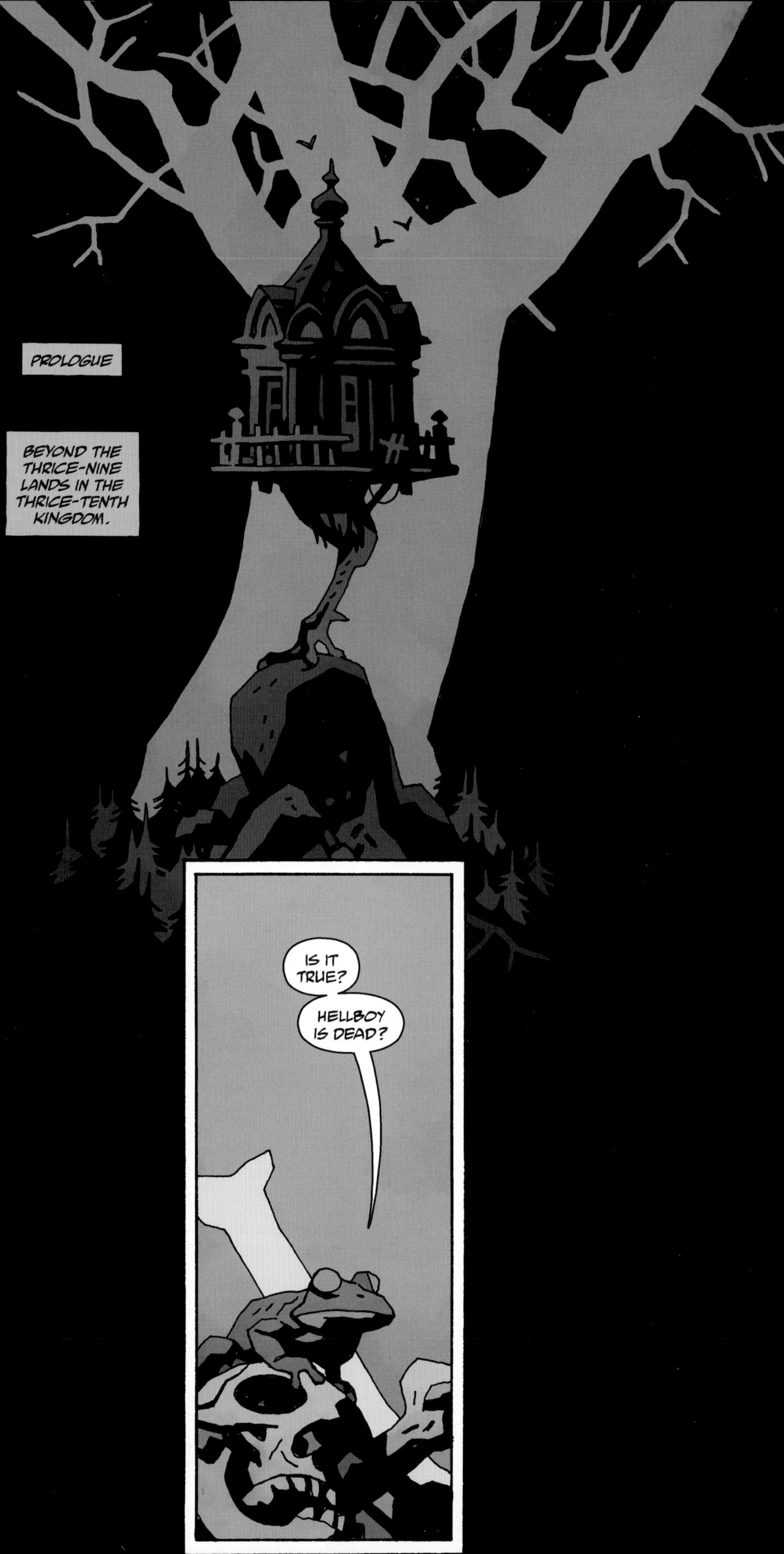
PROLOGUE
BEYOND THE THRICE-NINE LANDS IN THE THRICE-TENTH KINGDOM.
IS IT TRUE?
HELLBOY IS DEAD?

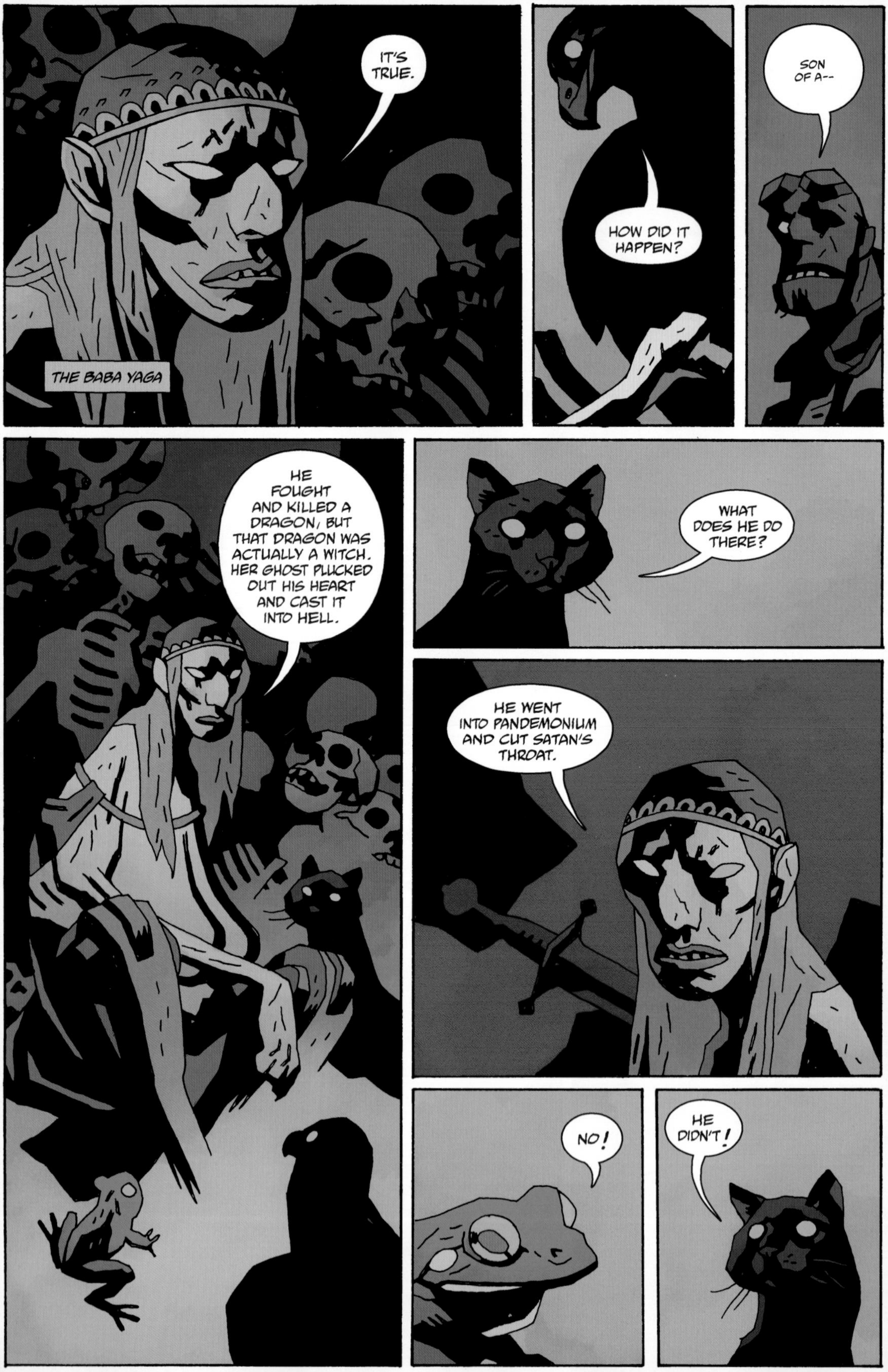
IT'S TRUE.
THE BABA YAGA
HOW DID IT HAPPEN?
SON OF A--
HE FOUGHT AND KILLED A DRAGON, BUT THAT DRAGON WAS ACTUALLY A WITCH. HER GHOST PLUCKED OUT HIS HEART AND CAST IT INTO HELL.
WHAT DOES HE DO THERE?
HE WENT INTO PANDEMONIUM AND CUT SATAN'S THROAT.
NO!
HE DIDN'T!

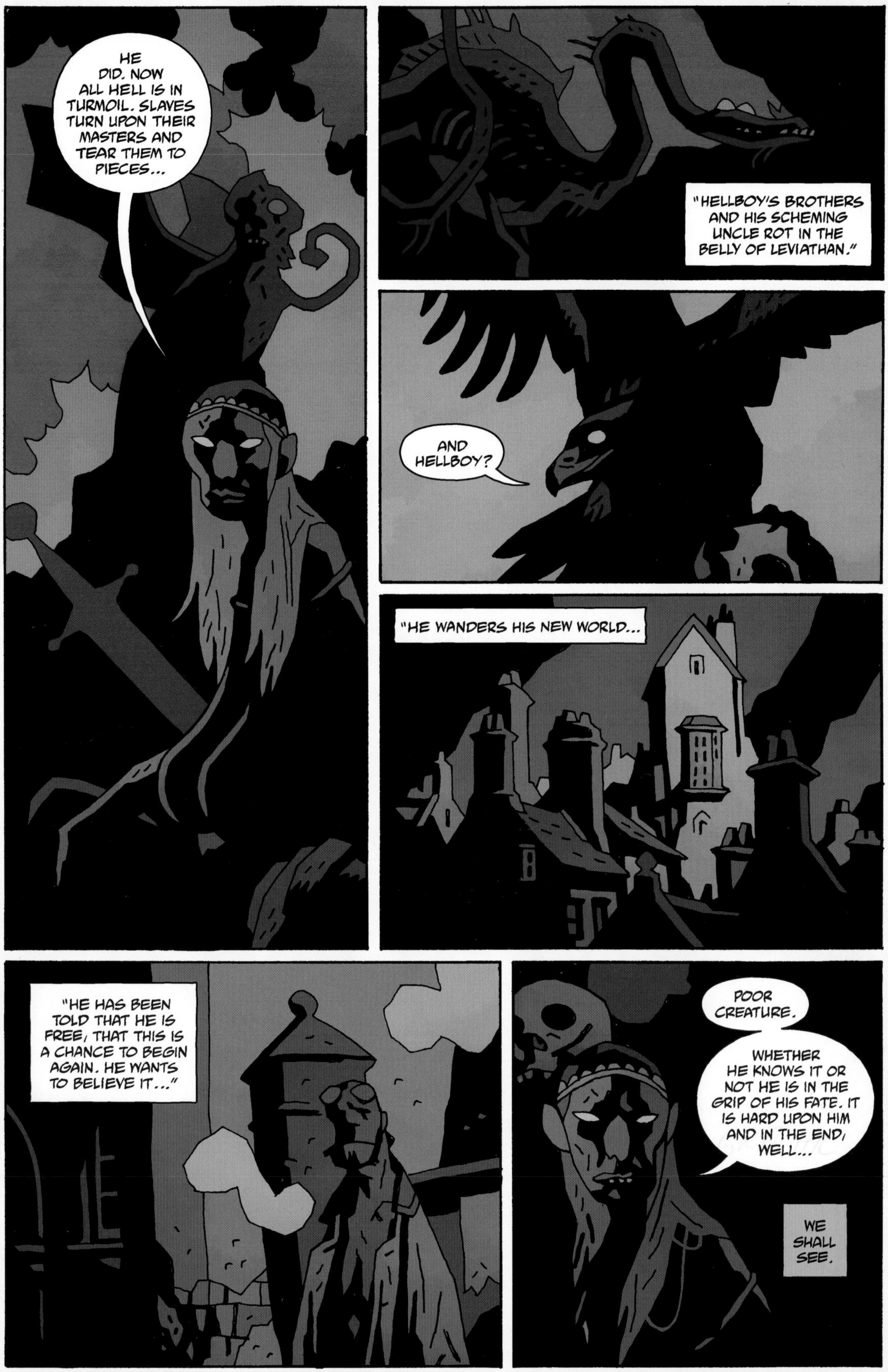
HE DID. NOW ALL HELL IS IN TURMOIL. SLAVES TURN UPON THEIR MASTERS AND TEAR THEM TO PIECES...
"HELLBOY'S BROTHERS AND HIS SCHEMING UNCLE ROT IN THE BELLY OF LEVIATHAN."
AND HELLBOY?
"HE WANDERS HIS NEW WORLD...
"HE HAS BEEN TOLD THAT HE IS FREE, THAT THIS IS A CHANCE TO BEGIN AGAIN. HE WANTS TO BELIEVE IT..."
POOR CREATURE.
WHETHER HE KNOWS IT OR NOT HE IS IN THE GRIP OF HIS FATE. IT IS HARD UPON HIM AND IN THE END, WELL...
WE SHALL SEE.

CHAPTER ONE

THE DEATH CARD

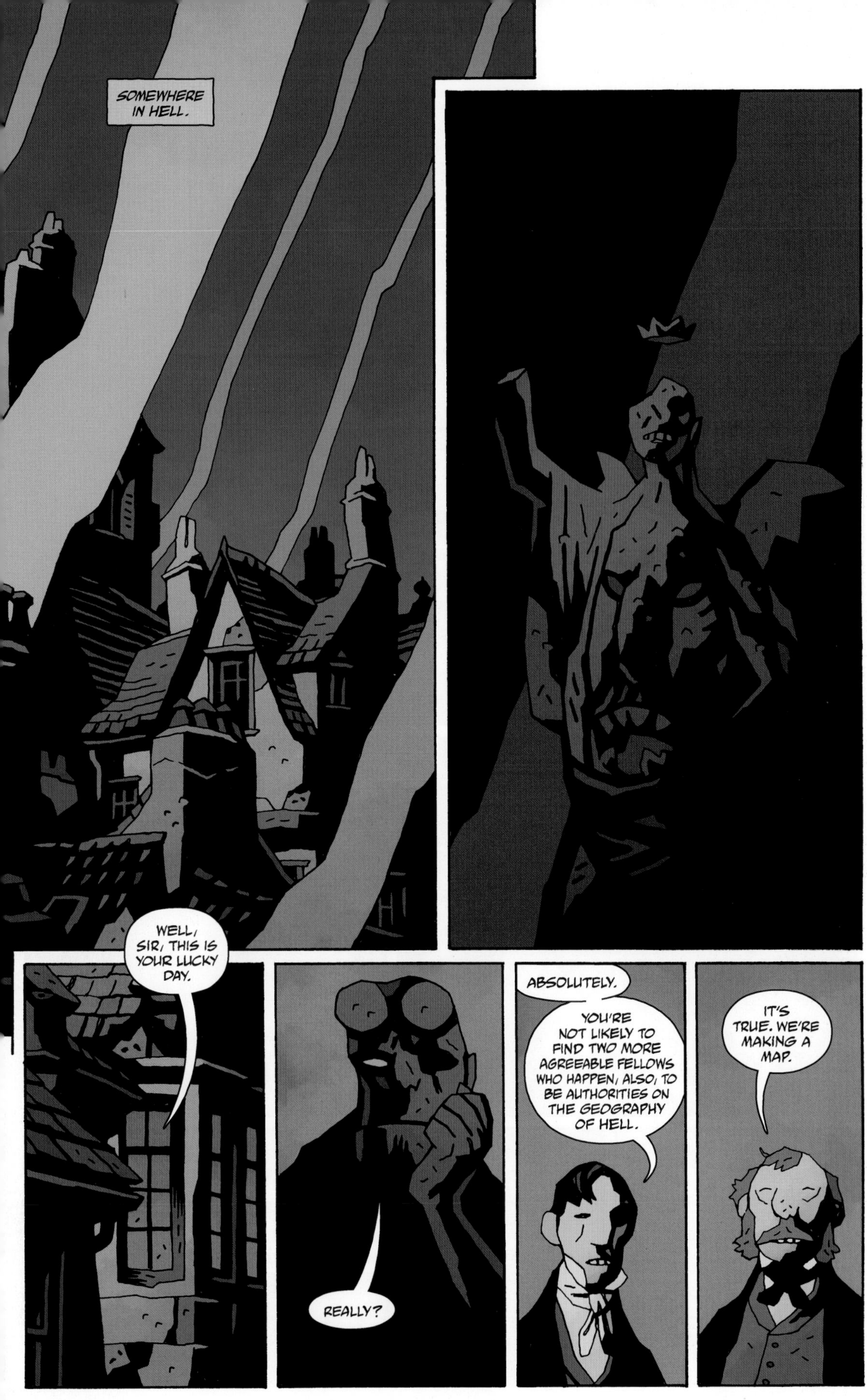
SOMEWHERE IN HELL.
WELL, SIR, THIS IS YOUR LUCKY DAY.
REALLY?
ABSOLUTELY.
YOU'RE NOT LIKELY TO FIND TWO MORE AGREEABLE FELLOWS WHO HAPPEN, ALSO, TO BE AUTHORITIES ON THE GEOGRAPHY OF HELL.
IT'S TRUE. WE'RE MAKING A MAP.

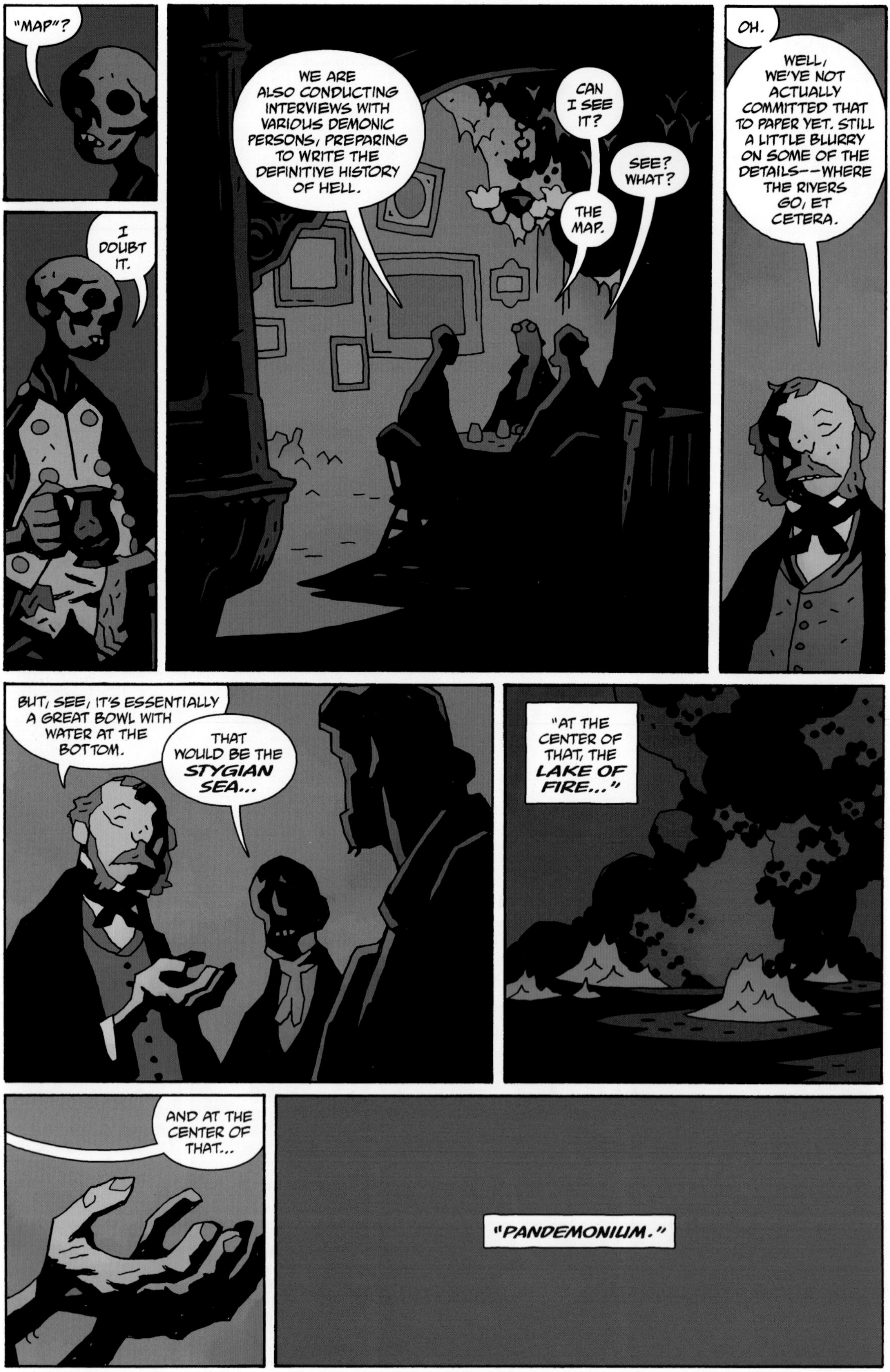
"MAP"?
I DOUBT IT.
WE ARE ALSO CONDUCTING INTERVIEWS WITH VARIOUS DEMONIC PERSONS, PREPARING TO WRITE THE DEFINITIVE HISTORY OF HELL.
CAN I SEE IT?
SEE? WHAT?
THE MAP.
OH.
WELL, WE'VE NOT ACTUALLY COMMITTED THAT TO PAPER YET. STILL A LITTLE BLURRY ON SOME OF THE DETAILS--WHERE THE RIVERS GO, ET CETERA.
BUT, SEE, IT'S ESSENTIALLY A GREAT BOWL WITH WATER AT THE BOTTOM.
THAT WOULD BE THE STYGIAN SEA...
"AT THE CENTER OF THAT, THE LAKE OF FIRE..."
AND AT THE CENTER OF THAT...
"PANDEMONIUM."

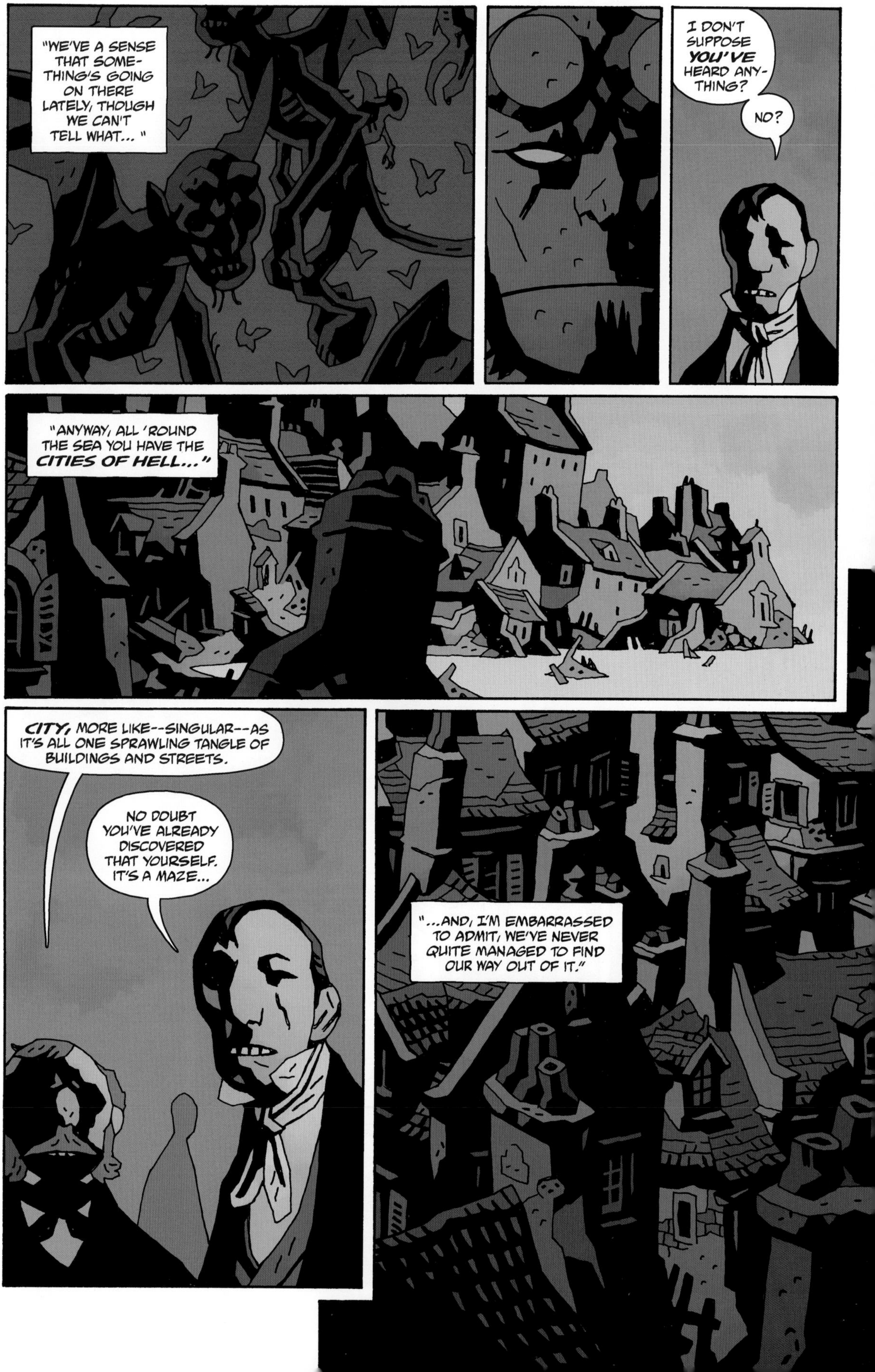
"WE'VE A SENSE THAT SOME-THING'S GOING ON THERE LATELY, THOUGH WE CAN'T TELL WHAT..."
I DON'T SUPPOSE YOU'VE HEARD ANY-THING?
NO?
"ANYWAY, ALL 'ROUND THE SEA YOU HAVE THE CITIES OF HELL..."
CITY, MORE LIKE--SINGULAR--AS IT'S ALL ONE SPRAWLING TANGLE OF BUILDINGS AND STREETS.
NO DOUBT YOU'VE ALREADY DISCOVERED THAT YOURSELF. IT'S A MAZE...
"...AND, I'M EMBARRASSED TO ADMIT, WE'VE NEVER QUITE MANAGED TO FIND OUR WAY OUT OF IT."

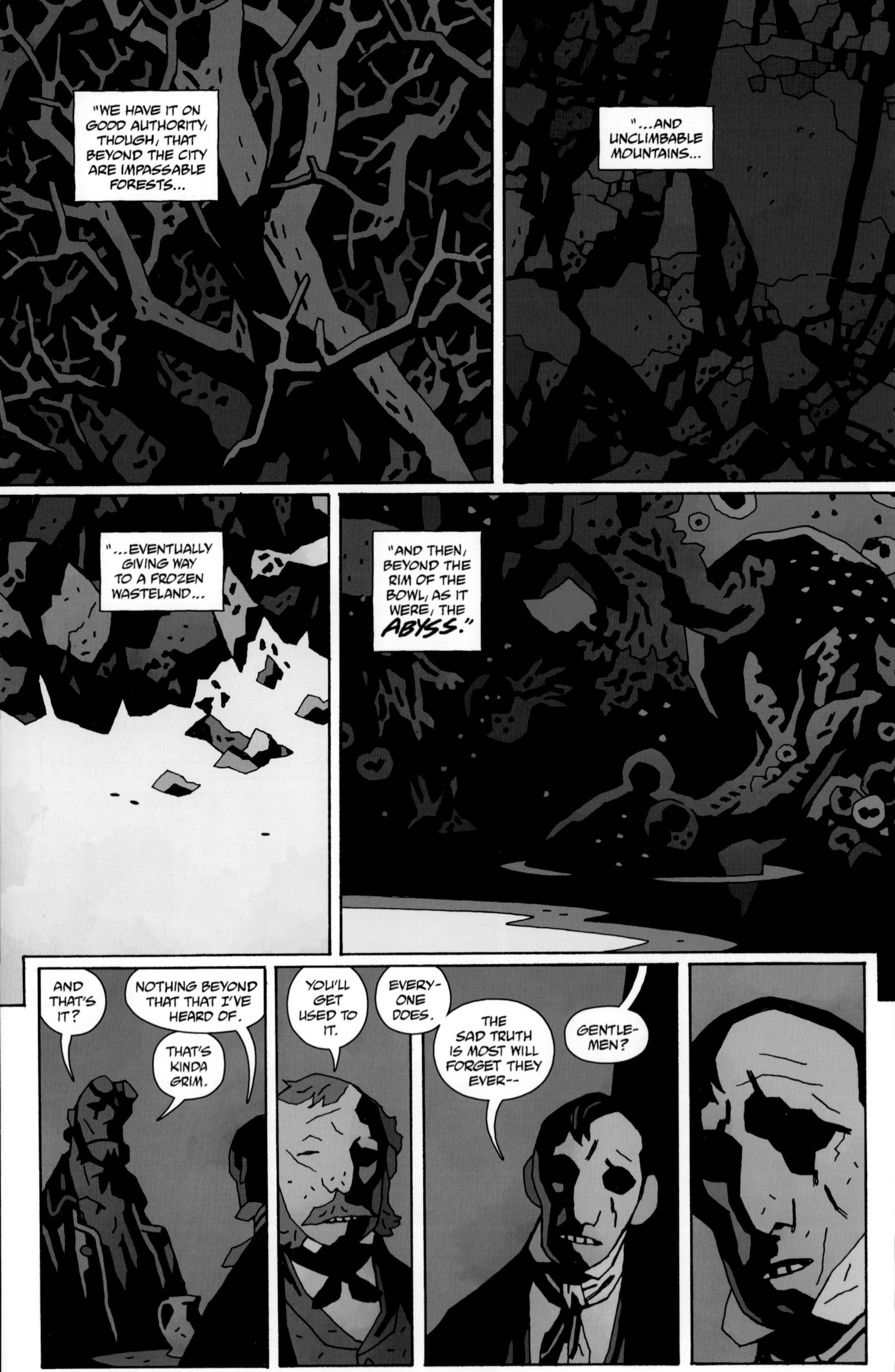

"WE HAVE IT ON GOOD AUTHORITY, THOUGH, THAT BEYOND THE CITY ARE IMPASSABLE FORESTS...
"...AND UNCLIMBABLE MOUNTAINS...
"...EVENTUALLY GIVING WAY TO A FROZEN WASTELAND...
"AND THEN, BEYOND THE RIM OF THE BOWL, AS IT WERE, THE ABYSS."
AND THAT'S IT?
NOTHING BEYOND THAT THAT I'VE HEARD OF.
THAT'S KINDA GRIM.
YOU'LL GET USED TO IT.
EVERY-ONE DOES.
THE SAD TRUTH IS MOST WILL FORGET THEY EVER--
GENTLE-MEN?

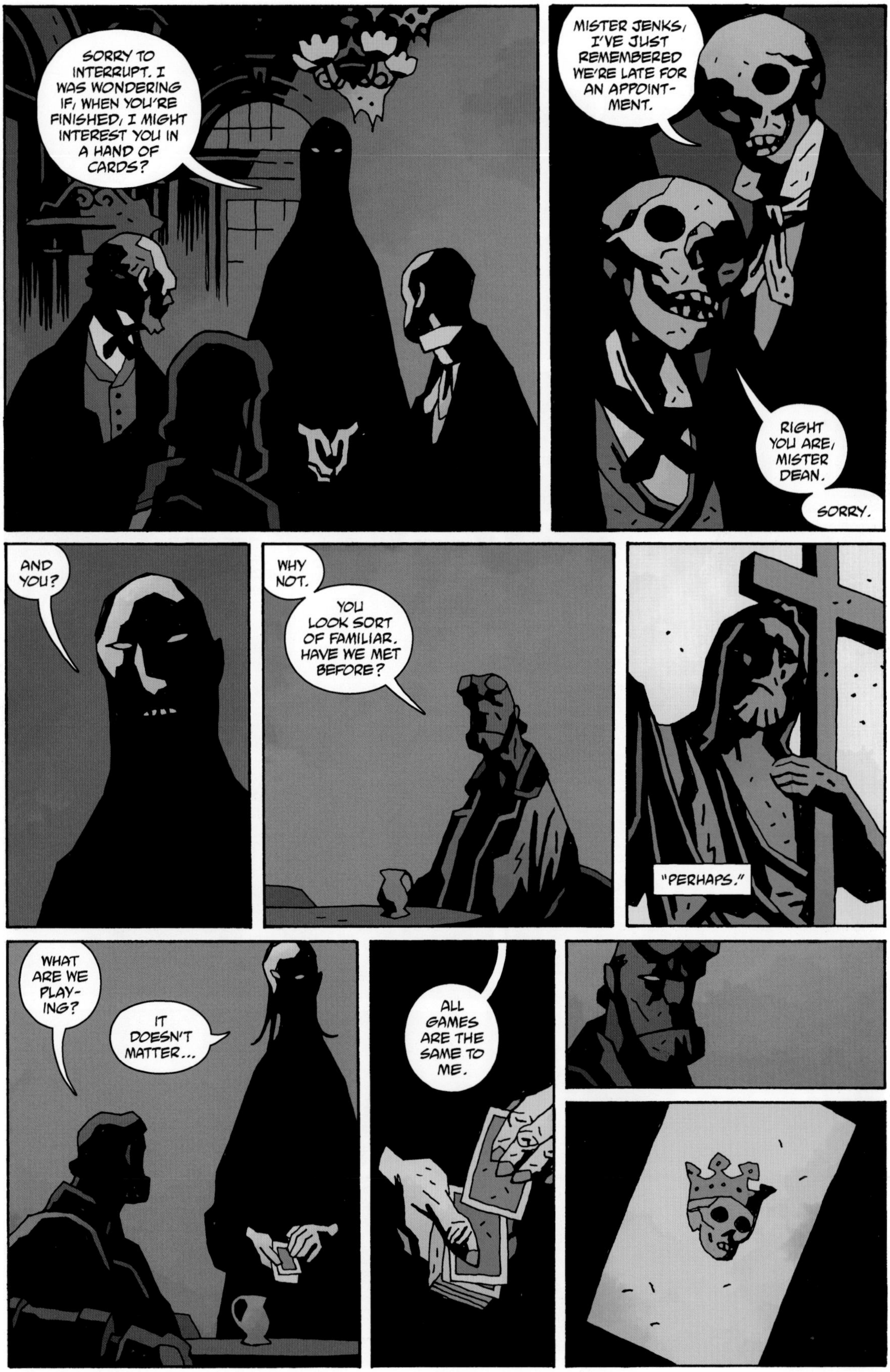
SORRY TO INTERRUPT. I WAS WONDERING IF, WHEN YOU'RE FINISHED, I MIGHT INTEREST YOU IN A HAND OF CARDS?
MISTER JENKS, I'VE JUST REMEMBERED WE'RE LATE FOR AN APPOINT-MENT.
RIGHT YOU ARE, MISTER DEAN.
SORRY.
AND YOU?
WHY NOT.
YOU LOOK SORT OF FAMILIAR. HAVE WE MET BEFORE?
"PERHAPS."
WHAT ARE WE PLAY-ING?
IT DOESN'T MATTER...
ALL GAMES ARE THE SAME TO ME.

SON OF A--

ACK!

YOU REMEMBER ME NOW?

BOOM

HELLBOY?

WHERE DID HE GO?

WHO KNOWS.

THAT OTHER ONE COMES IN HERE SOMETIMES AND THERE'S ALWAYS TROUBLE.

WHO IS HE?

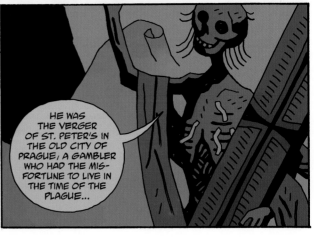

HE WAS THE VERGER OF ST. PETER'S IN THE OLD CITY OF PRAGUE, A GAMBLER WHO HAD THE MISFORTUNE TO LIVE IN THE TIME OF THE PLAGUE...

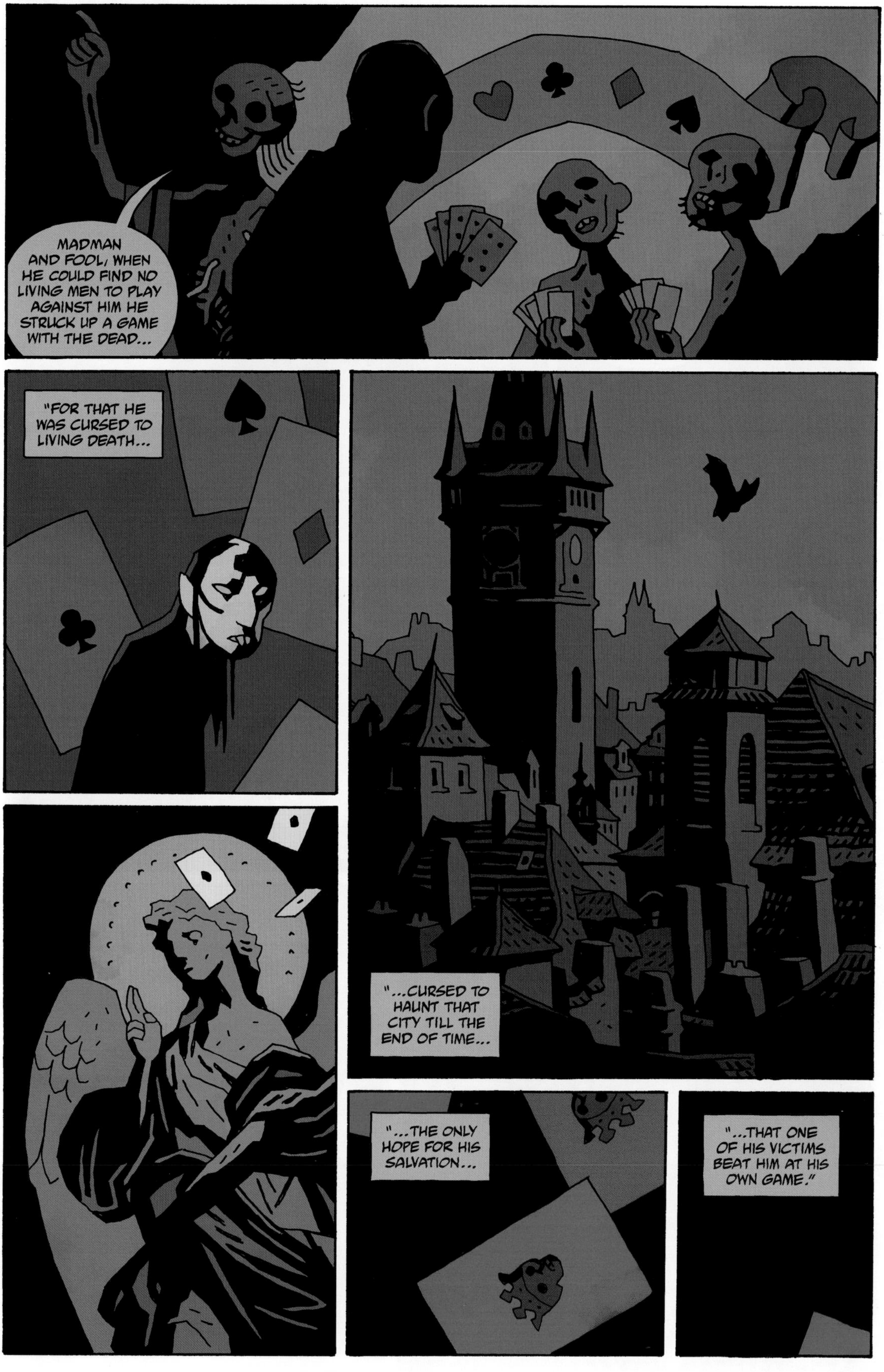
MADMAN AND FOOL, WHEN HE COULD FIND NO LIVING MEN TO PLAY AGAINST HIM HE STRUCK UP A GAME WITH THE DEAD...
"FOR THAT HE WAS CURSED TO LIVING DEATH...
"...CURSED TO HAUNT THAT CITY TILL THE END OF TIME...
"...THE ONLY HOPE FOR HIS SALVATION...
"...THAT ONE OF HIS VICTIMS BEAT HIM AT HIS OWN GAME."

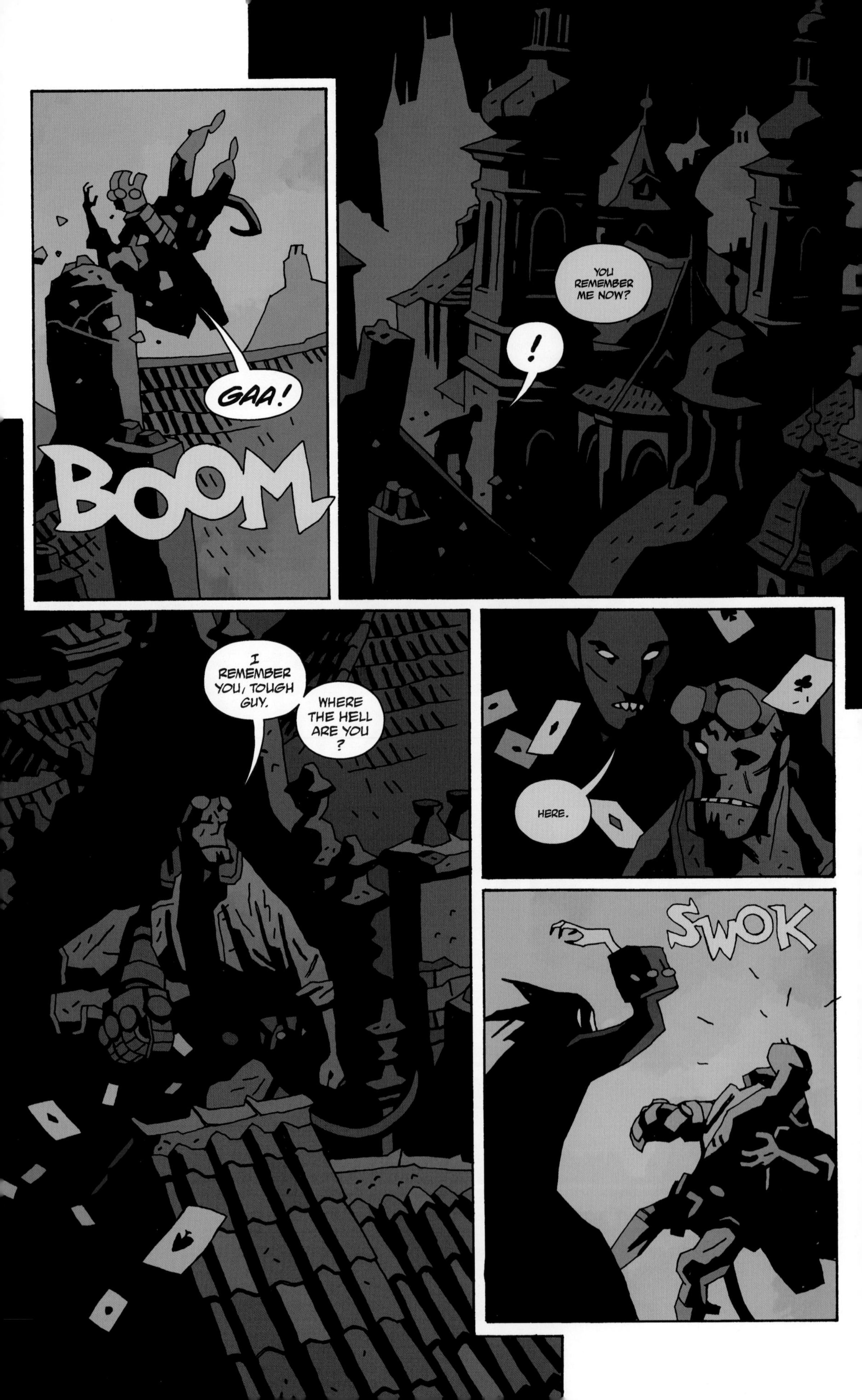
GAA!
BOOM
YOU REMEMBER ME NOW?
!
I REMEMBER YOU, TOUGH GUY.
WHERE THE HELL ARE YOU ?
HERE.
SWOK

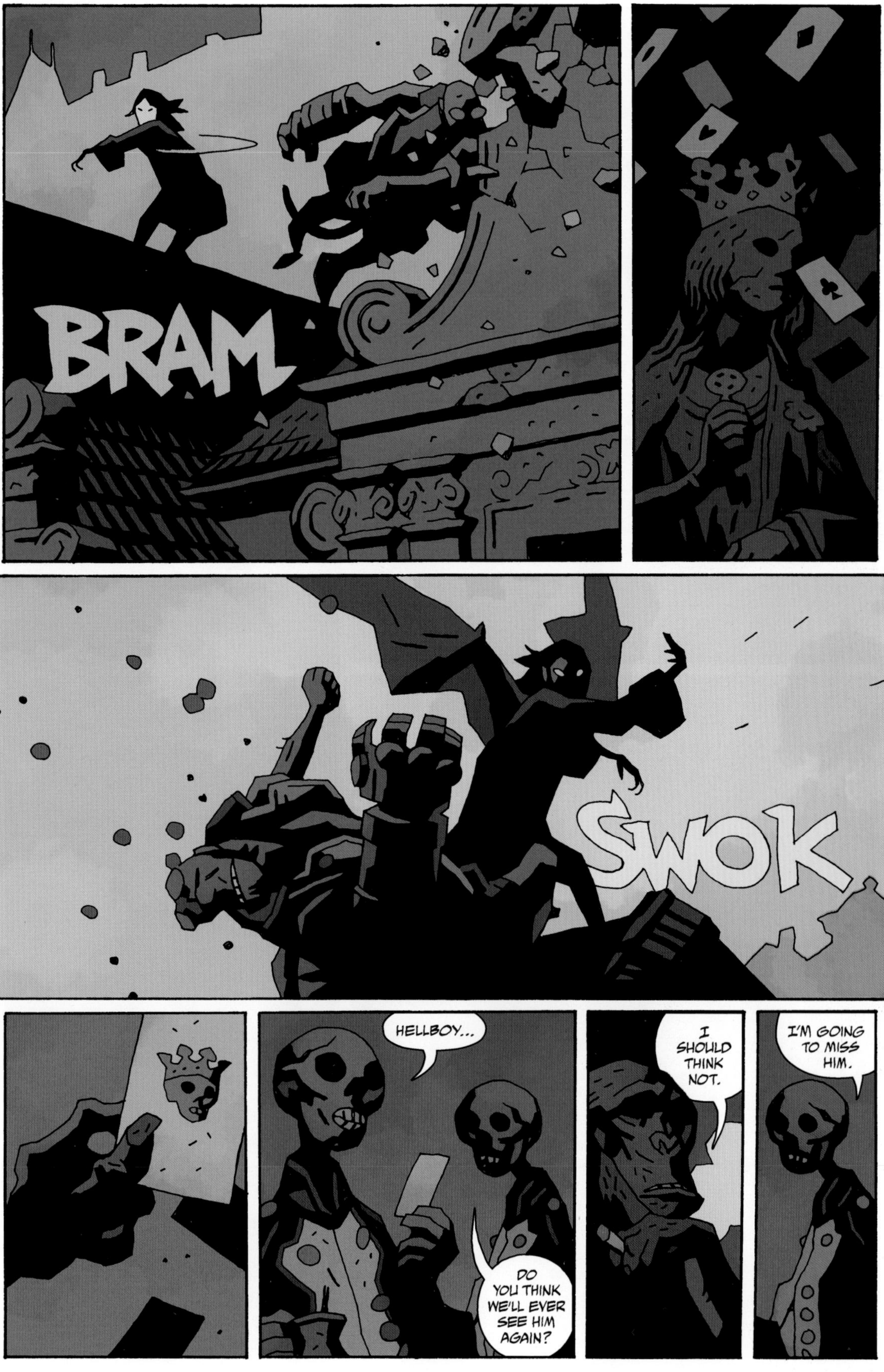

BRAM
SWOK
HELLBOY...
DO YOU THINK WE'LL EVER SEE HIM AGAIN?
I SHOULD THINK NOT.
I'M GOING TO MISS HIM.

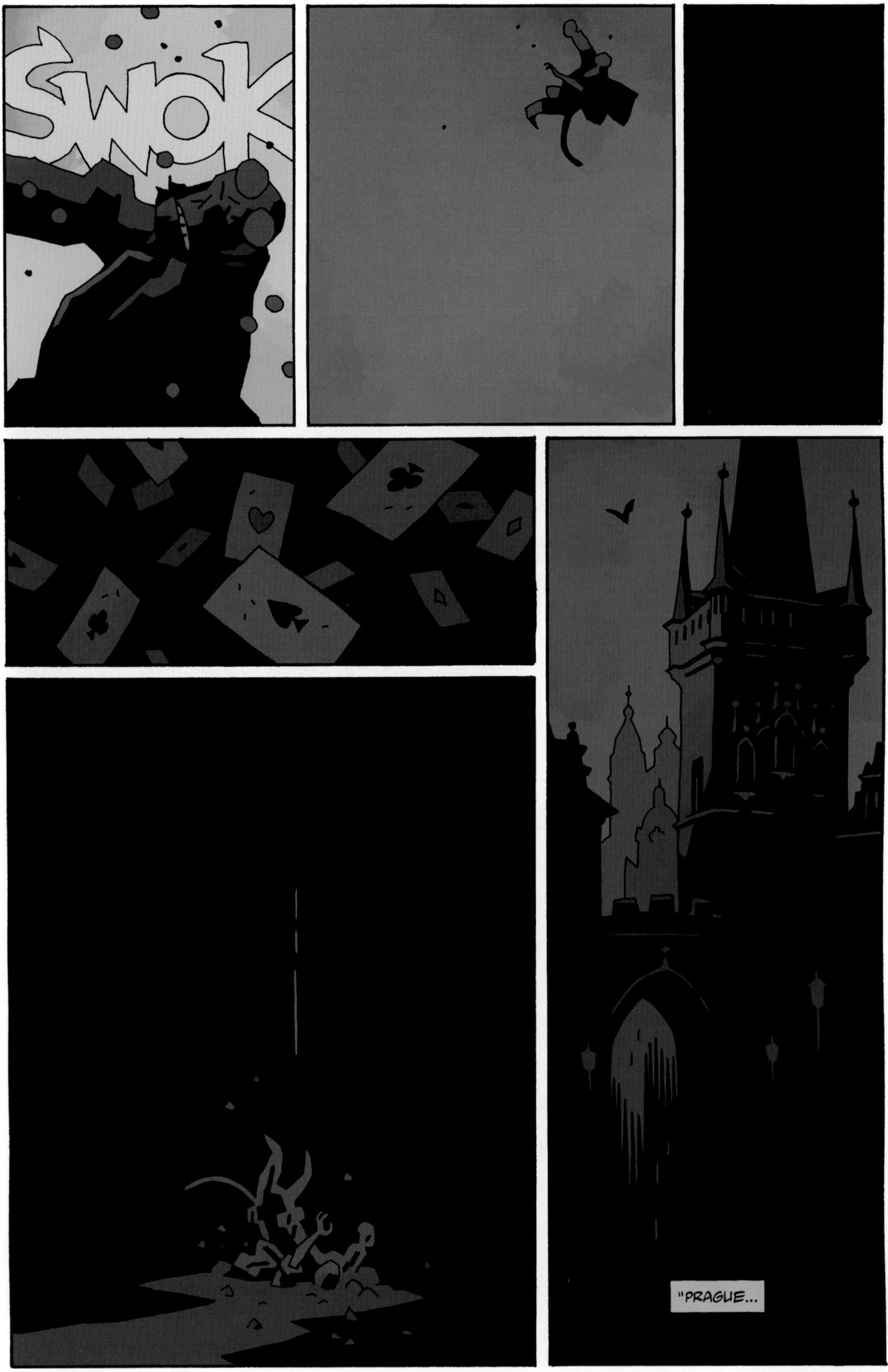
SWOK
"PRAGUE...

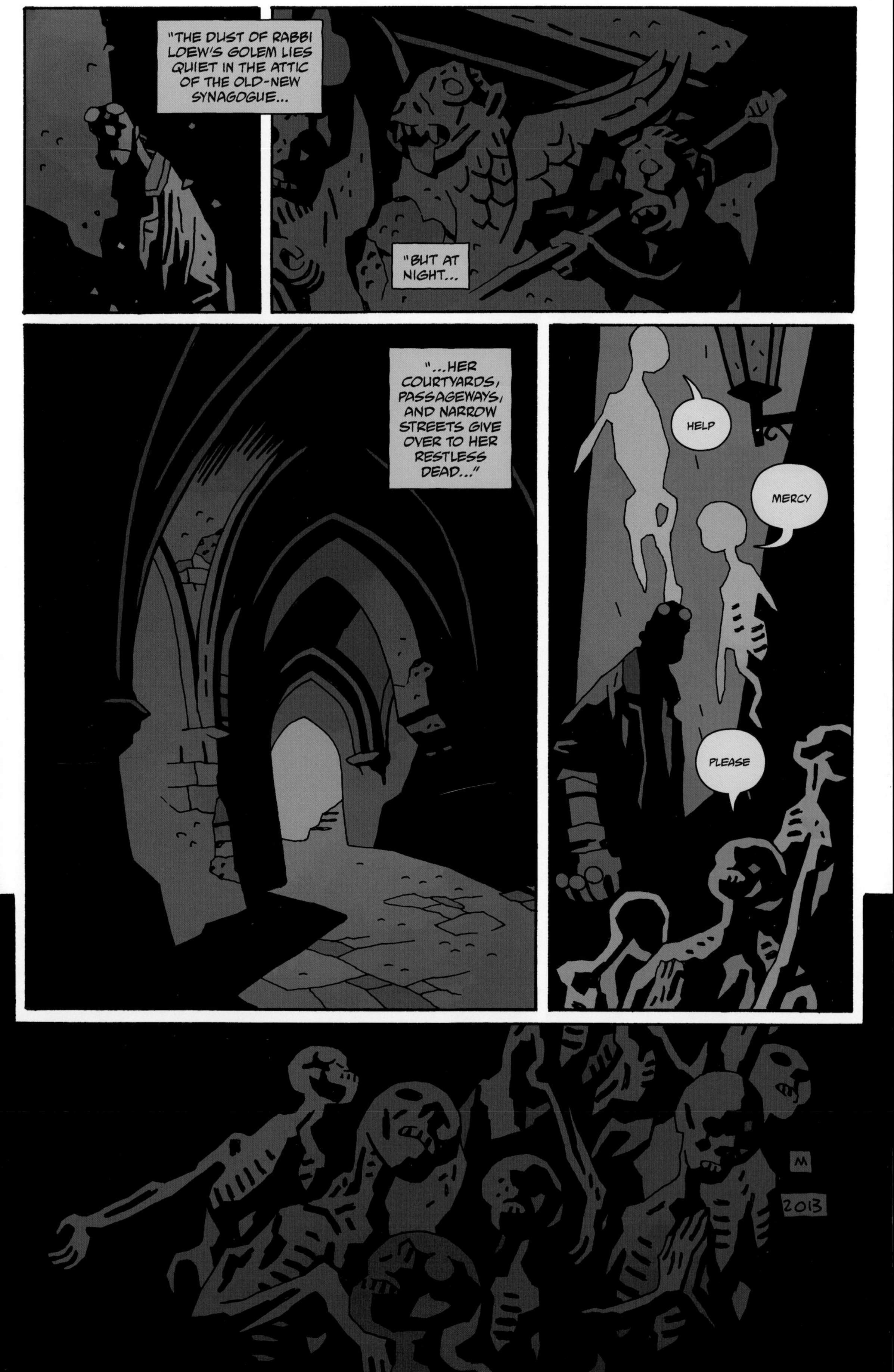
"THE DUST OF RABBI LOEW'S GOLEM LIES QUIET IN THE ATTIC OF THE OLD-NEW SYNAGOGUE...
"BUT AT NIGHT...
"...HER COURTYARDS, PASSAGEWAYS, AND NARROW STREETS GIVE OVER TO HER RESTLESS DEAD..."
HELP
MERCY
PLEASE
M
2013

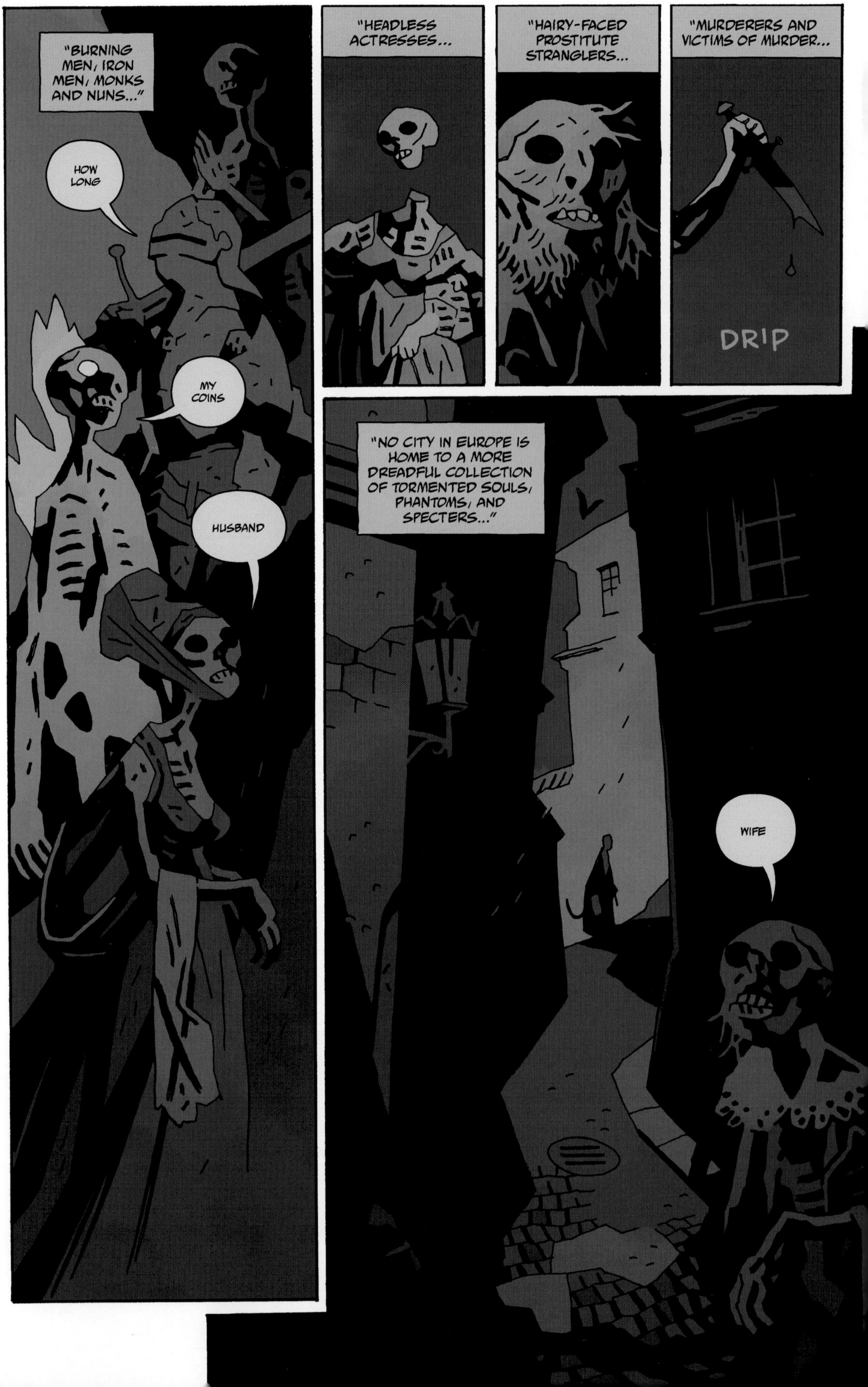
"BURNING MEN, IRON MEN, MONKS AND NUNS..."
HOW LONG
MY COINS
HUSBAND
"HEADLESS ACTRESSES...
"HAIRY-FACED PROSTITUTE STRANGLERS...
"MURDERERS AND VICTIMS OF MURDER...
DRIP
"NO CITY IN EUROPE IS HOME TO A MORE DREADFUL COLLECTION OF TORMENTED SOULS, PHANTOMS, AND SPECTERS..."
WIFE

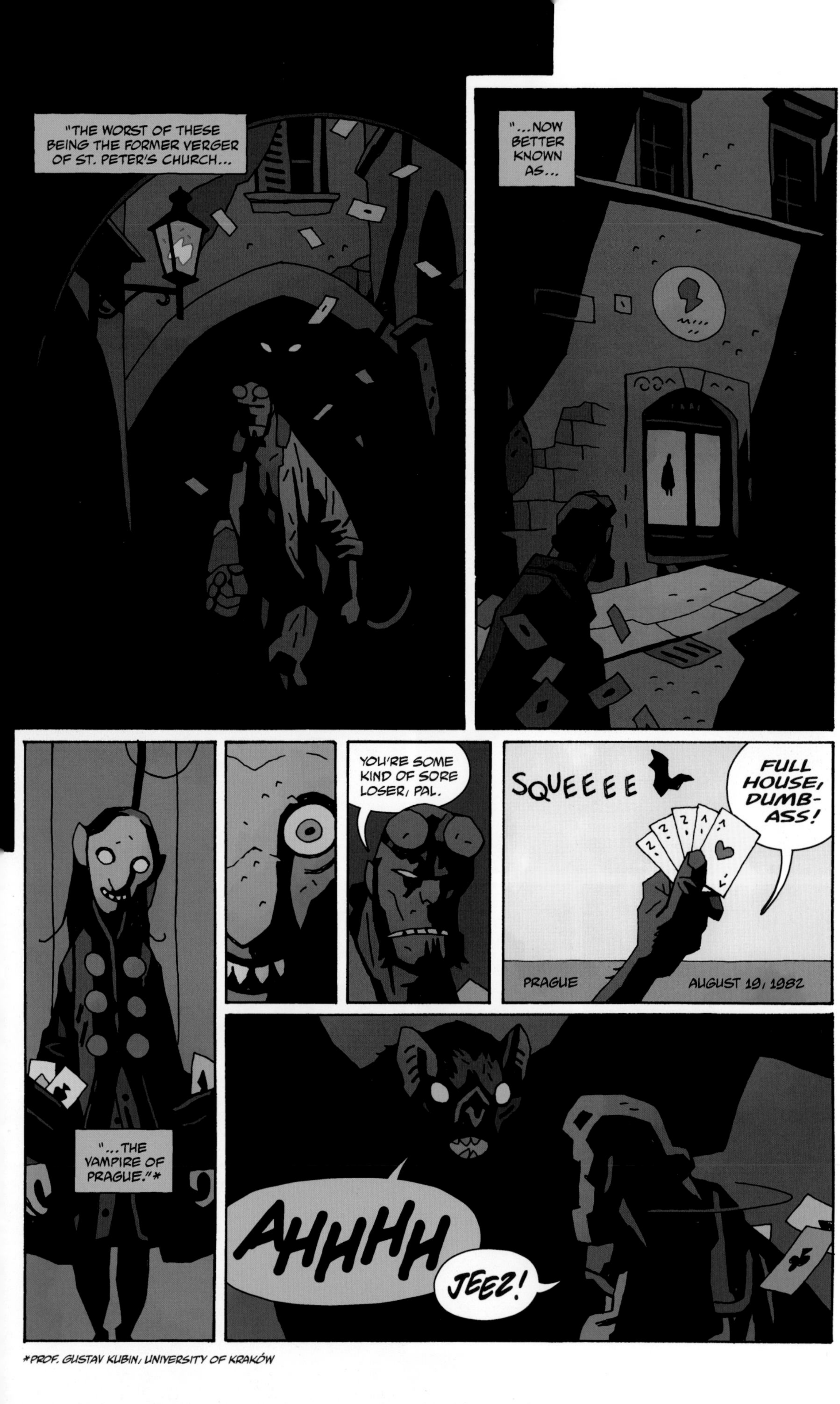
"THE WORST OF THESE BEING THE FORMER VERGER OF ST. PETER'S CHURCH...
"...NOW BETTER KNOWN AS...
"...THE VAMPIRE OF PRAGUE."*
YOU'RE SOME KIND OF SORE LOSER, PAL.
SQUEEEEE
FULL HOUSE, DUMB-ASS!
PRAGUE
AUGUST 19, 1982
AHHHH
JEEZ!

*PROF. GUSTAV KUBIN, UNIVERSITY OF KRAKÓW

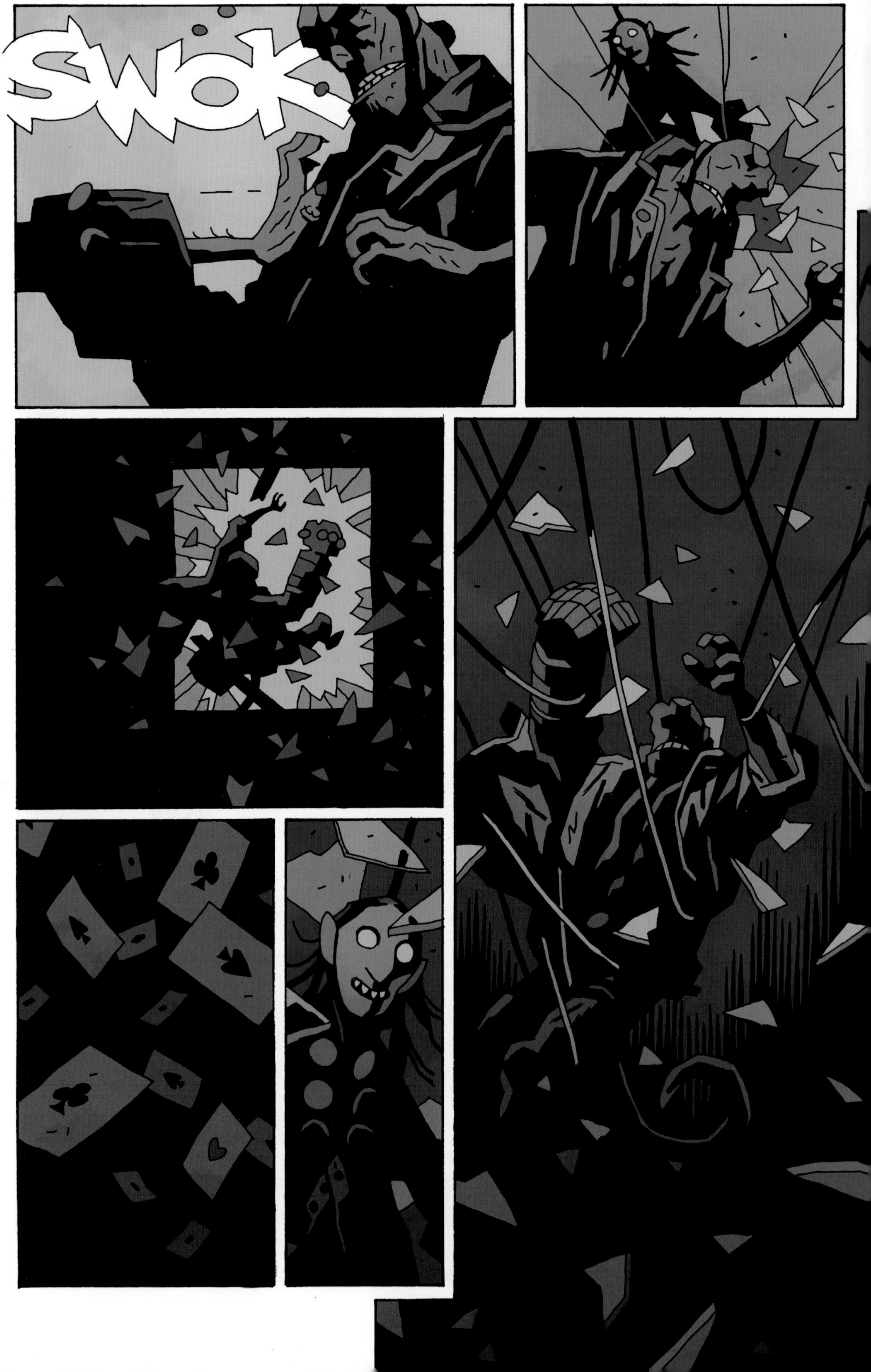
SWOK

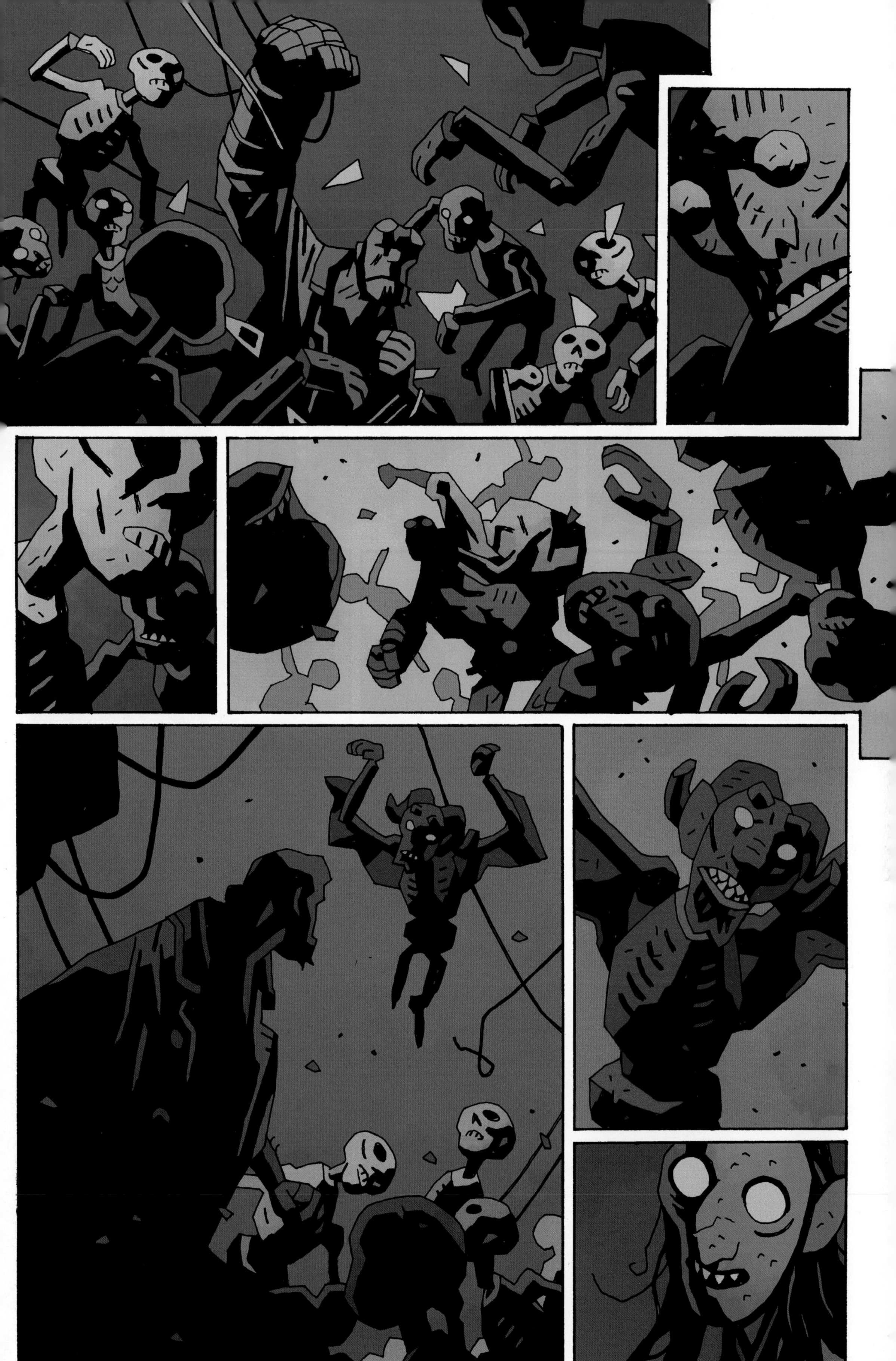

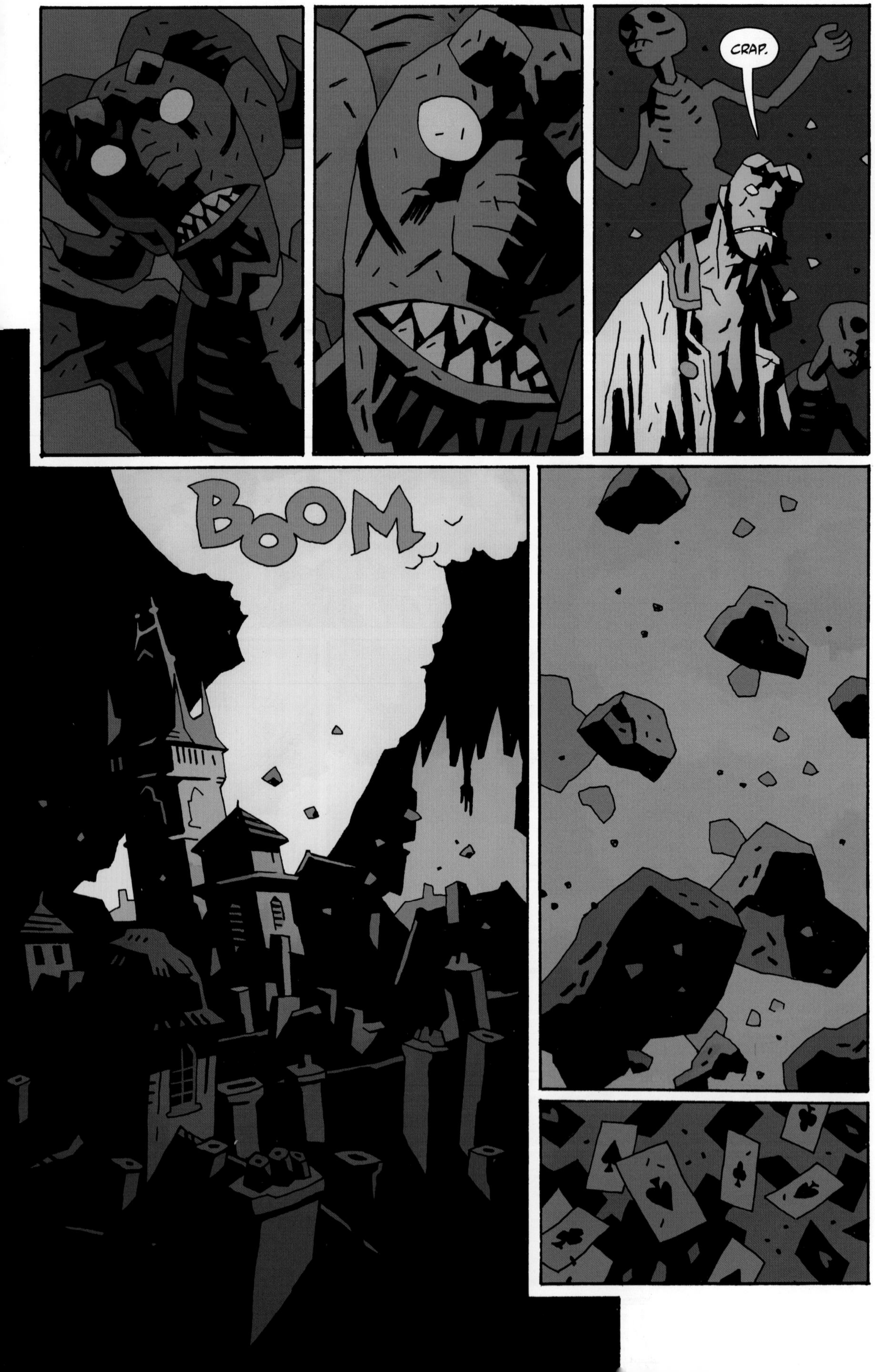
CRAP.
BOOM

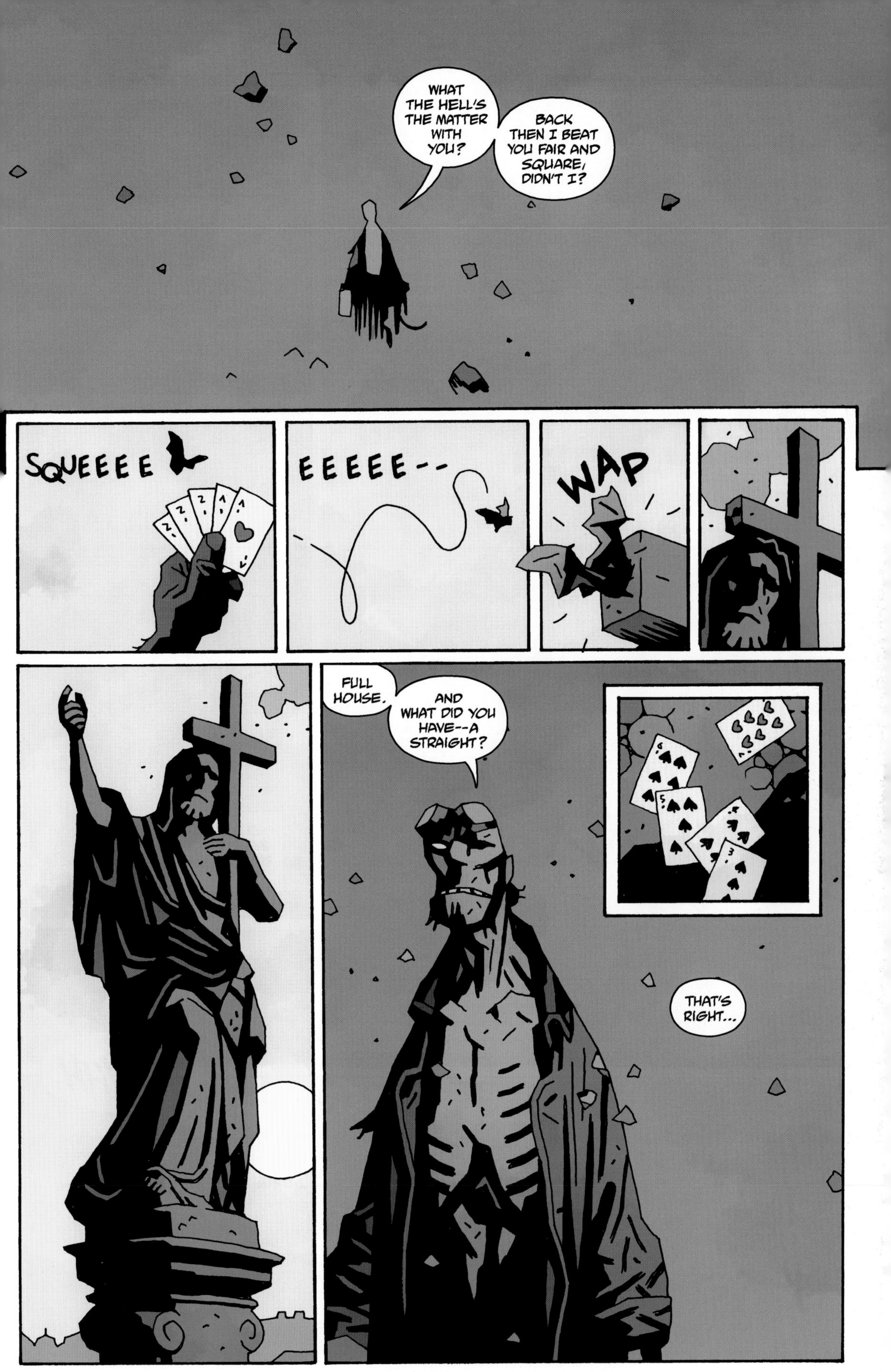
WHAT THE HELL'S THE MATTER WITH YOU?
BACK THEN I BEAT YOU FAIR AND SQUARE, DIDN'T I?
SQUEEEEE
EEEEE--
WAP
FULL HOUSE.
AND WHAT DID YOU HAVE--A STRAIGHT?
THAT'S RIGHT...

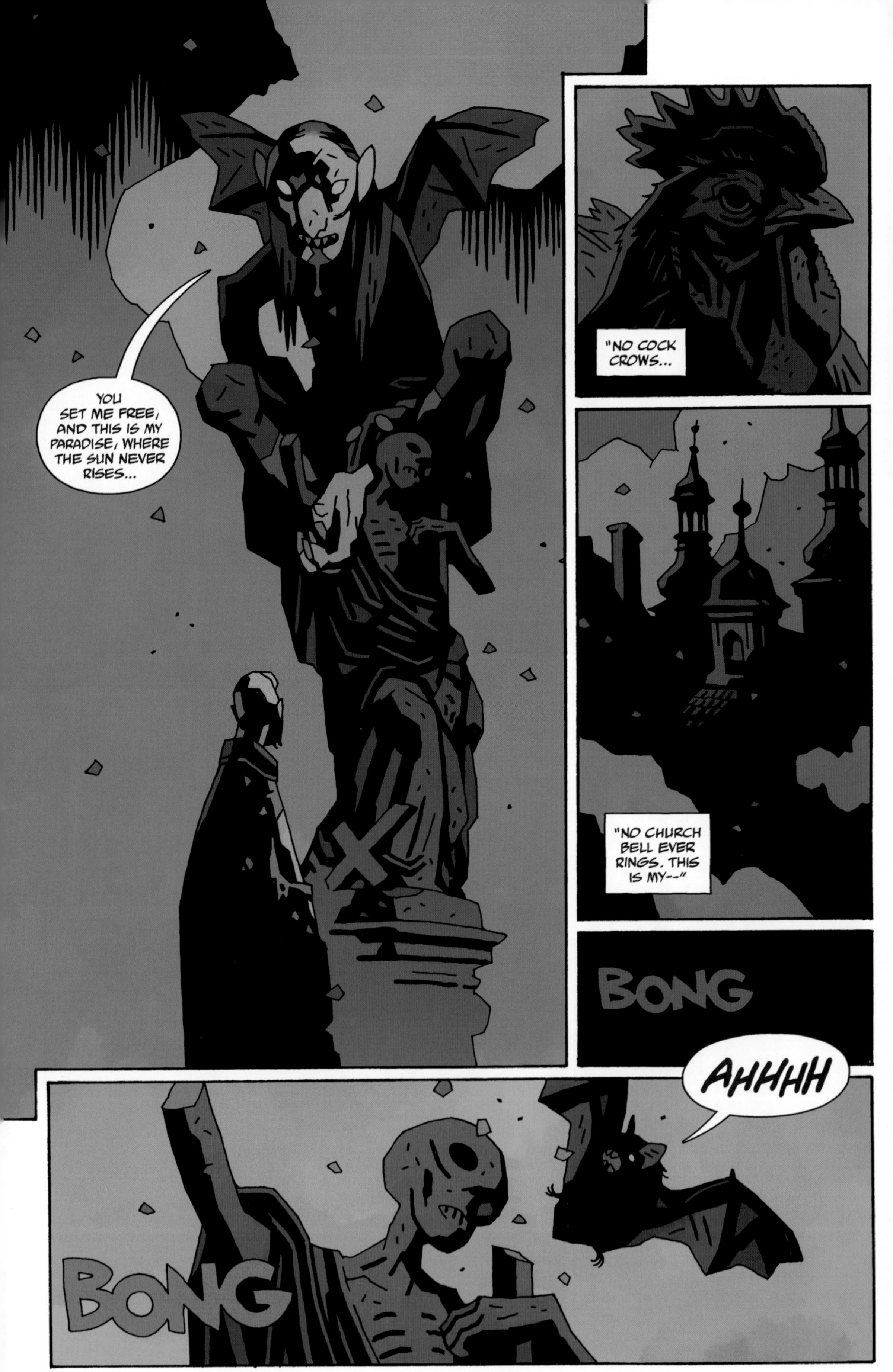
YOU SET ME FREE, AND THIS IS MY PARADISE, WHERE THE SUN NEVER RISES...
"NO COCK CROWS...
"NO CHURCH BELL EVER RINGS. THIS IS MY--"
BONG
AHHHH
BONG

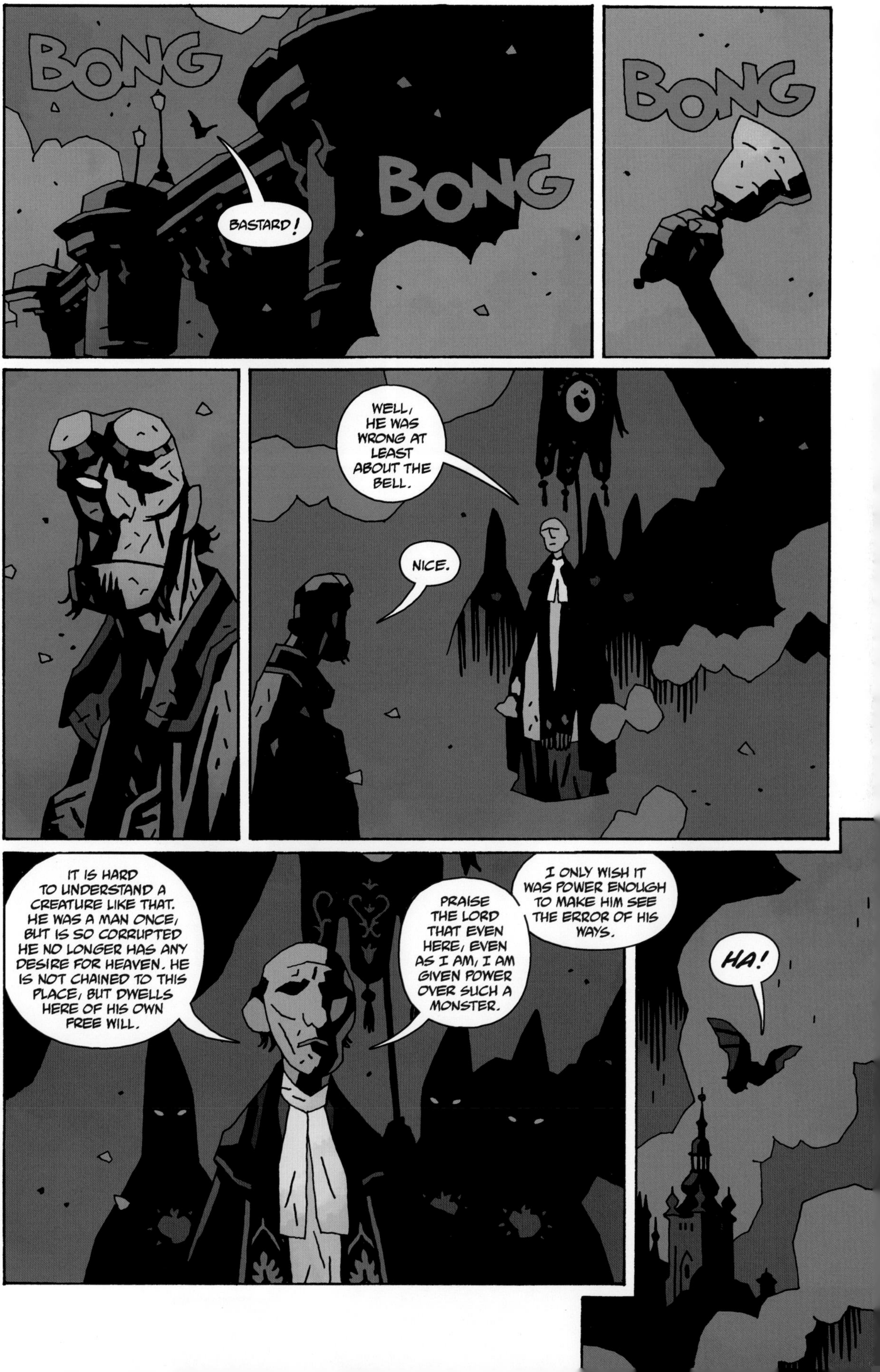
BONG
BASTARD!
BONG
BONG
WELL, HE WAS WRONG AT LEAST ABOUT THE BELL.
NICE.
IT IS HARD TO UNDERSTAND A CREATURE LIKE THAT. HE WAS A MAN ONCE, BUT IS SO CORRUPTED HE NO LONGER HAS ANY DESIRE FOR HEAVEN. HE IS NOT CHAINED TO THIS PLACE, BUT DWELLS HERE OF HIS OWN FREE WILL.
PRAISE THE LORD THAT EVEN HERE, EVEN AS I AM, I AM GIVEN POWER OVER SUCH A MONSTER.
I ONLY WISH IT WAS POWER ENOUGH TO MAKE HIM SEE THE ERROR OF HIS WAYS.
HA!

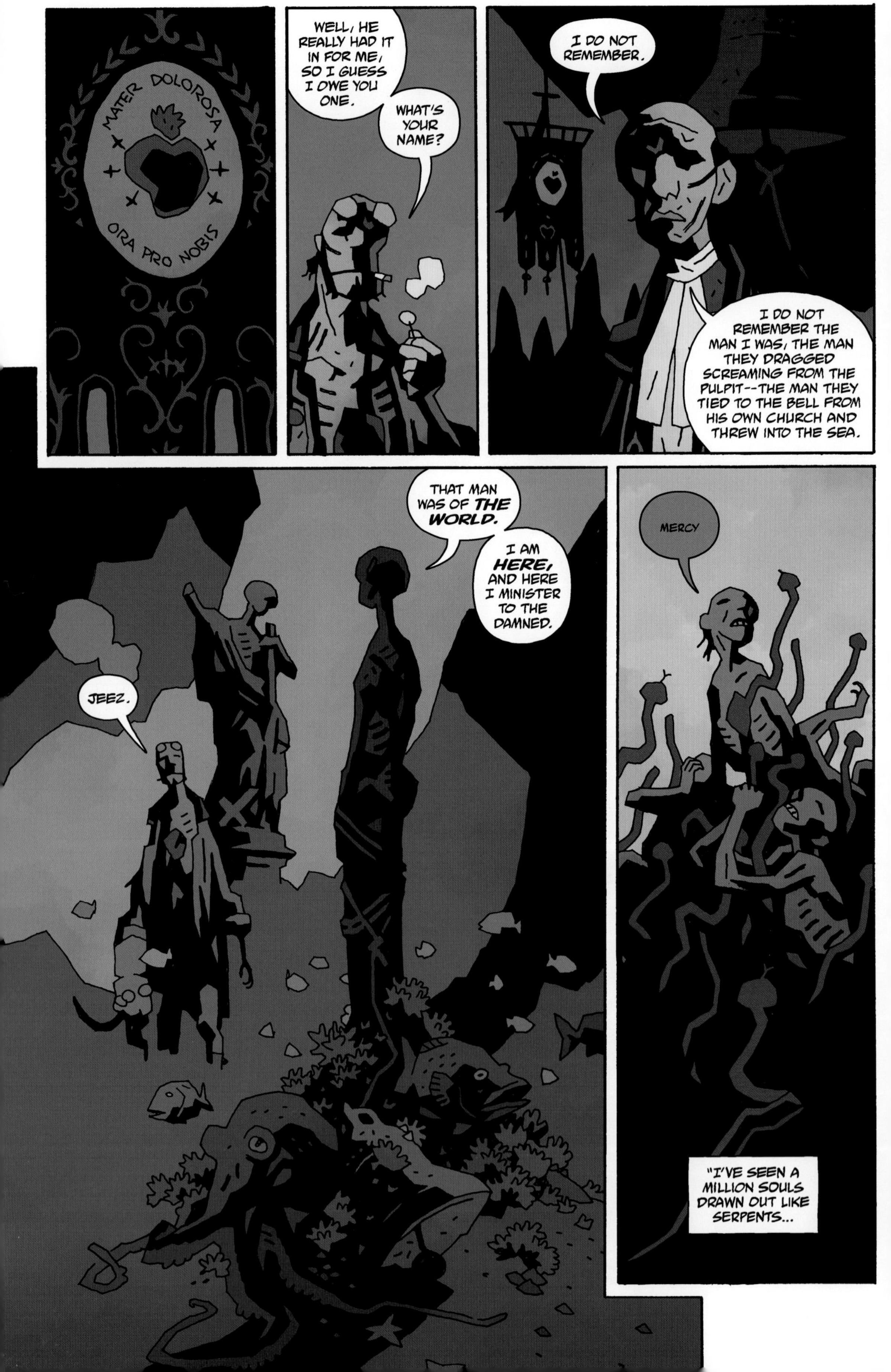
MATER DOLOROSA
ORA PRO NOBIS
WELL, HE REALLY HAD IT IN FOR ME, SO I GUESS I OWE YOU ONE.
WHAT'S YOUR NAME?
I DO NOT REMEMBER.
I DO NOT REMEMBER THE MAN I WAS, THE MAN THEY DRAGGED SCREAMING FROM THE PULPIT--THE MAN THEY TIED TO THE BELL FROM HIS OWN CHURCH AND THREW INTO THE SEA.
JEEZ.
THAT MAN WAS OF THE WORLD.
I AM HERE, AND HERE I MINISTER TO THE DAMNED.
MERCY
"I'VE SEEN A MILLION SOULS DRAWN OUT LIKE SERPENTS...

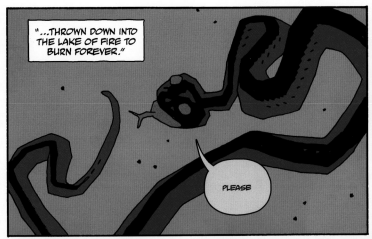

"...THROWN DOWN INTO THE LAKE OF FIRE TO BURN FOREVER."

PLEASE

BUT LATELY I HAVE SEEN THE OTHER AS WELL.

FORGIVE ME

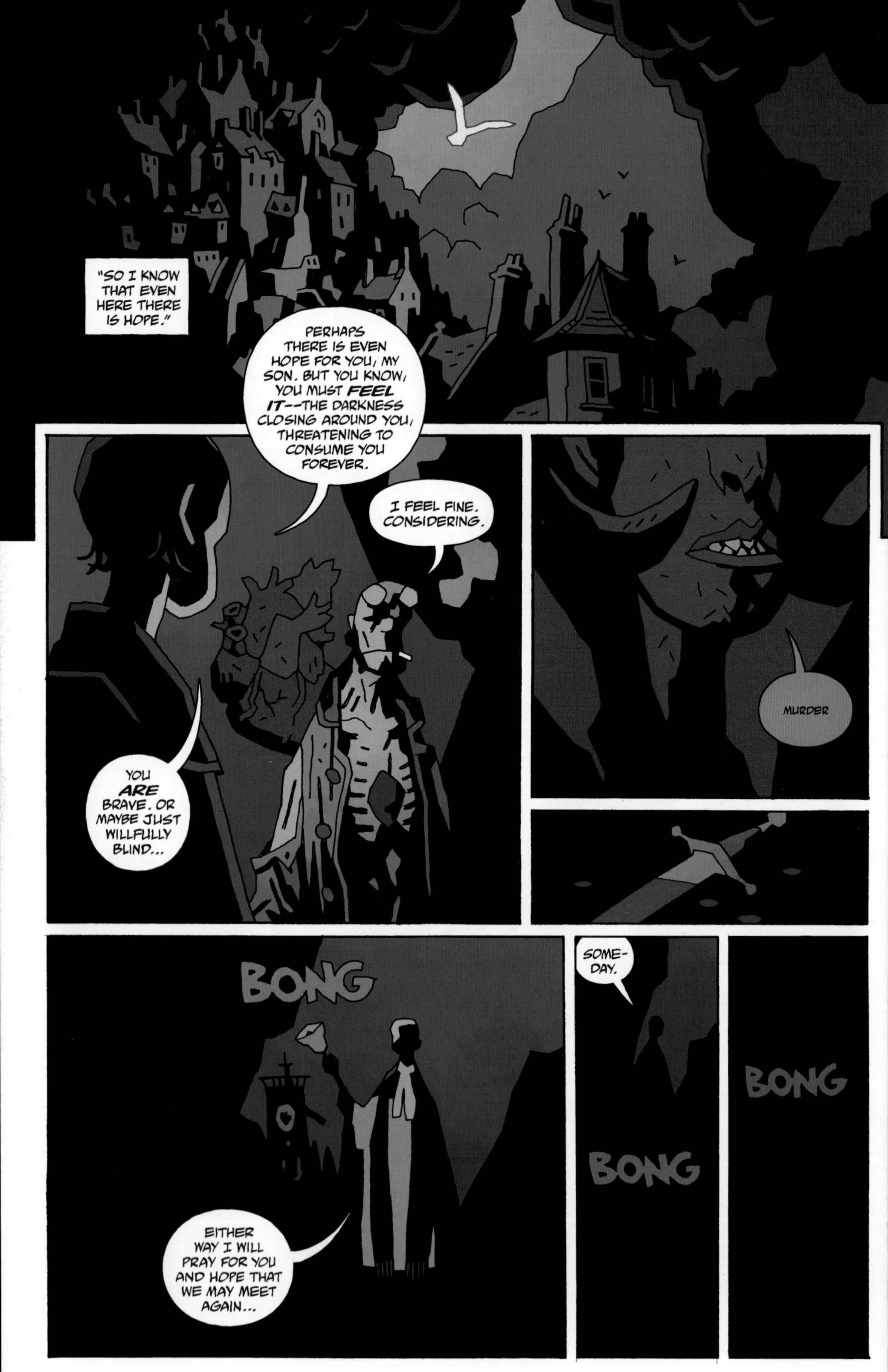
"SO I KNOW THAT EVEN HERE THERE IS HOPE."
PERHAPS THERE IS EVEN HOPE FOR YOU, MY SON. BUT YOU KNOW, YOU MUST FEEL IT--THE DARKNESS CLOSING AROUND YOU, THREATENING TO CONSUME YOU FOREVER.
I FEEL FINE. CONSIDERING.
YOU ARE BRAVE. OR MAYBE JUST WILLFULLY BLIND...
MURDER
BONG
EITHER WAY I WILL PRAY FOR YOU AND HOPE THAT WE MAY MEET AGAIN...
SOME-DAY.
BONG
BONG

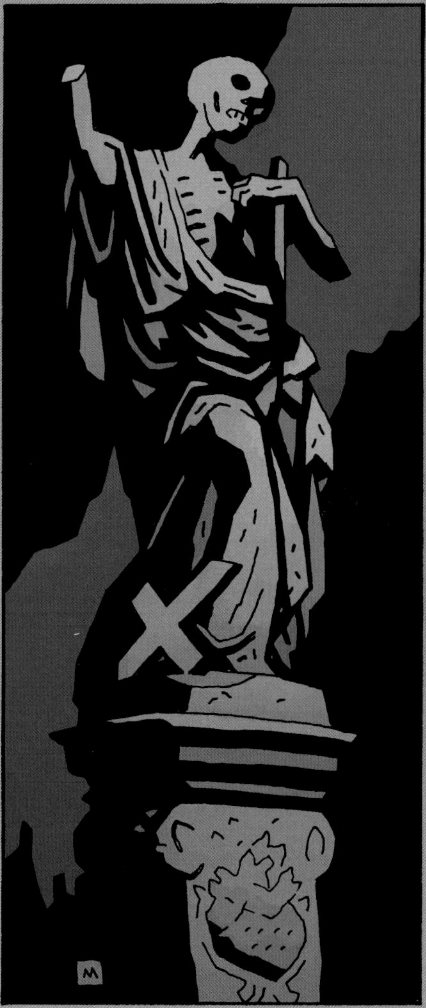

CHAPTER TWO
THE TRIALS OF DR. HOFFMANN

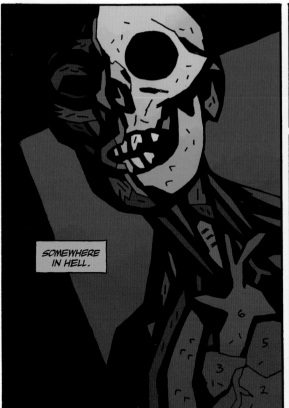

SOMEWHERE
IN HELL.

BONG

UGH...

WE'RE
DOCTORS.

WHAT
THE--?

Shhh.
DRINK
THIS.

IT'S ALL
RIGHT...

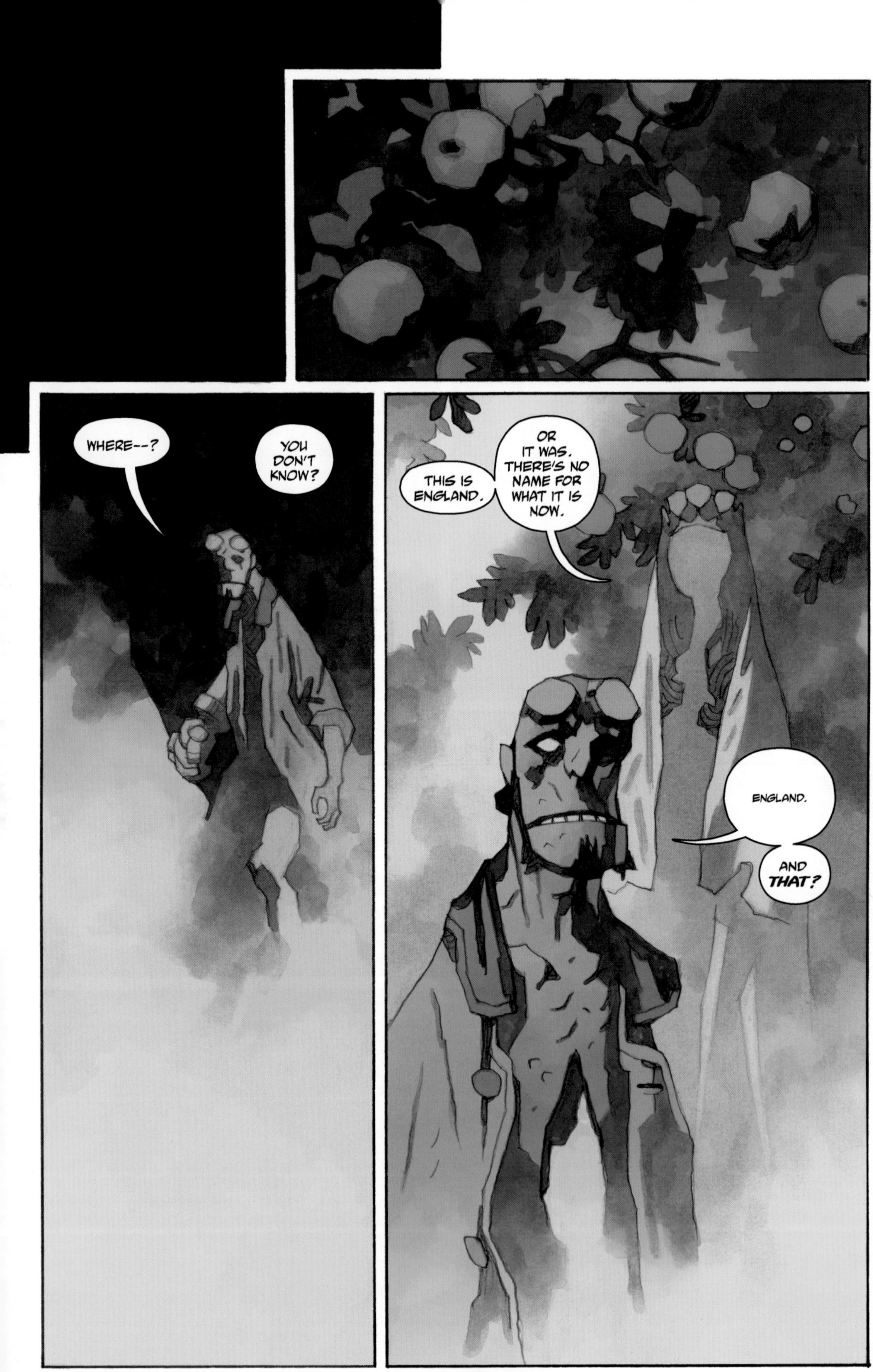
WHERE--?
YOU DON'T KNOW?
THIS IS ENGLAND.
OR IT WAS. THERE'S NO NAME FOR WHAT IT IS NOW.
ENGLAND.
AND *THAT?*

THE WORLD TREE--THE **NEW** WORLD TREE, SPRUNG UP FROM YOUR BLOOD, YOUR SACRIFICE. WHEN IT'S GROWN IT WILL BE THE TREE FOR THE **NEW** **WORLD.**

THE OLD TREE IS DYING. CREATURES IN HELL GNAW AT ITS ROOTS, AND SOMETHING WORSE IS COMING...

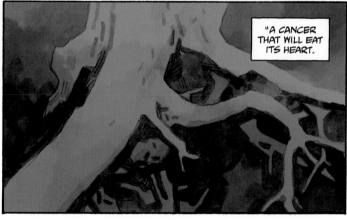

"A CANCER THAT WILL EAT ITS HEART.

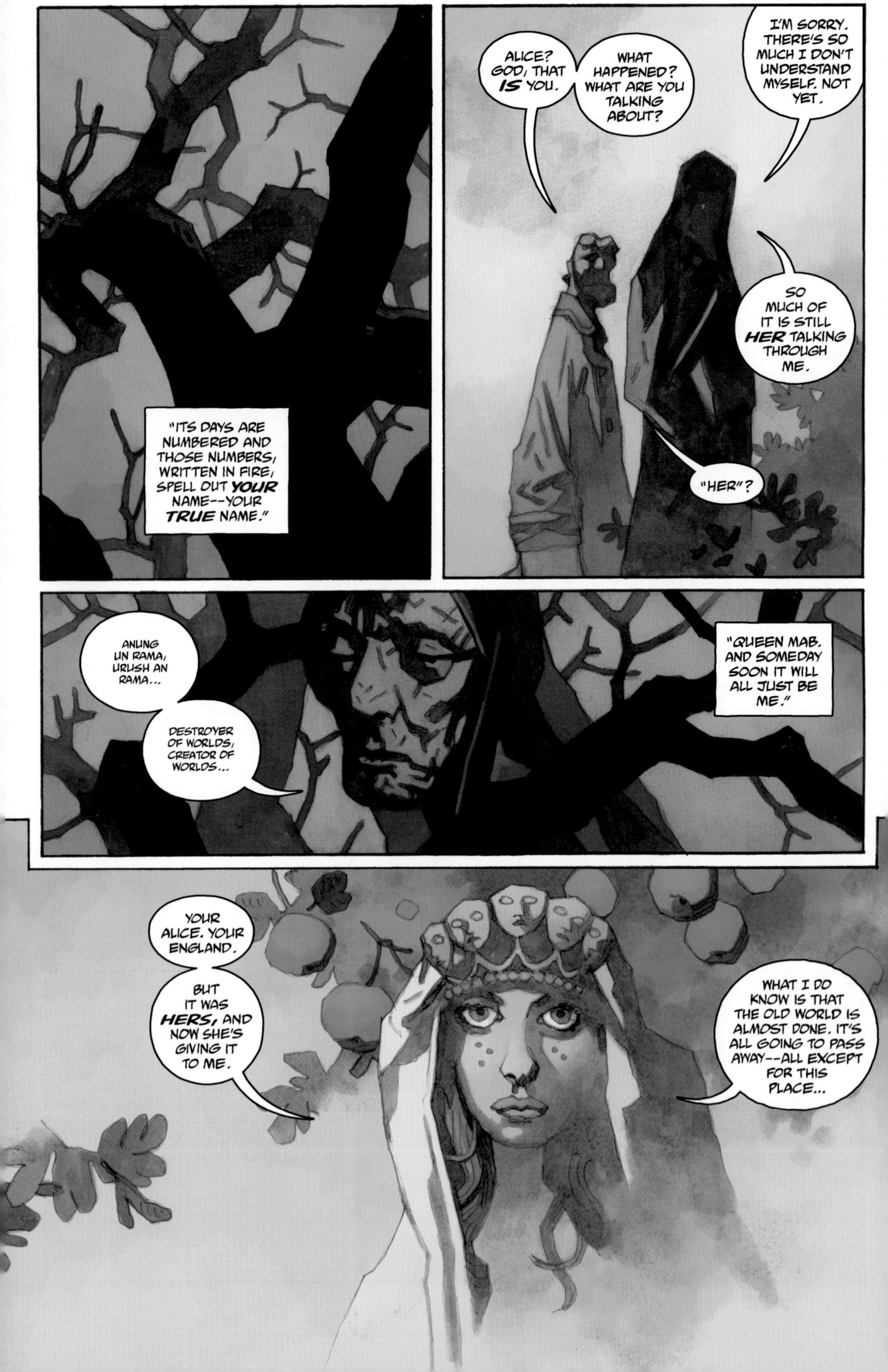
"ITS DAYS ARE NUMBERED AND THOSE NUMBERS, WRITTEN IN FIRE, SPELL OUT YOUR NAME--YOUR TRUE NAME."
ALICE? GOD, THAT IS YOU.
WHAT HAPPENED? WHAT ARE YOU TALKING ABOUT?
I'M SORRY. THERE'S SO MUCH I DON'T UNDERSTAND MYSELF. NOT YET.
SO MUCH OF IT IS STILL HER TALKING THROUGH ME.
"HER"?
ANUNG UN RAMA, URUSH AN RAMA...
DESTROYER OF WORLDS, CREATOR OF WORLDS...
"QUEEN MAB. AND SOMEDAY SOON IT WILL ALL JUST BE ME."
YOUR ALICE. YOUR ENGLAND.
BUT IT WAS HERS, AND NOW SHE'S GIVING IT TO ME.
WHAT I DO KNOW IS THAT THE OLD WORLD IS ALMOST DONE. IT'S ALL GOING TO PASS AWAY--ALL EXCEPT FOR THIS PLACE...

"AND HERE IT ALL BEGINS AGAIN."

WHATEVER IT IS... IT'S BEAUTIFUL.

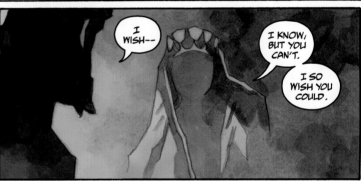

I WISH--

I KNOW, BUT YOU CAN'T.

I SO WISH YOU COULD.

MAYBE I CAN. MAYBE--

NO.

YOU CAN'T.

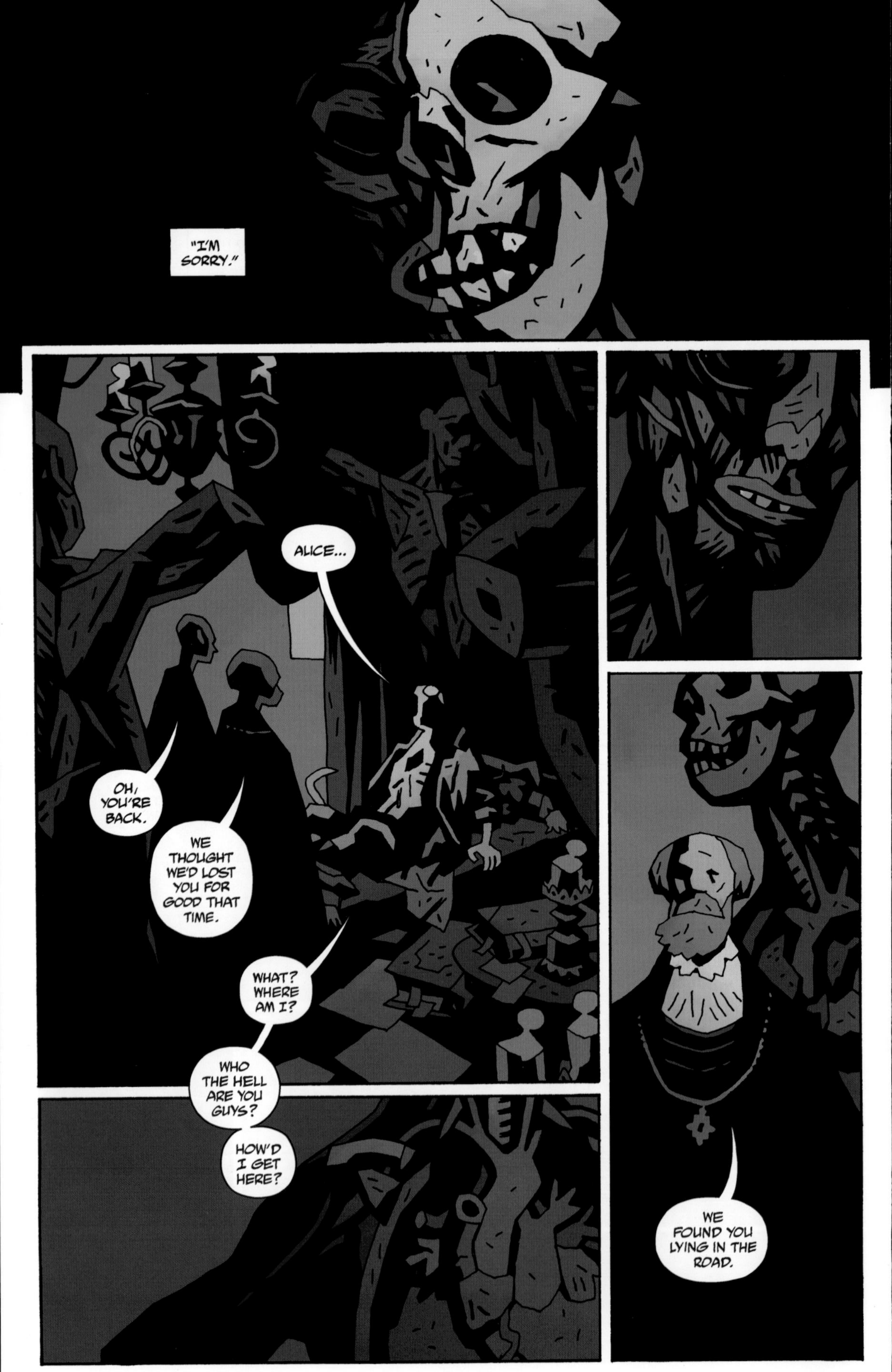
"I'M SORRY."
ALICE...
OH, YOU'RE BACK.
WE THOUGHT WE'D LOST YOU FOR GOOD THAT TIME.
WHAT? WHERE AM I?
WHO THE HELL ARE YOU GUYS?
HOW'D I GET HERE?
WE FOUND YOU LYING IN THE ROAD.

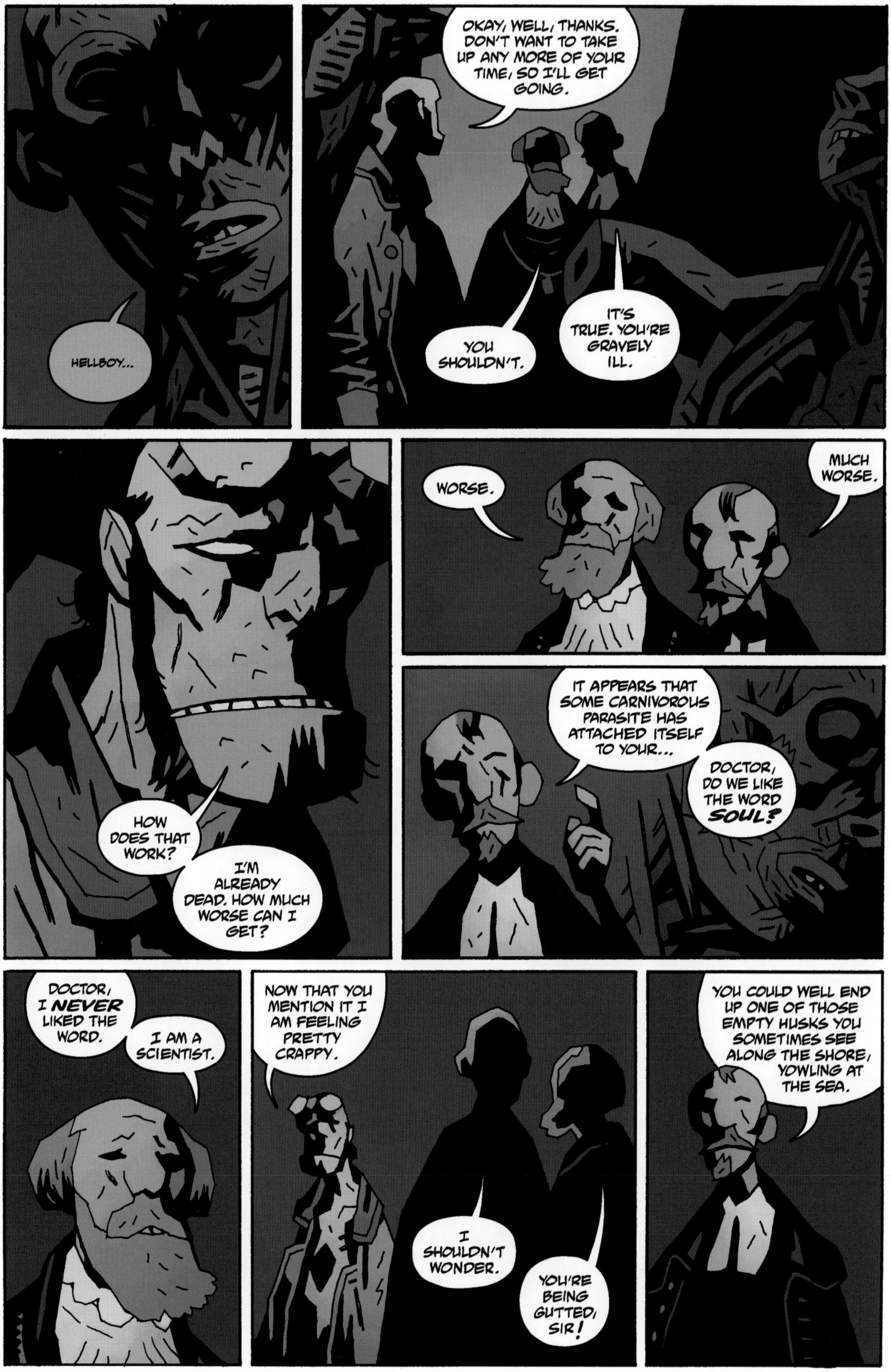
HELLBOY...
OKAY, WELL, THANKS. DON'T WANT TO TAKE UP ANY MORE OF YOUR TIME, SO I'LL GET GOING.
YOU SHOULDN'T.
IT'S TRUE. YOU'RE GRAVELY ILL.
HOW DOES THAT WORK?
I'M ALREADY DEAD. HOW MUCH WORSE CAN I GET?
WORSE.
MUCH WORSE.
IT APPEARS THAT SOME CARNIVOROUS PARASITE HAS ATTACHED ITSELF TO YOUR...
DOCTOR, DO WE LIKE THE WORD SOUL?
DOCTOR, I NEVER LIKED THE WORD.
I AM A SCIENTIST.
NOW THAT YOU MENTION IT I AM FEELING PRETTY CRAPPY.
I SHOULDN'T WONDER.
YOU'RE BEING GUTTED, SIR!
YOU COULD WELL END UP ONE OF THOSE EMPTY HUSKS YOU SOMETIMES SEE ALONG THE SHORE, YOWLING AT THE SEA.

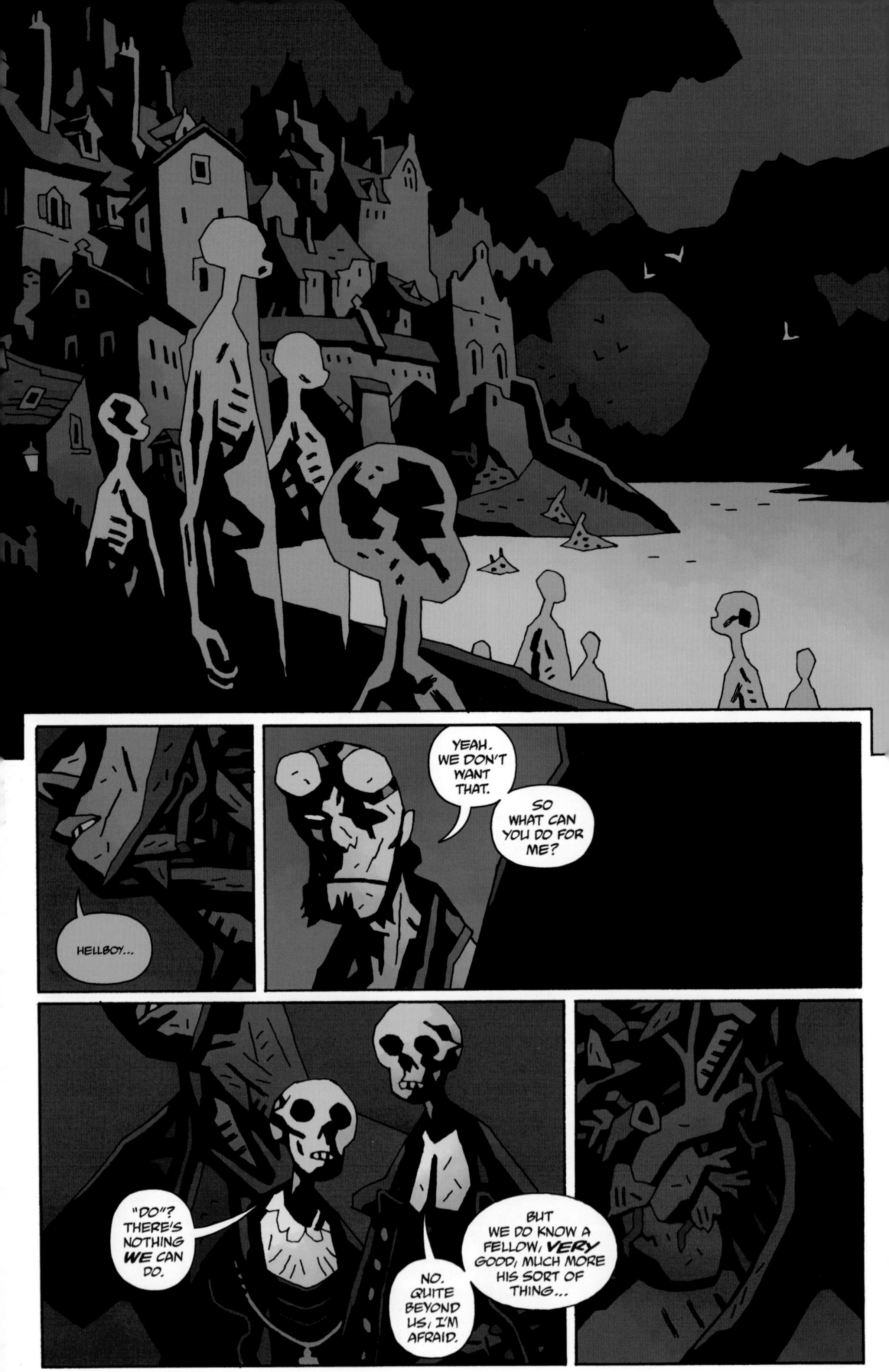
HELLBOY...
YEAH. WE DON'T WANT THAT.
SO WHAT CAN YOU DO FOR ME?
"DO"? THERE'S NOTHING WE CAN DO.
NO. QUITE BEYOND US, I'M AFRAID.
BUT WE DO KNOW A FELLOW, VERY GOOD, MUCH MORE HIS SORT OF THING...

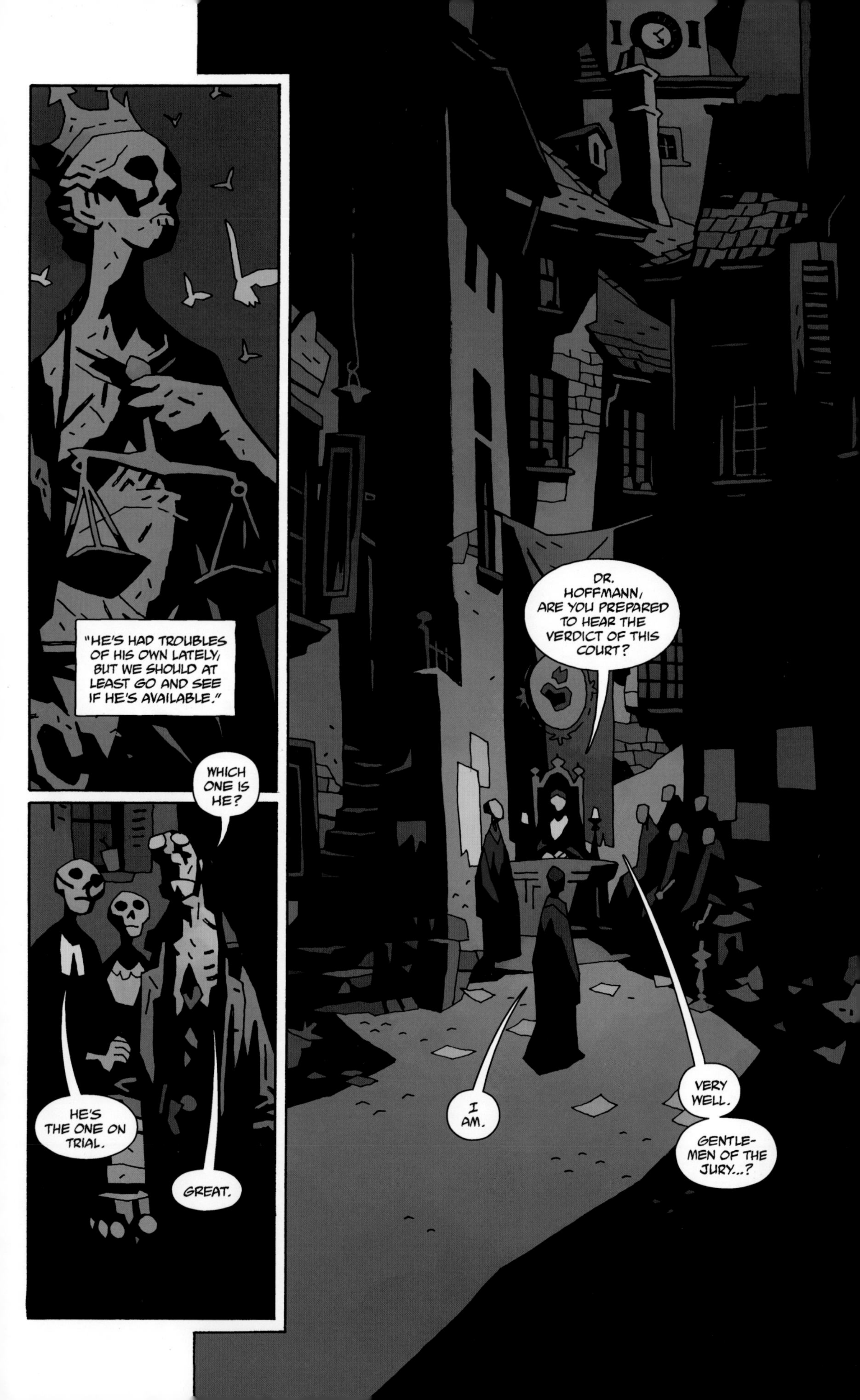

"HE'S HAD TROUBLES OF HIS OWN LATELY, BUT WE SHOULD AT LEAST GO AND SEE IF HE'S AVAILABLE."
WHICH ONE IS HE?
HE'S THE ONE ON TRIAL.
GREAT.
DR. HOFFMANN, ARE YOU PREPARED TO HEAR THE VERDICT OF THIS COURT?
I AM.
VERY WELL.
GENTLE-MEN OF THE JURY...?

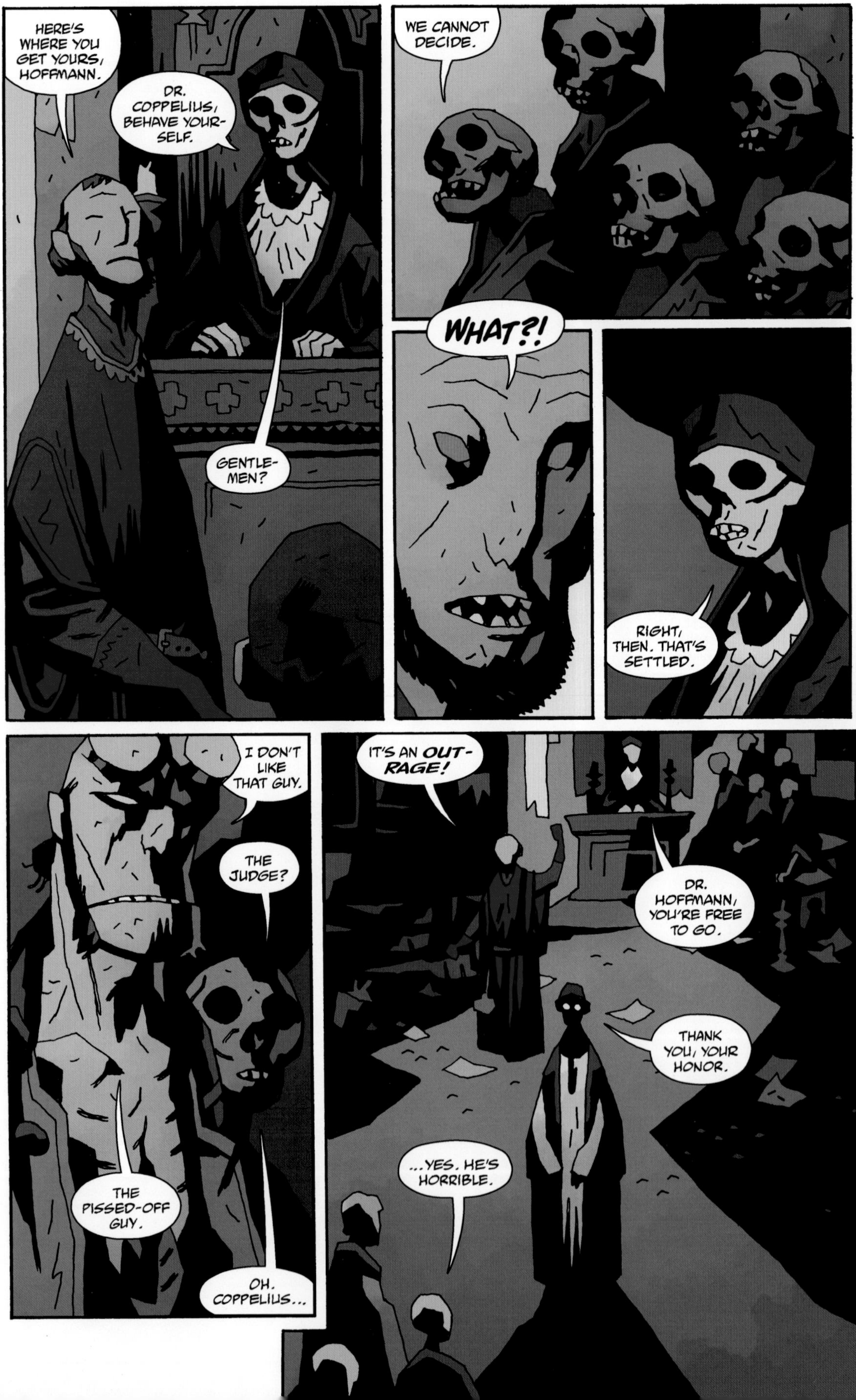
HERE'S WHERE YOU GET YOURS, HOFFMANN.
DR. COPPELIUS, BEHAVE YOURSELF.
GENTLEMEN?
WE CANNOT DECIDE.
WHAT?!
RIGHT, THEN. THAT'S SETTLED.
I DON'T LIKE THAT GUY.
THE JUDGE?
THE PISSED-OFF GUY.
OH. COPPELIUS...
IT'S AN OUTRAGE!
DR. HOFFMANN, YOU'RE FREE TO GO.
THANK YOU, YOUR HONOR.
...YES. HE'S HORRIBLE.

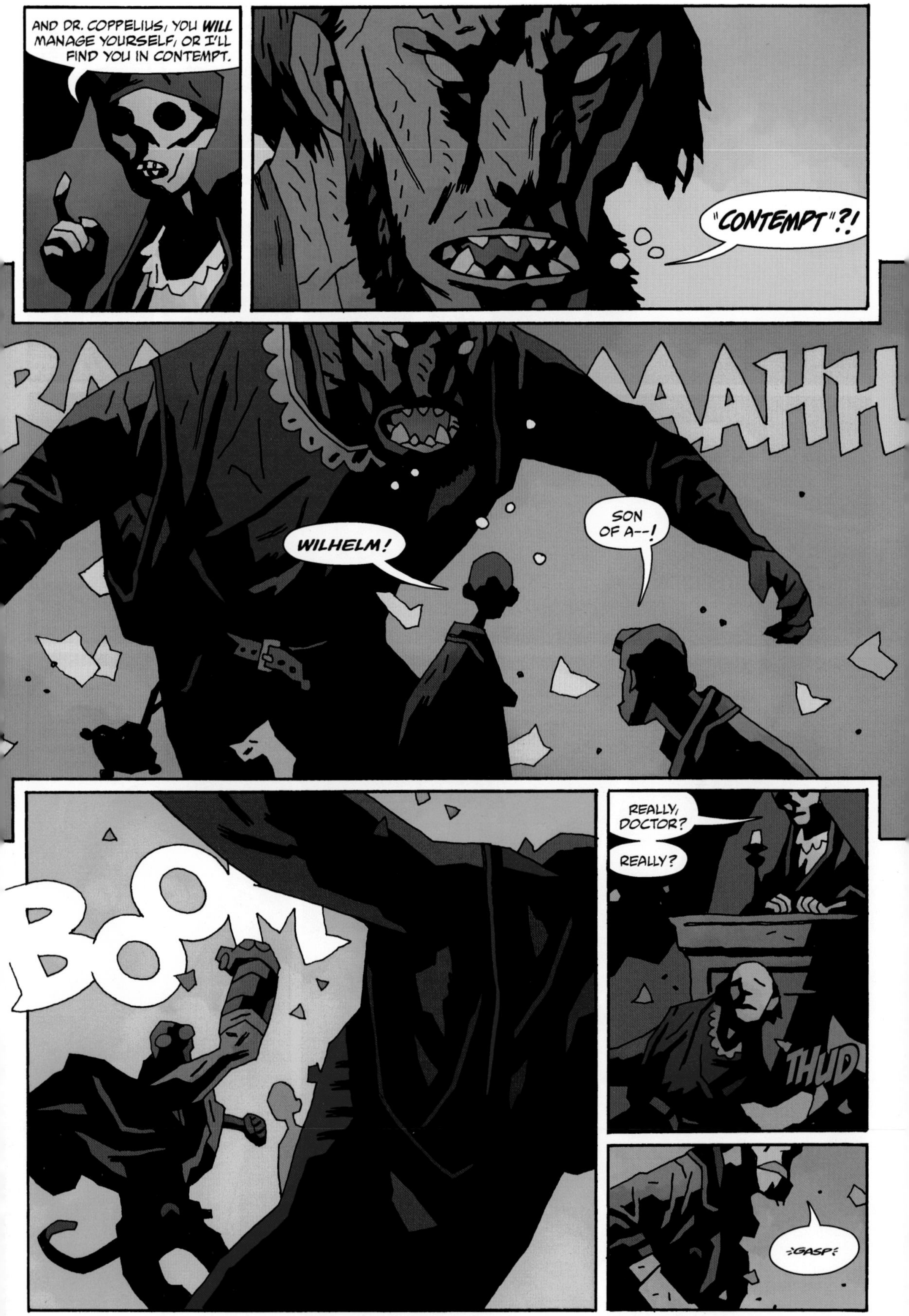
AND DR. COPPELIUS, YOU **WILL** MANAGE YOURSELF, OR I'LL FIND YOU IN CONTEMPT.
"CONTEMPT"?!
RAAAAAHH
WILHELM!
SON OF A--!
BOOM
REALLY, DOCTOR?
REALLY?
THUD
GASP

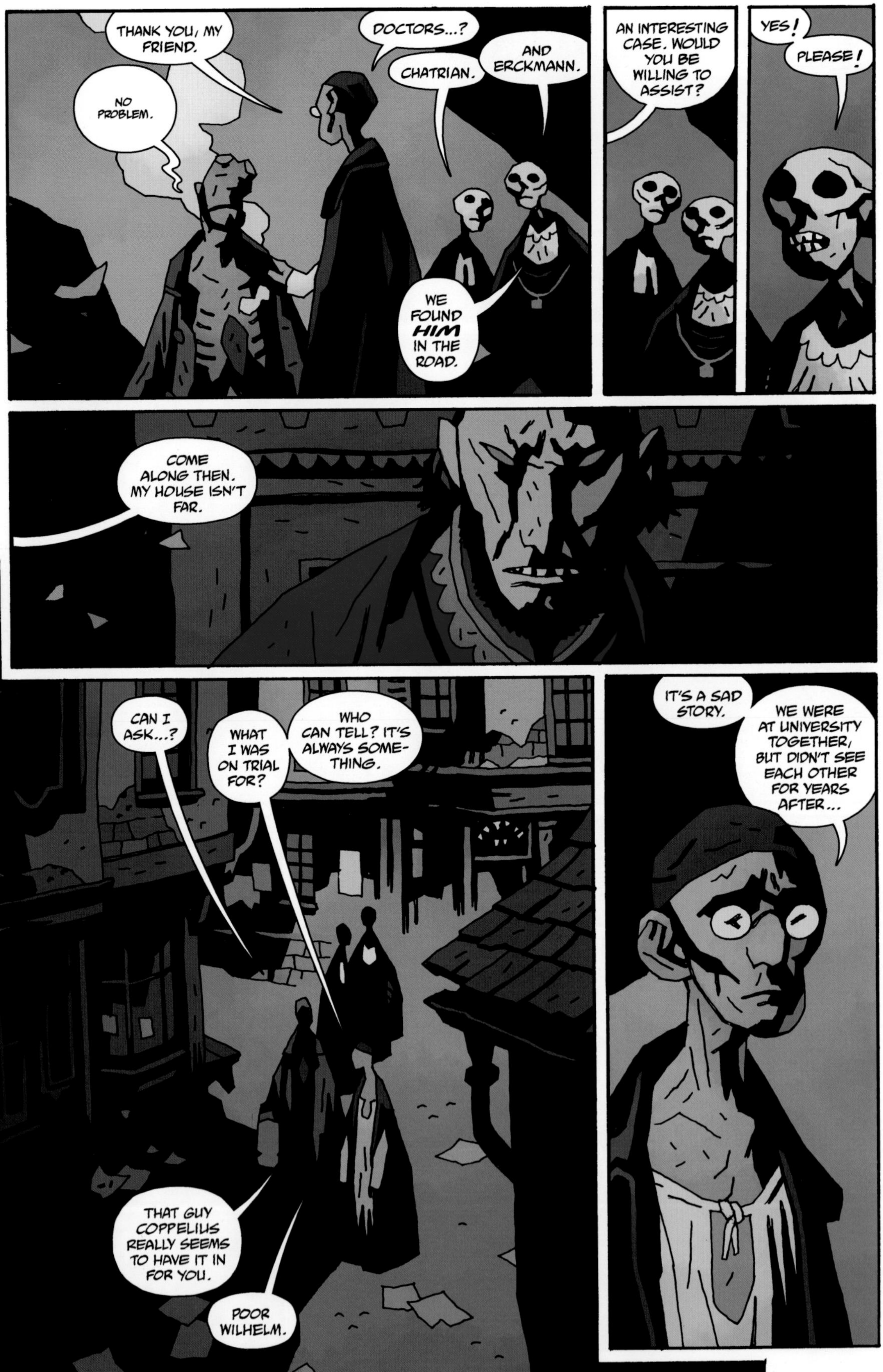
THANK YOU, MY FRIEND.
NO PROBLEM.
DOCTORS...?
CHATRIAN.
AND ERCKMANN.
WE FOUND HIM IN THE ROAD.
AN INTERESTING CASE. WOULD YOU BE WILLING TO ASSIST?
YES!
PLEASE!
COME ALONG THEN. MY HOUSE ISN'T FAR.
CAN I ASK...?
WHAT I WAS ON TRIAL FOR?
WHO CAN TELL? IT'S ALWAYS SOME-THING.
THAT GUY COPPELIUS REALLY SEEMS TO HAVE IT IN FOR YOU.
POOR WILHELM.
IT'S A SAD STORY.
WE WERE AT UNIVERSITY TOGETHER, BUT DIDN'T SEE EACH OTHER FOR YEARS AFTER...

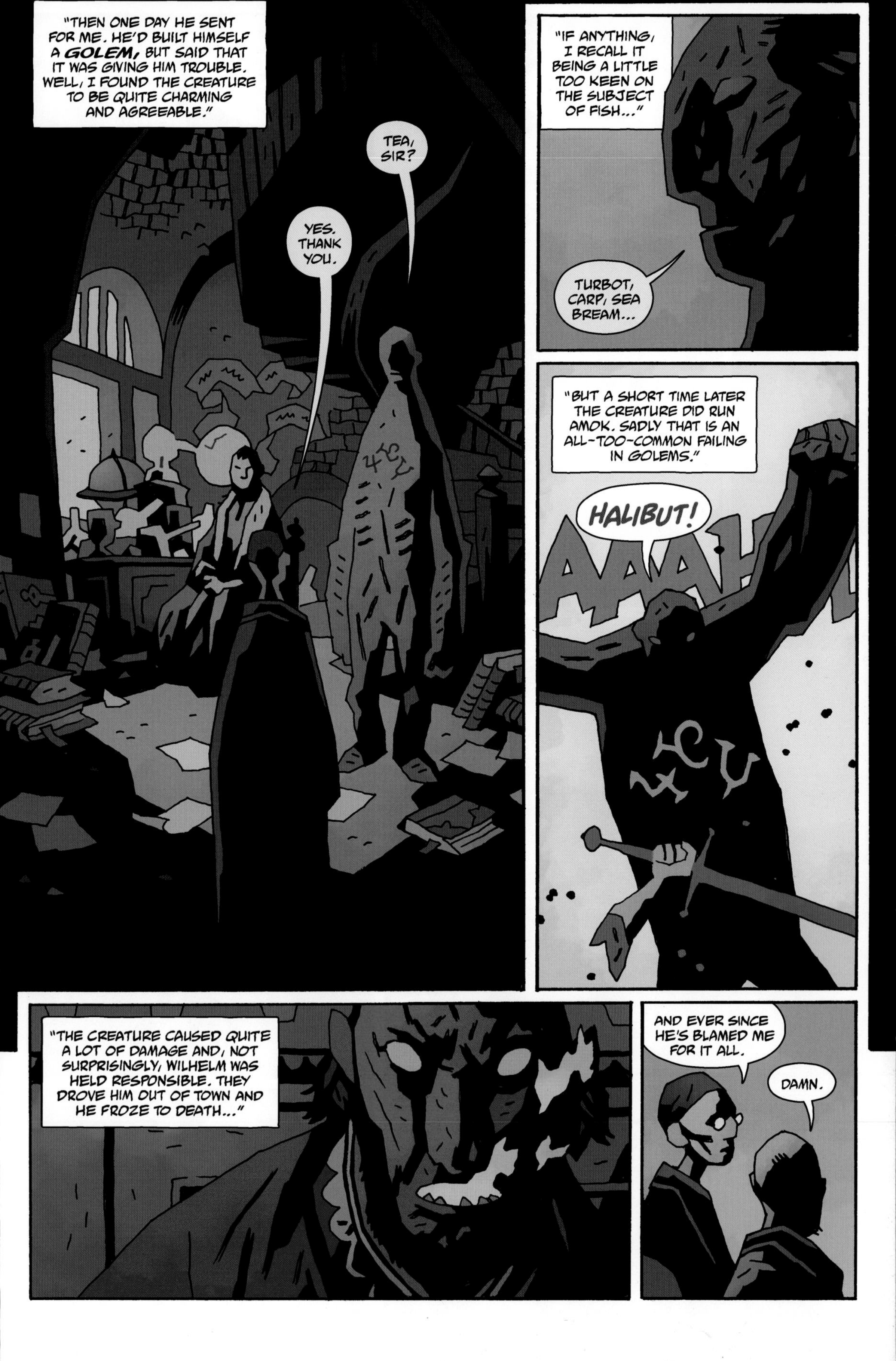
"THEN ONE DAY HE SENT FOR ME. HE'D BUILT HIMSELF A GOLEM, BUT SAID THAT IT WAS GIVING HIM TROUBLE. WELL, I FOUND THE CREATURE TO BE QUITE CHARMING AND AGREEABLE."
TEA, SIR?
YES. THANK YOU.
"IF ANYTHING, I RECALL IT BEING A LITTLE TOO KEEN ON THE SUBJECT OF FISH..."
TURBOT, CARP, SEA BREAM...
"BUT A SHORT TIME LATER THE CREATURE DID RUN AMOK. SADLY THAT IS AN ALL-TOO-COMMON FAILING IN GOLEMS."
HALIBUT!
AAAH
"THE CREATURE CAUSED QUITE A LOT OF DAMAGE AND, NOT SURPRISINGLY, WILHELM WAS HELD RESPONSIBLE. THEY DROVE HIM OUT OF TOWN AND HE FROZE TO DEATH..."
AND EVER SINCE HE'S BLAMED ME FOR IT ALL.
DAMN.

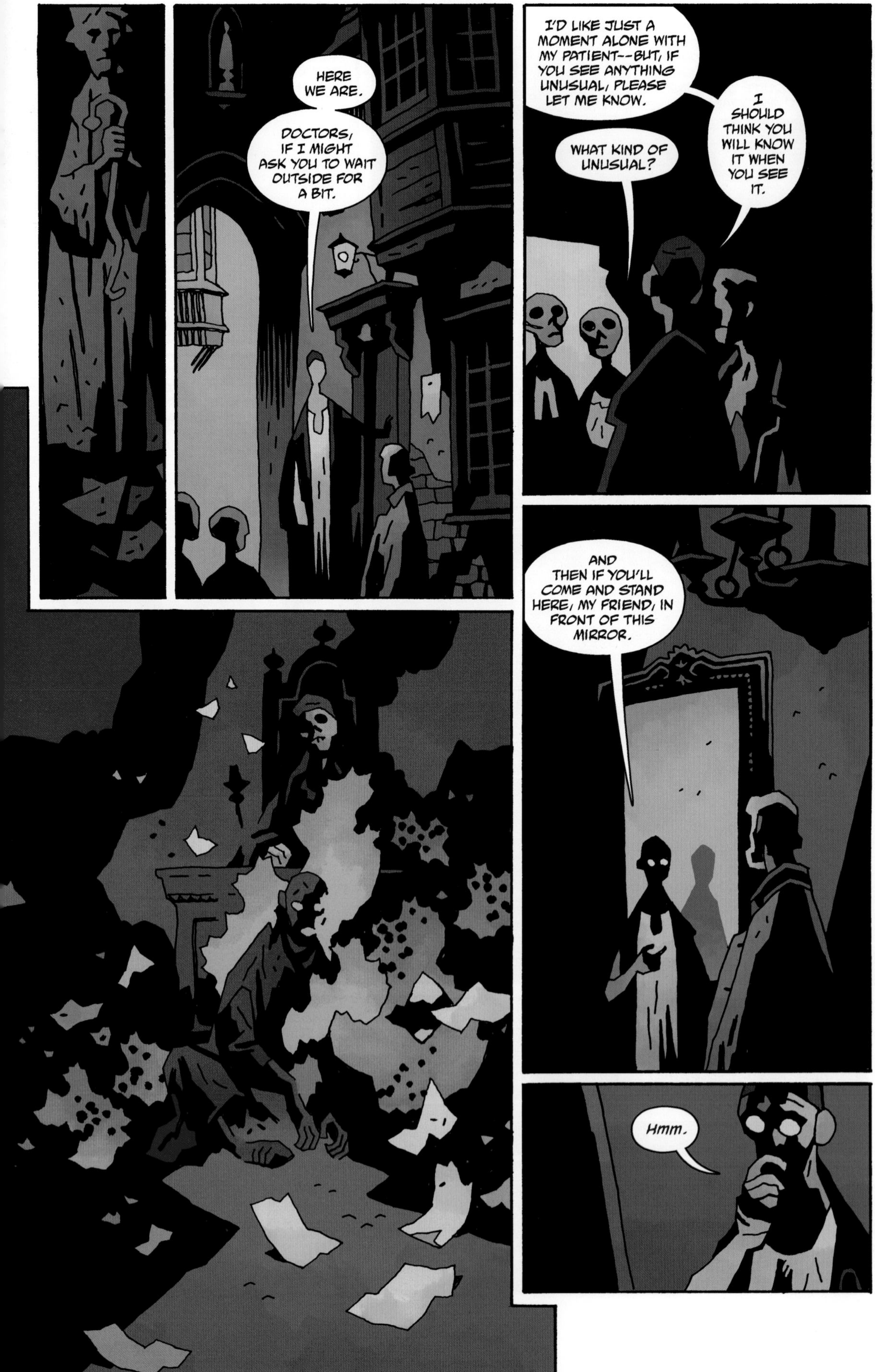
HERE WE ARE.
DOCTORS, IF I MIGHT ASK YOU TO WAIT OUTSIDE FOR A BIT.
I'D LIKE JUST A MOMENT ALONE WITH MY PATIENT--BUT, IF YOU SEE ANYTHING UNUSUAL, PLEASE LET ME KNOW.
WHAT KIND OF UNUSUAL?
I SHOULD THINK YOU WILL KNOW IT WHEN YOU SEE IT.
AND THEN IF YOU'LL COME AND STAND HERE, MY FRIEND, IN FRONT OF THIS MIRROR.
Hmm.

MATER DOLOROSA
ORA PRO NO
IS IT BAD?
I'M AFRAID SO.
DRINK THIS.
NOT A CURE, BUT IT SHOULD HOLD YOU OVER TILL YOUR SITUATION CAN BE PROPERLY DEALT WITH.
MATER DOLORO
UGH.
IT'S DISGUSTING.

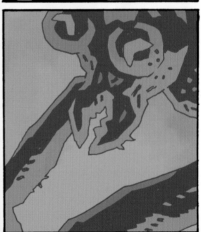

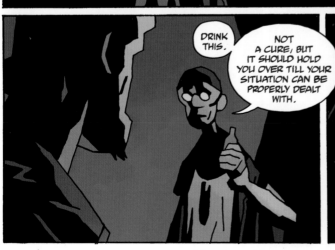

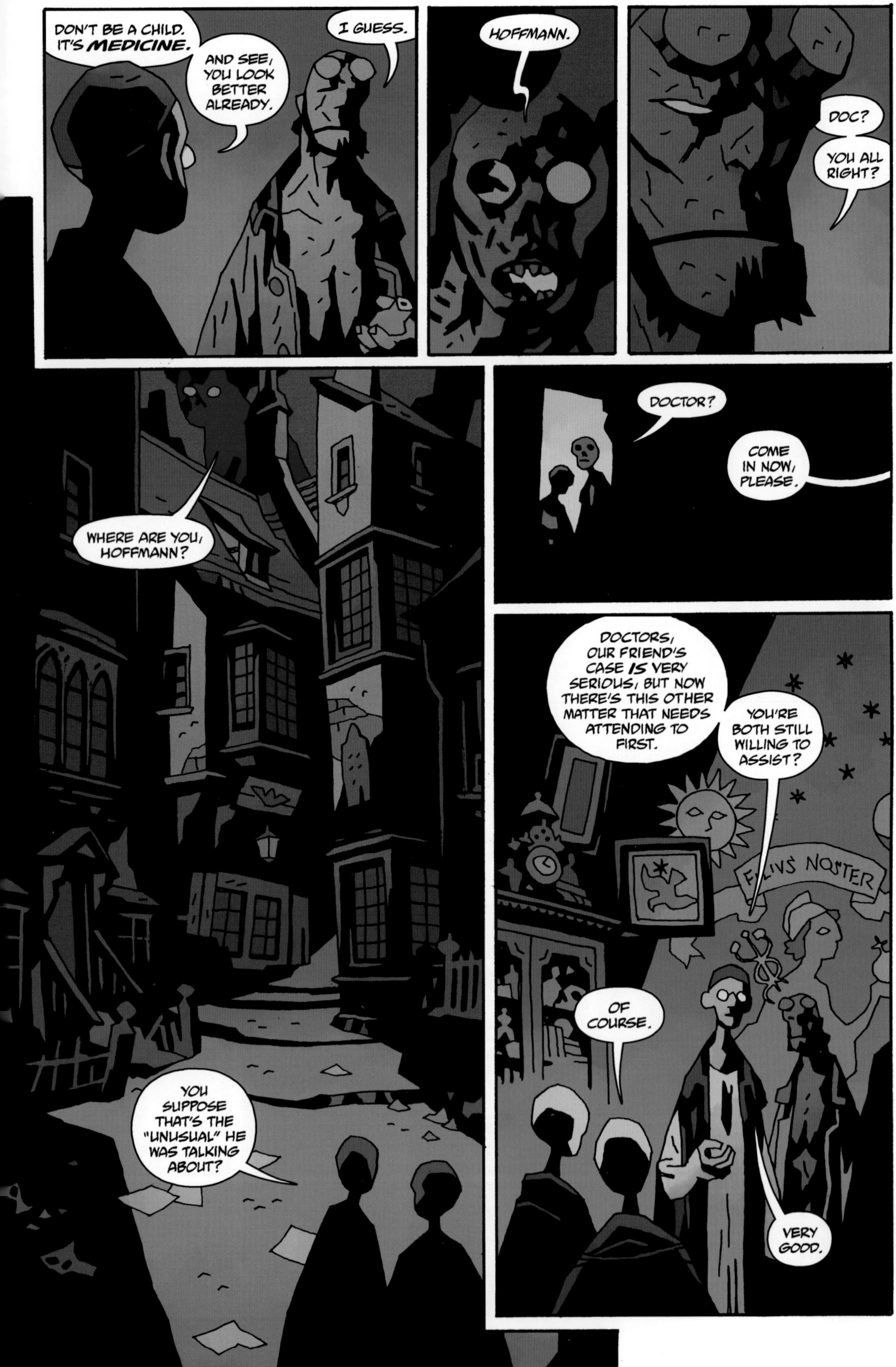
DON'T BE A CHILD. IT'S MEDICINE.
AND SEE, YOU LOOK BETTER ALREADY.
I GUESS.
HOFFMANN.
DOC?
YOU ALL RIGHT?
WHERE ARE YOU, HOFFMANN?
YOU SUPPOSE THAT'S THE "UNUSUAL" HE WAS TALKING ABOUT?
DOCTOR?
COME IN NOW, PLEASE.
DOCTORS, OUR FRIEND'S CASE IS VERY SERIOUS, BUT NOW THERE'S THIS OTHER MATTER THAT NEEDS ATTENDING TO FIRST.
YOU'RE BOTH STILL WILLING TO ASSIST?
OF COURSE.
VERY GOOD.

HOFFMANN!

DR. CHATRIAN, IF YOU'LL FETCH THAT DEAD CAT OFF THAT SHELF THERE...

AND DR. ERCKMANN.

IN THAT CABINET THERE, THIRD DRAWER FROM THE RIGHT, YOU'LL FIND A PIECE OF RED STRING.

?

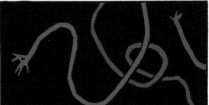

AND YOU--HOW ARE YOU FEELING?

PRETTY GOOD.

EXCELLENT. IN THAT ROOM OVER THERE YOU'LL FIND A LARGE TRUNK...

IF YOU'LL PLEASE DRAG THAT OUT BACK TO THE COURT-YARD.

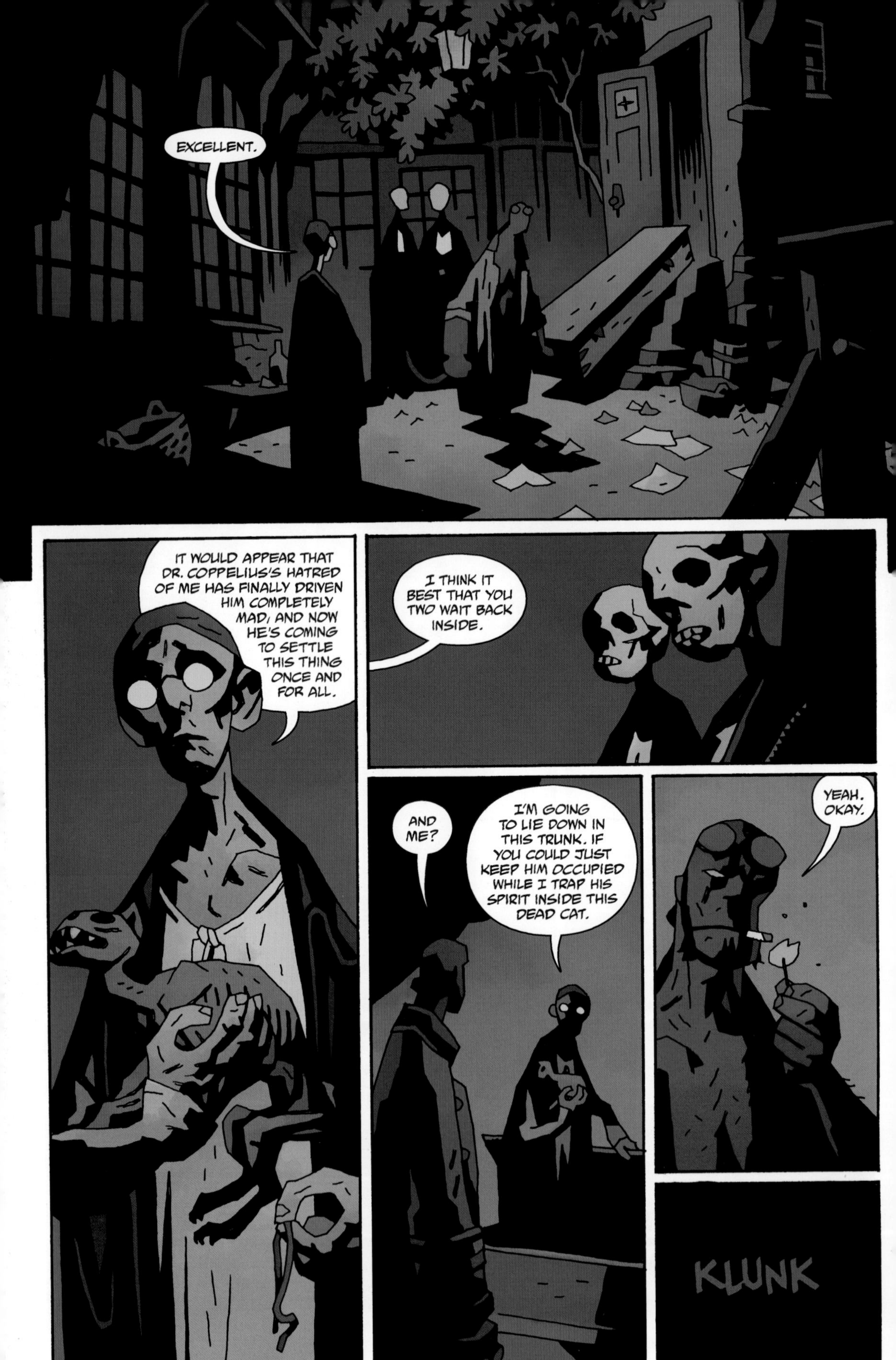
EXCELLENT.
IT WOULD APPEAR THAT DR. COPPELIUS'S HATRED OF ME HAS FINALLY DRIVEN HIM COMPLETELY MAD; AND NOW HE'S COMING TO SETTLE THIS THING ONCE AND FOR ALL.
I THINK IT BEST THAT YOU TWO WAIT BACK INSIDE.
AND ME?
I'M GOING TO LIE DOWN IN THIS TRUNK. IF YOU COULD JUST KEEP HIM OCCUPIED WHILE I TRAP HIS SPIRIT INSIDE THIS DEAD CAT.
YEAH. OKAY.
KLUNK

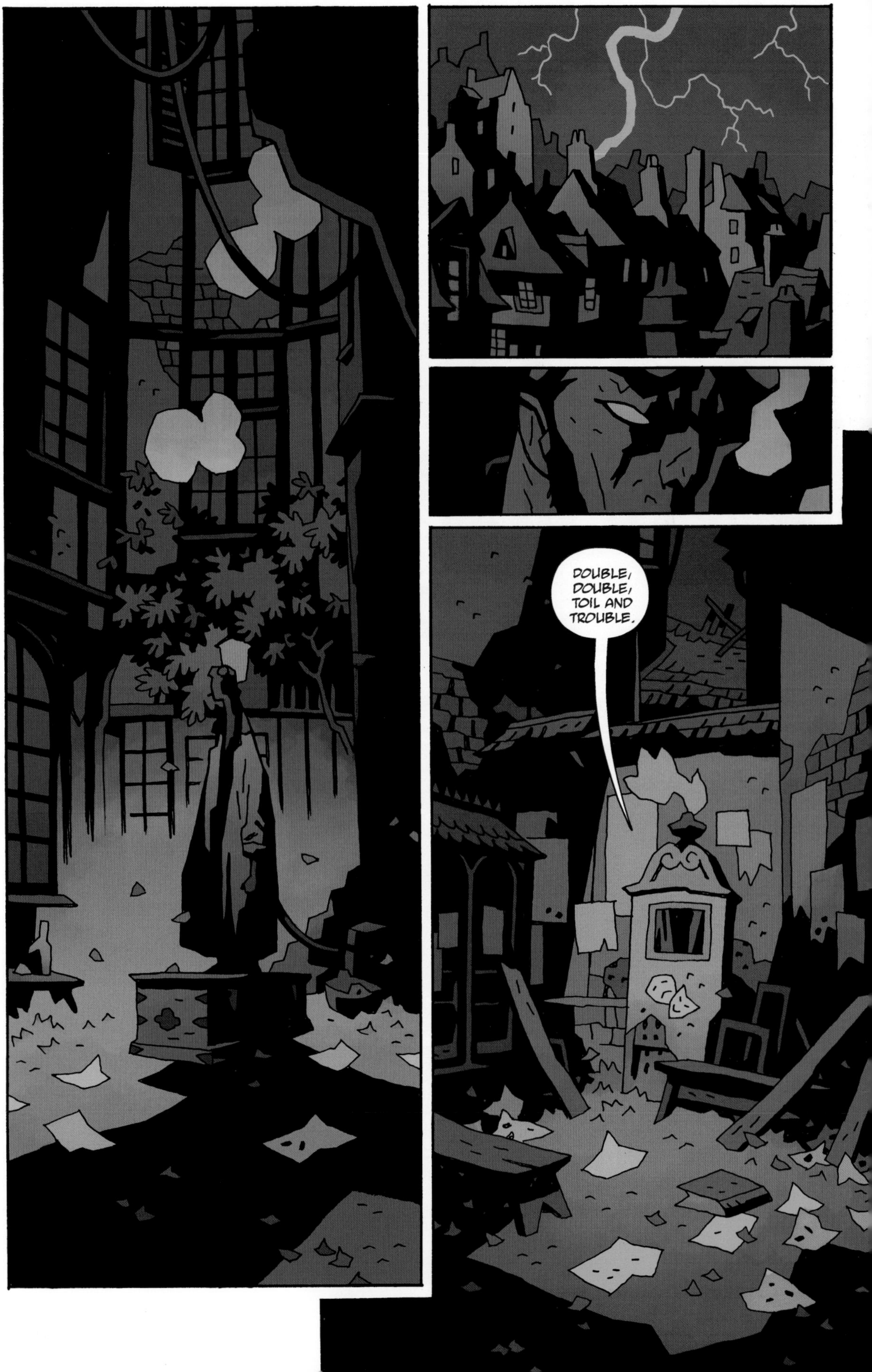
DOUBLE, DOUBLE, TOIL AND TROUBLE.

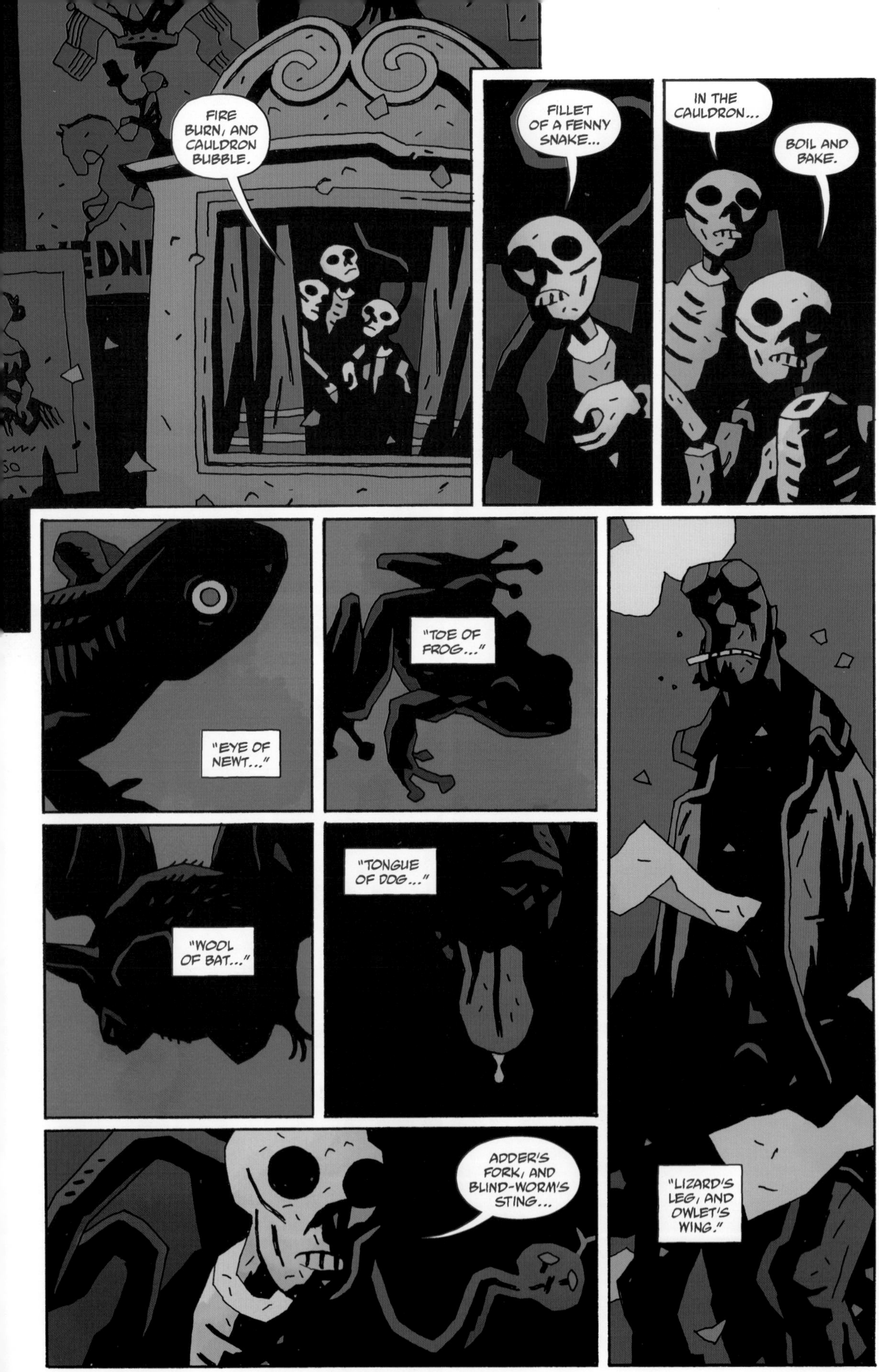

FIRE BURN, AND CAULDRON BUBBLE.
FILLET OF A FENNY SNAKE...
IN THE CAULDRON...
BOIL AND BAKE.
"EYE OF NEWT..."
"TOE OF FROG..."
"WOOL OF BAT..."
"TONGUE OF DOG..."
ADDER'S FORK, AND BLIND-WORM'S STING...
"LIZARD'S LEG, AND OWLET'S WING."

DOUBLE, DOUBLE...

TOIL AND TROUBLE.

"LIKE A HELL BROTH BOIL AND BUBBLE."

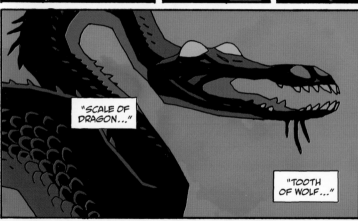

"SCALE OF DRAGON..."

"TOOTH OF WOLF..."

BY THE PRICKING OF MY THUMBS...

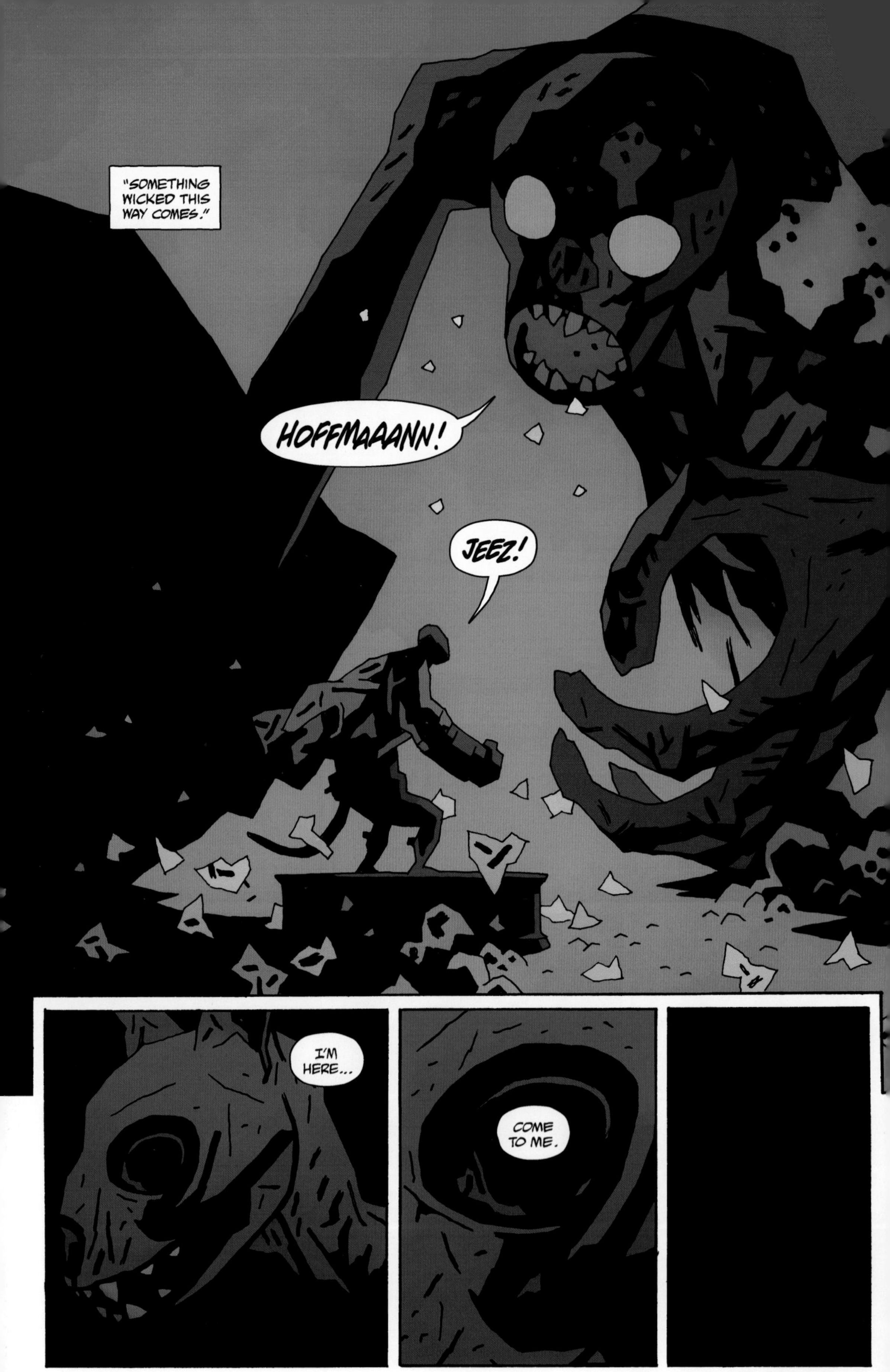
"SOMETHING WICKED THIS WAY COMES."
HOFFMAAANN!
JEEZ!
I'M HERE...
COME TO ME.

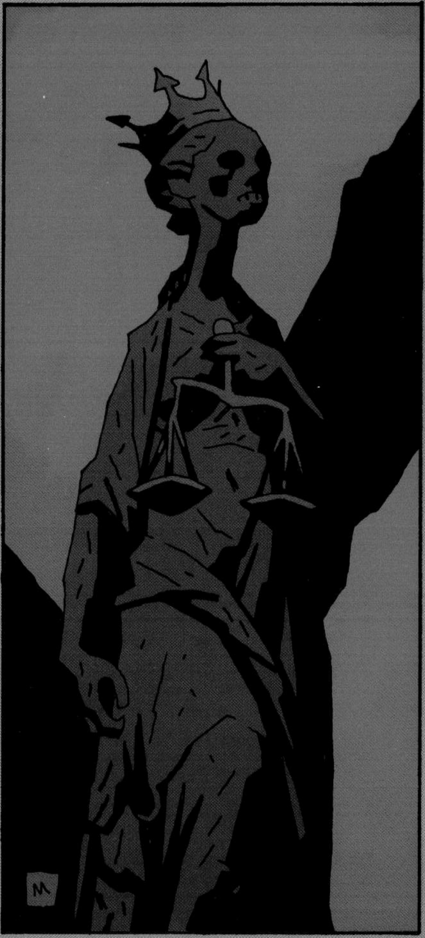

CHAPTER THREE

THE HOUNDS OF PLUTO

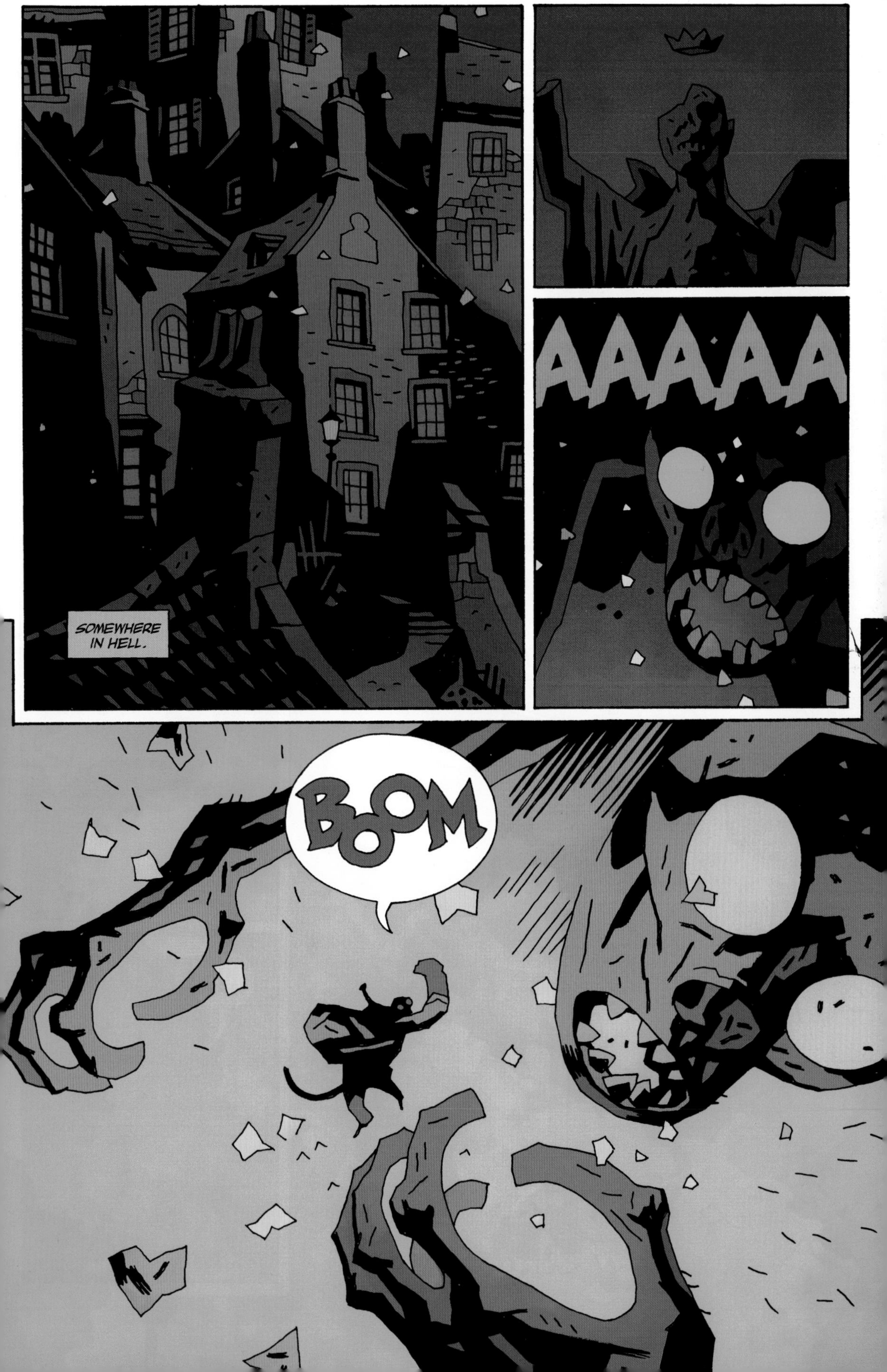
SOMEWHERE IN HELL.
AAAAA
BOOOM

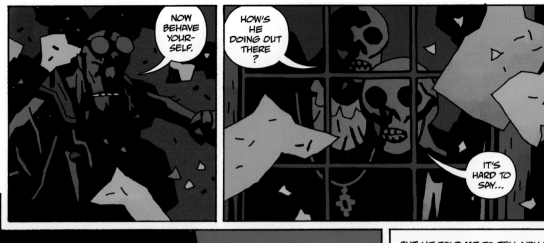

NOW BEHAVE YOURSELF.

HOW'S HE DOING OUT THERE?

IT'S HARD TO SAY...

BUT HE TOLD ME TO TELL YOU TO STICK AROUND UNTIL HE--

AAAA

HOFFMAANN!

RELAX.

I THINK HE WENT NEXT DOOR TO BORROW A MANDRAKE ROOT.

WILHELM.

I'M. HERE.

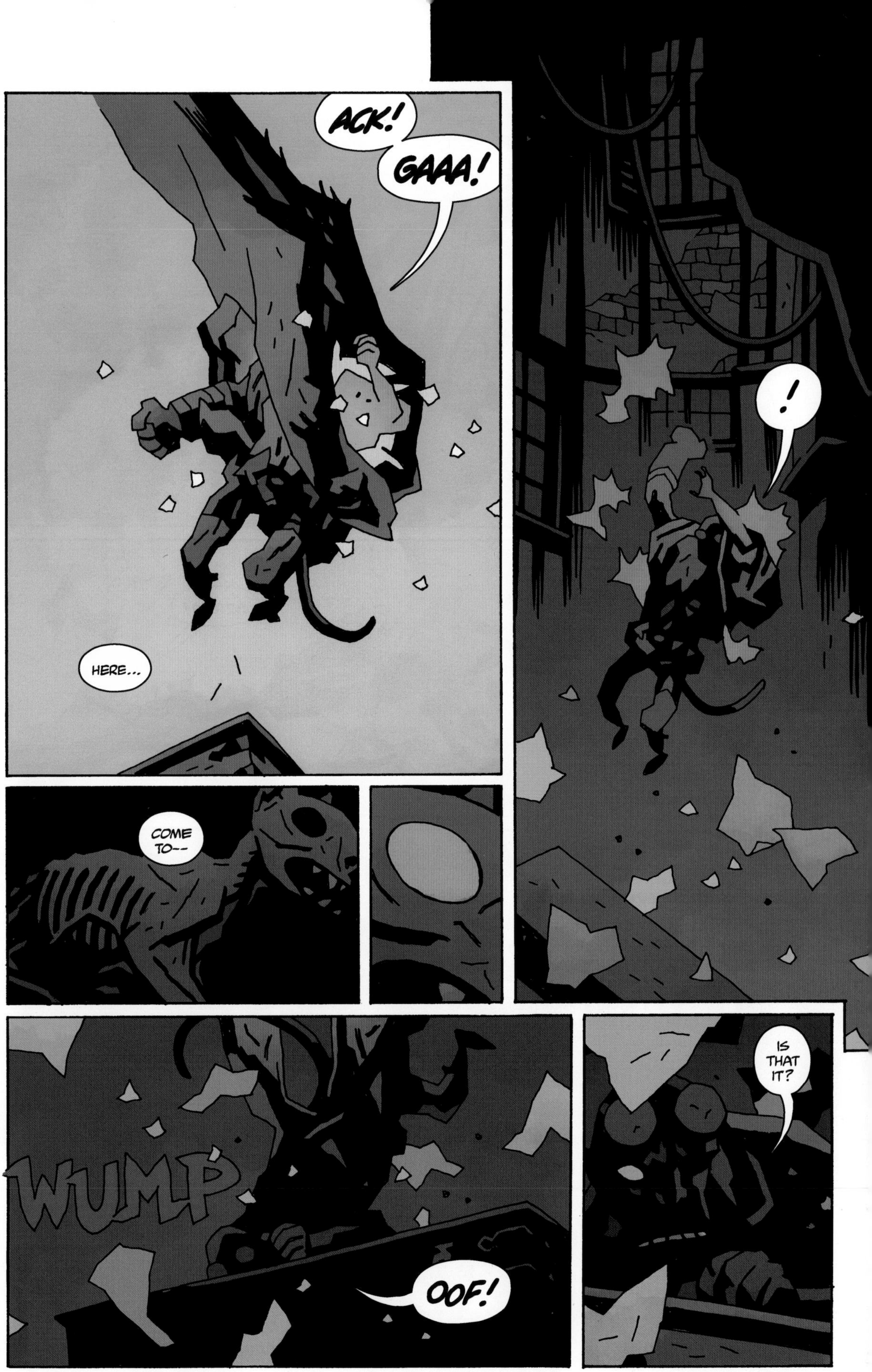
ACK!
GAAA!
HERE...
!
COME TO--
WUMP
OOF!
IS THAT IT?

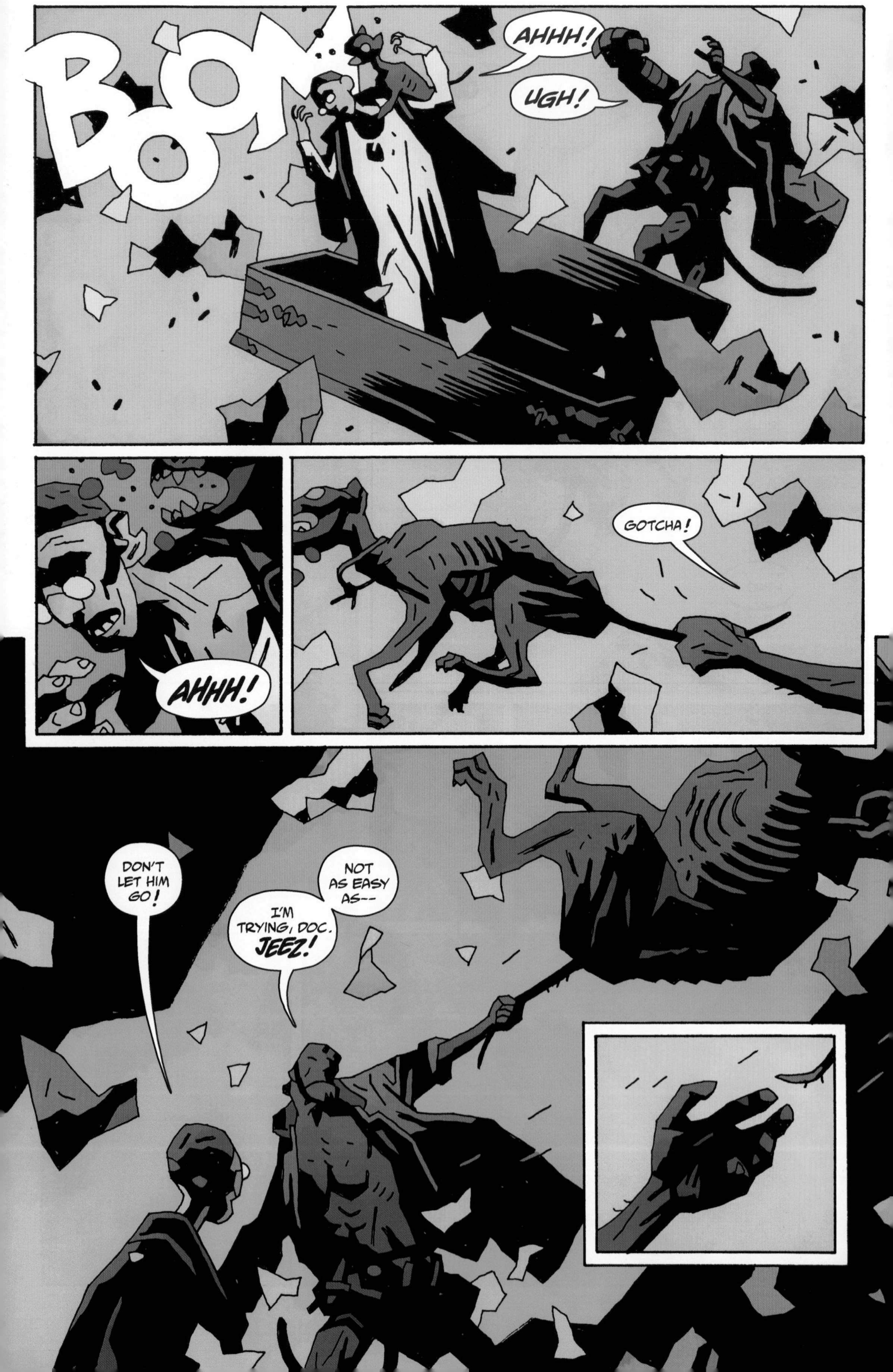
BOOM
AHHH!
UGH!
AHHH!
GOTCHA!
DON'T LET HIM GO!
NOT AS EASY AS--
I'M TRYING, DOC. JEEZ!

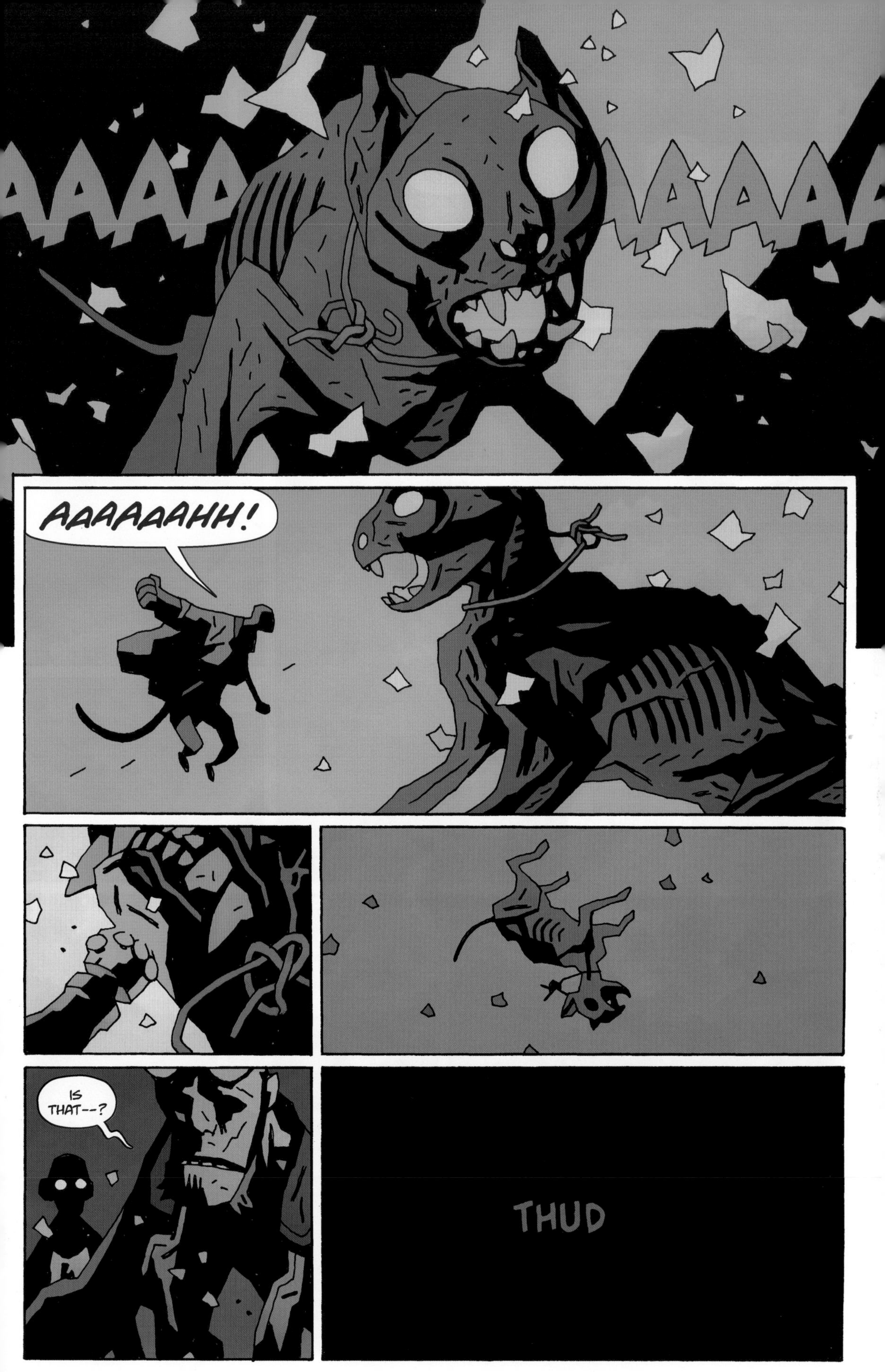
AAAAAAAAAAAA
AAAAAAHH!
IS THAT--?
THUD

HE'S
OFF
AGAIN.

IS
HE--?

NO.
BRING HIM
INSIDE.

CRAP...

I'M **SO** SORRY, MY
FRIEND. I WAS RUSHED
AND DIDN'T HAVE THE
STRING 'ROUND THE
CAT'S NECK QUITE TIGHT
ENOUGH. BUT NOT TO
WORRY, IT'S ALL
PROPERLY DONE
NOW.

AND
HOW ARE
YOU
FEELING
?

I COULD USE SOME
MORE OF THAT MEDICINE
OF YOURS.

I'M
AFRAID
IT'S TOO LATE
FOR THAT TO
DO YOU ANY
GOOD.

DAMN.

DON'T
WORRY. I'M
NOW ABLE TO
GIVE YOUR
CASE MY FULL
ATTENTION.

HOFFMANN...

I'M
ALL
YOURS,
DOC.

GOOD.

AND, DOCTORS,
I'M HAPPY TO HAVE
YOU COME WITH US,
BUT I MUST WARN YOU,
THERE COULD BE
CONSIDERABLE
DANGER.

OH.

SKRITCH

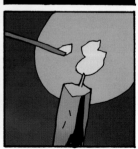

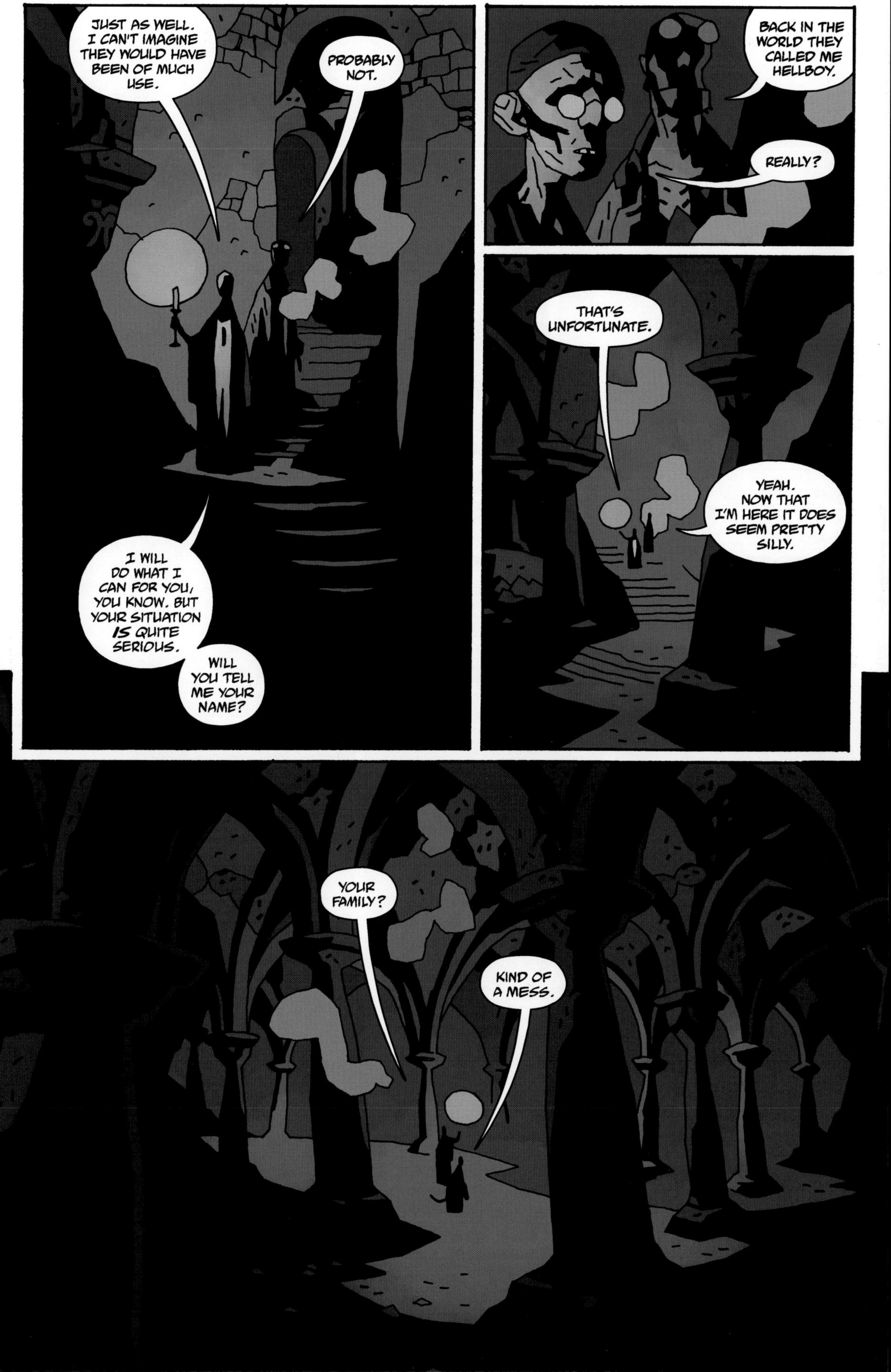
JUST AS WELL. I CAN'T IMAGINE THEY WOULD HAVE BEEN OF MUCH USE.
PROBABLY NOT.
I WILL DO WHAT I CAN FOR YOU, YOU KNOW. BUT YOUR SITUATION *IS* QUITE SERIOUS.
WILL YOU TELL ME YOUR NAME?
BACK IN THE WORLD THEY CALLED ME HELLBOY.
REALLY?
THAT'S UNFORTUNATE.
YEAH. NOW THAT I'M HERE IT DOES SEEM PRETTY SILLY.
YOUR FAMILY?
KIND OF A MESS.

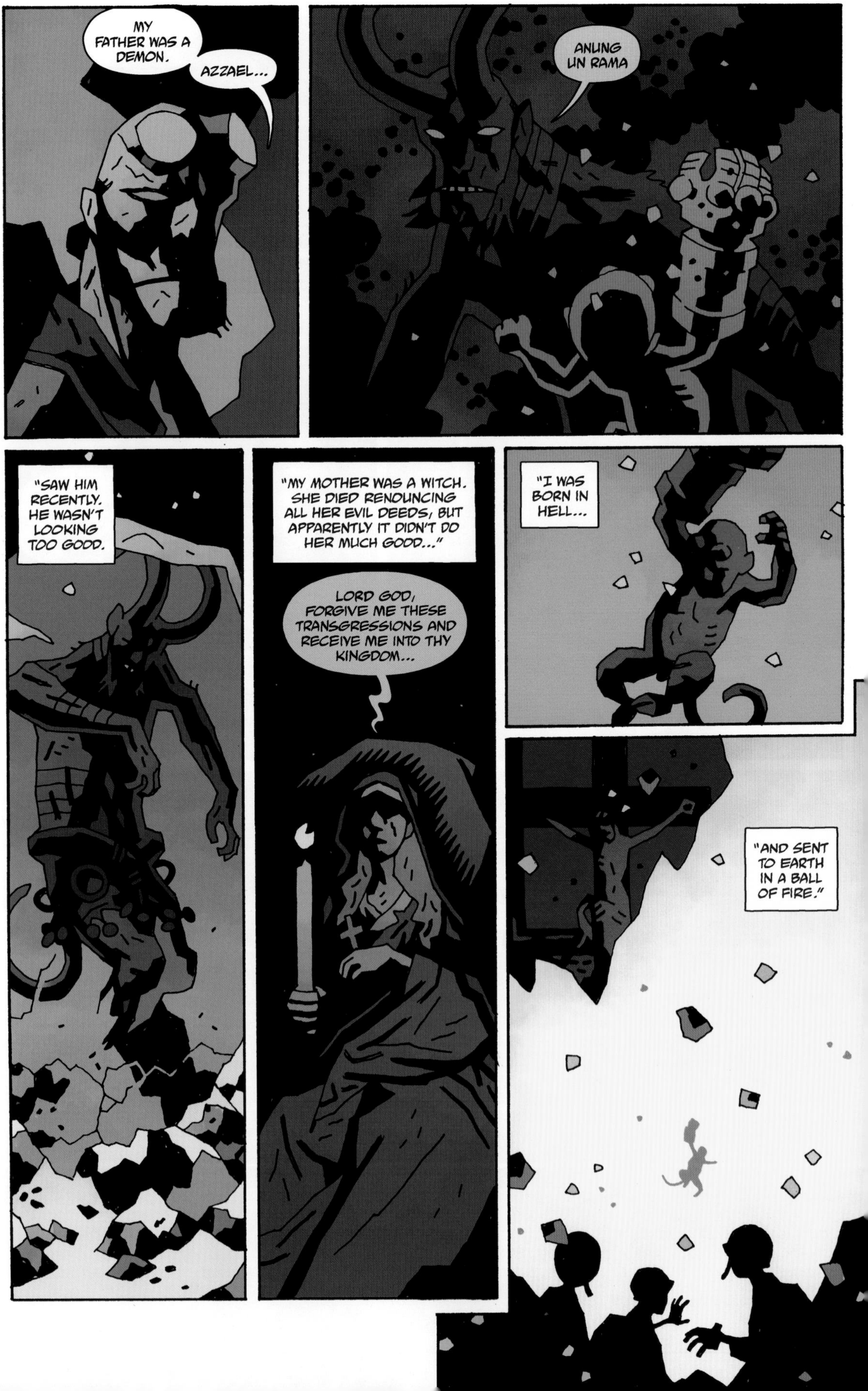
MY FATHER WAS A DEMON.
AZZAEL...
ANUNG UN RAMA
"SAW HIM RECENTLY. HE WASN'T LOOKING TOO GOOD.
"MY MOTHER WAS A WITCH. SHE DIED RENOUNCING ALL HER EVIL DEEDS, BUT APPARENTLY IT DIDN'T DO HER MUCH GOOD..."
LORD GOD, FORGIVE ME THESE TRANSGRESSIONS AND RECEIVE ME INTO THY KINGDOM...
"I WAS BORN IN HELL...
"AND SENT TO EARTH IN A BALL OF FIRE."

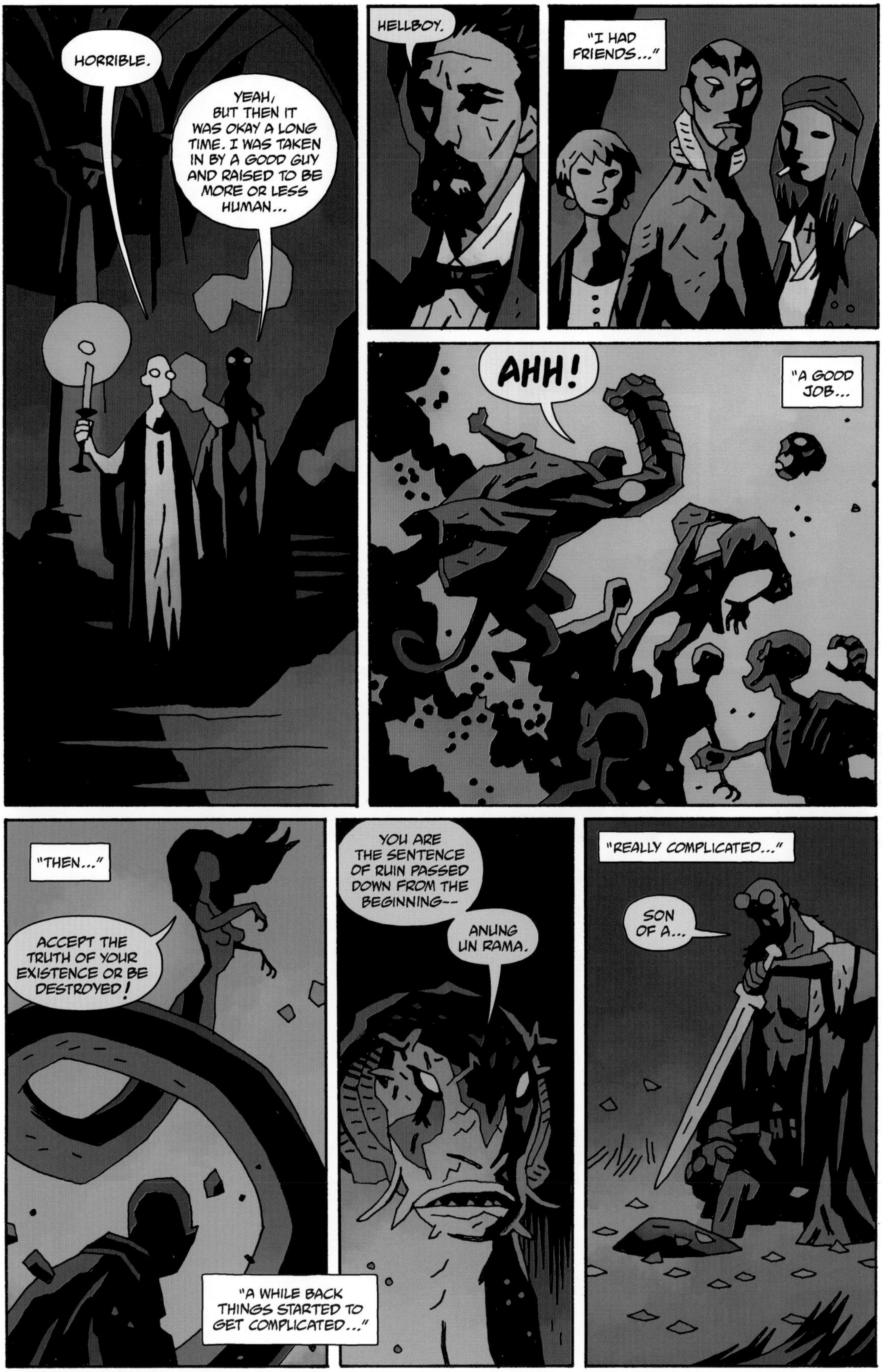
HORRIBLE.
YEAH, BUT THEN IT WAS OKAY A LONG TIME. I WAS TAKEN IN BY A GOOD GUY AND RAISED TO BE MORE OR LESS HUMAN...
HELLBOY.
"I HAD FRIENDS..."
AHH!
"A GOOD JOB...
"THEN..."
ACCEPT THE TRUTH OF YOUR EXISTENCE OR BE DESTROYED!
YOU ARE THE SENTENCE OF RUIN PASSED DOWN FROM THE BEGINNING--
ANUNG UN RAMA.
"A WHILE BACK THINGS STARTED TO GET COMPLICATED..."
"REALLY COMPLICATED..."
SON OF A...

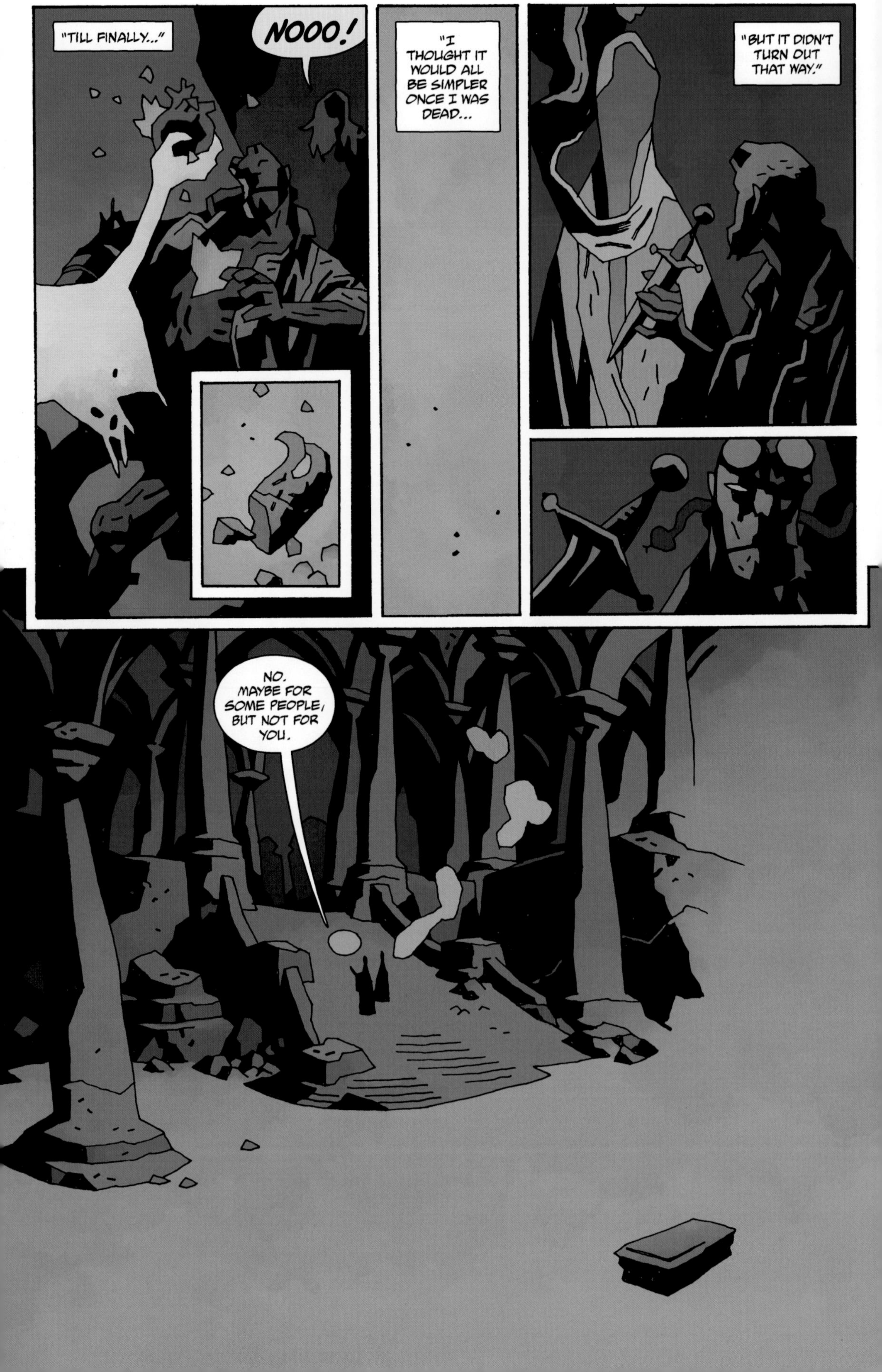
"TILL FINALLY..."
NOOO!
"I THOUGHT IT WOULD ALL BE SIMPLER ONCE I WAS DEAD...
"BUT IT DIDN'T TURN OUT THAT WAY."
NO. MAYBE FOR SOME PEOPLE, BUT NOT FOR YOU.

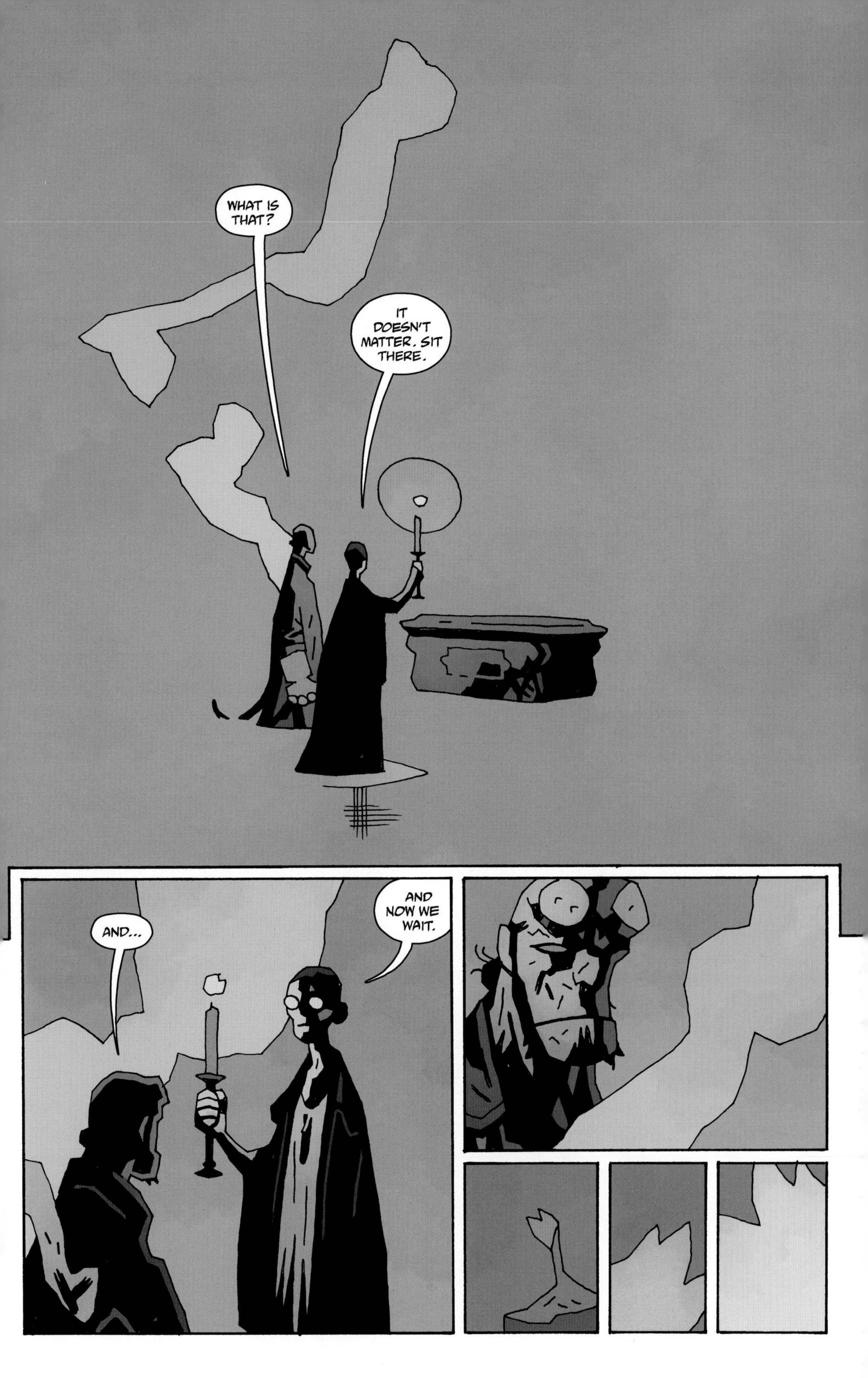
WHAT IS THAT?
IT DOESN'T MATTER. SIT THERE.
AND...
AND NOW WE WAIT.

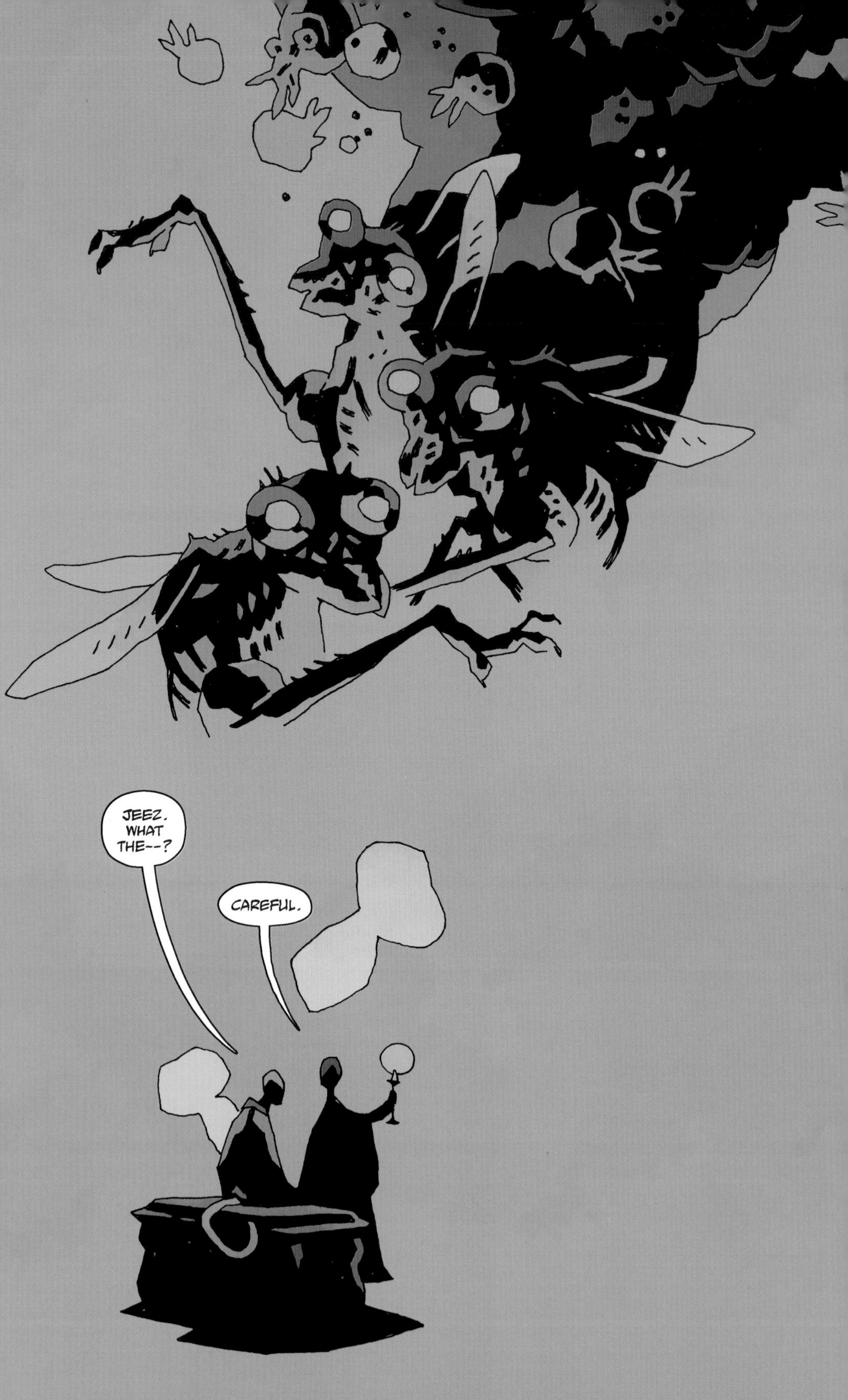
JEEZ. WHAT THE--?
CAREFUL.

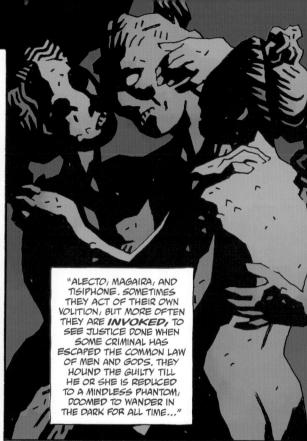

WHATEVER HAPPENS NOW, LET ME DO THE TALKING.

OKAY, BUT WHAT ARE THEY?

THE ERINYES, SOMETIMES CALLED THE FURIES...

"ALECTO, MAGAIRA, AND TISIPHONE. SOMETIMES THEY ACT OF THEIR OWN VOLITION, BUT MORE OFTEN THEY ARE *INVOKED*, TO SEE JUSTICE DONE WHEN SOME CRIMINAL HAS ESCAPED THE COMMON LAW OF MEN AND GODS. THEY HOUND THE GUILTY TILL HE OR SHE IS REDUCED TO A MINDLESS PHANTOM, DOOMED TO WANDER IN THE DARK FOR ALL TIME..."

INVISIBLE TILL NOW, THESE ARE THE CREATURES THAT HAVE BEEN HOUNDING *YOU*, GNAWING AWAY AT YOUR SOUL.

WHY ME?

IT'S A FAIR QUESTION. WHAT HAS THIS MAN DONE?

MURDER.

MURDER.

MURDER.

HE WILL NOT DENY THE CHARGE.

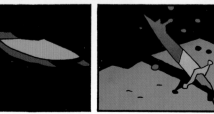

CLANG

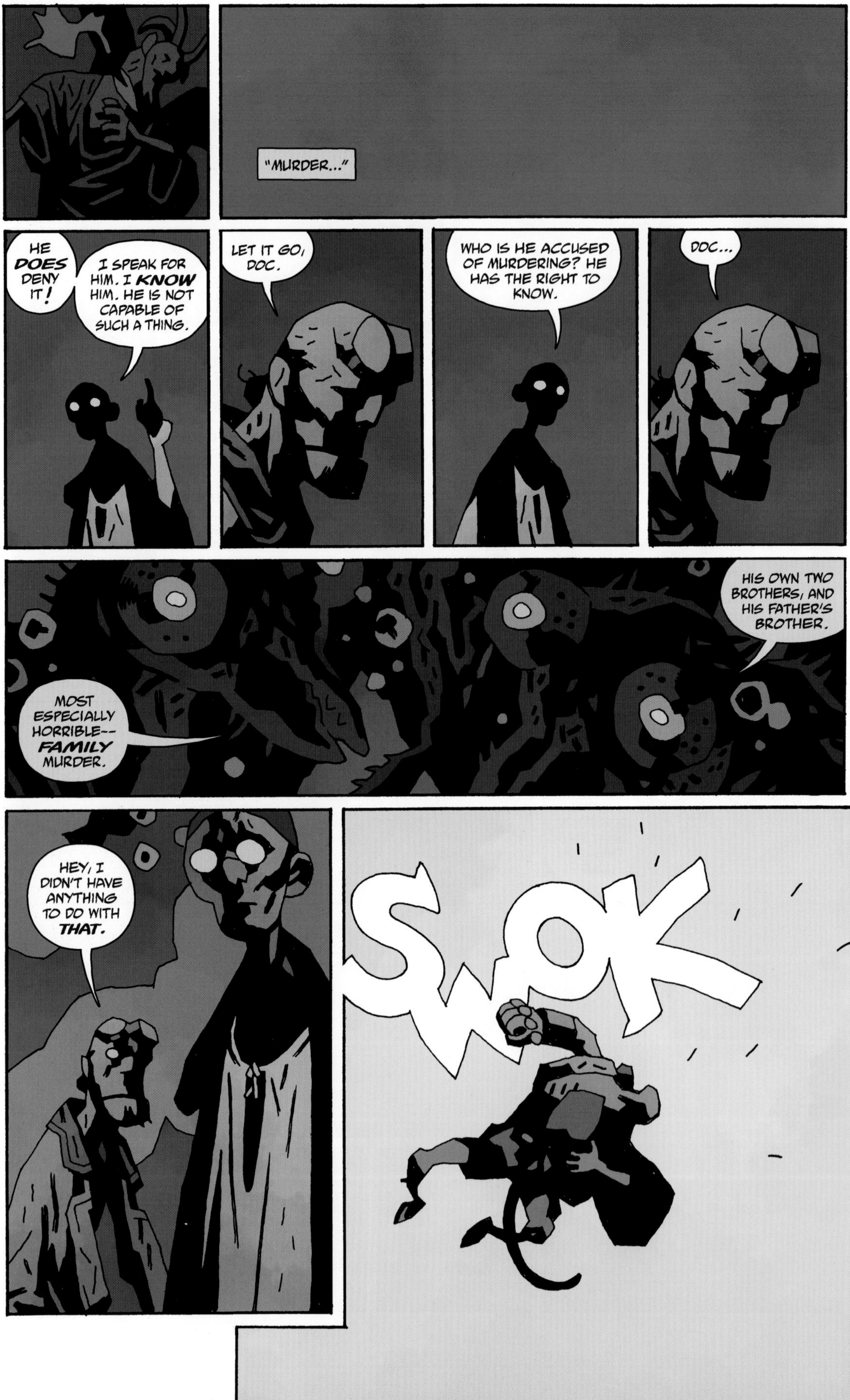
"MURDER..."
HE DOES DENY IT!
I SPEAK FOR HIM. I KNOW HIM. HE IS NOT CAPABLE OF SUCH A THING.
LET IT GO, DOC.
WHO IS HE ACCUSED OF MURDERING? HE HAS THE RIGHT TO KNOW.
DOC...
HIS OWN TWO BROTHERS, AND HIS FATHER'S BROTHER.
MOST ESPECIALLY HORRIBLE-- FAMILY MURDER.
HEY, I DIDN'T HAVE ANYTHING TO DO WITH THAT.
SWOK

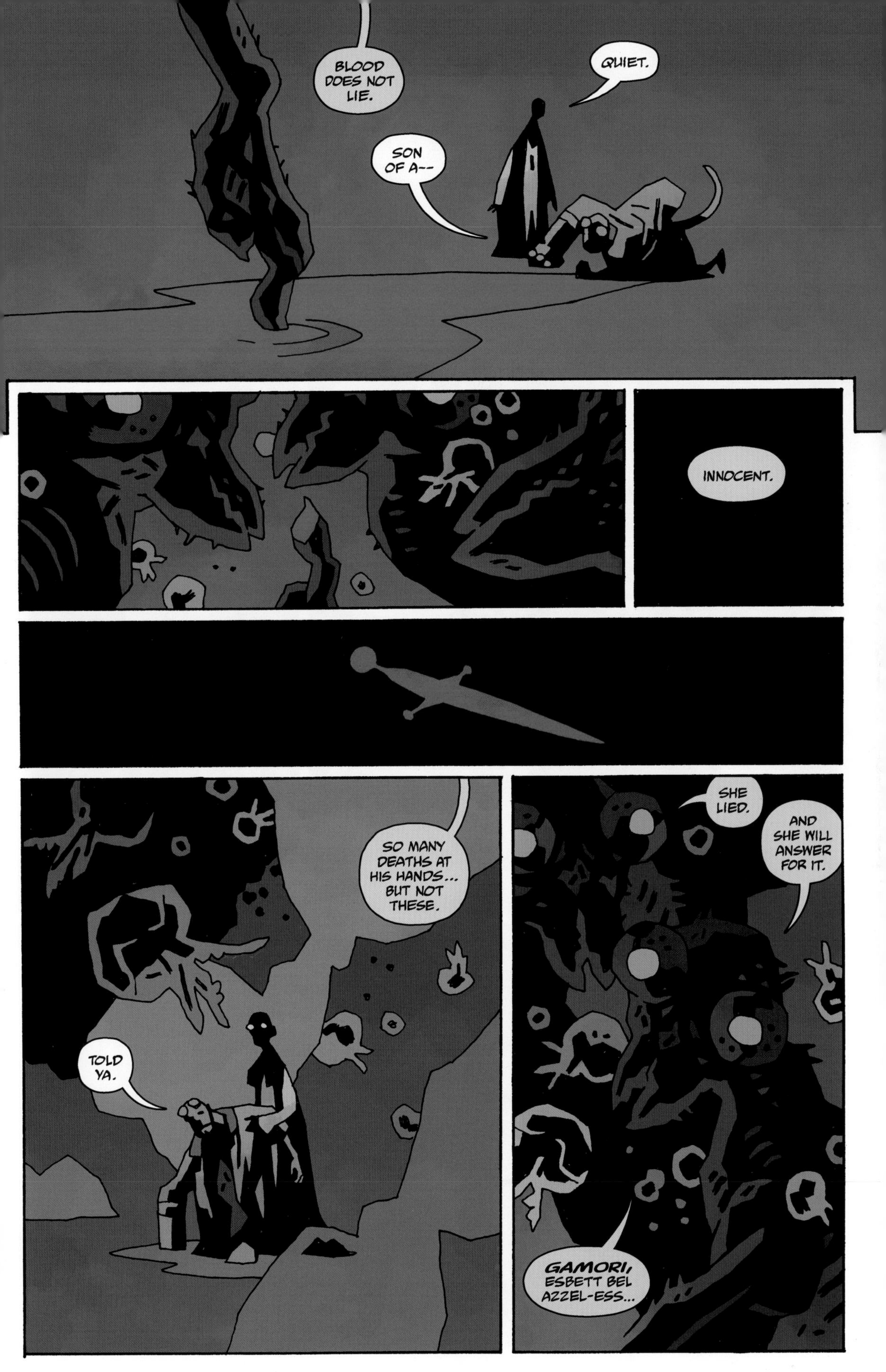
BLOOD DOES NOT LIE.
QUIET.
SON OF A--
INNOCENT.
SO MANY DEATHS AT HIS HANDS... BUT NOT THESE.
TOLD YA.
SHE LIED.
AND SHE WILL ANSWER FOR IT.
GAMORI, ESBETT BEL AZZEL-ESS...

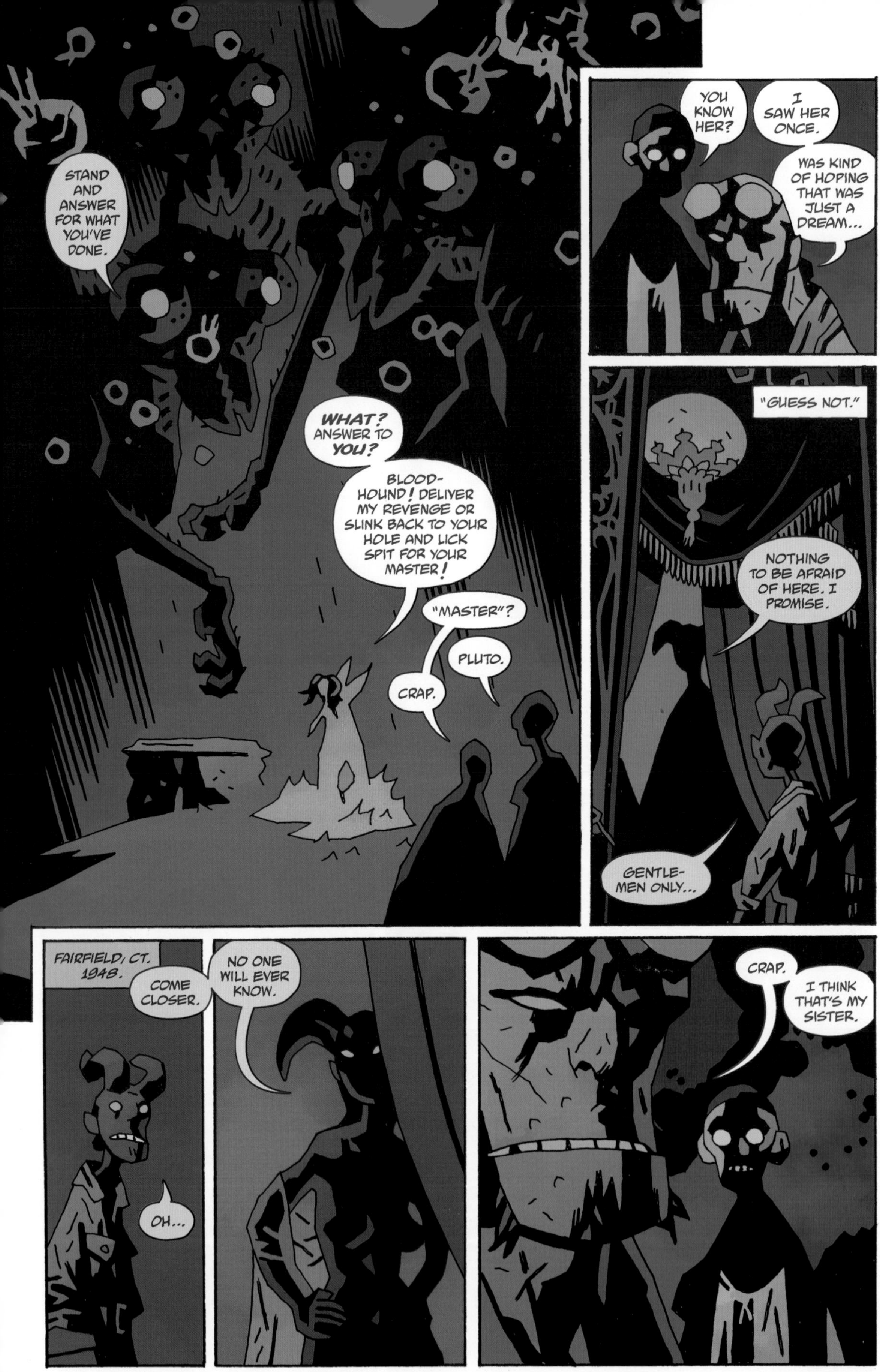
STAND AND ANSWER FOR WHAT YOU'VE DONE.
WHAT? ANSWER TO YOU?
BLOOD-HOUND! DELIVER MY REVENGE OR SLINK BACK TO YOUR HOLE AND LICK SPIT FOR YOUR MASTER!
"MASTER"?
PLUTO.
CRAP.
YOU KNOW HER?
I SAW HER ONCE.
WAS KIND OF HOPING THAT WAS JUST A DREAM...
"GUESS NOT."
NOTHING TO BE AFRAID OF HERE. I PROMISE.
GENTLE-MEN ONLY...
FAIRFIELD, CT. 1948.
COME CLOSER.
OH...
NO ONE WILL EVER KNOW.
CRAP.
I THINK THAT'S MY SISTER.

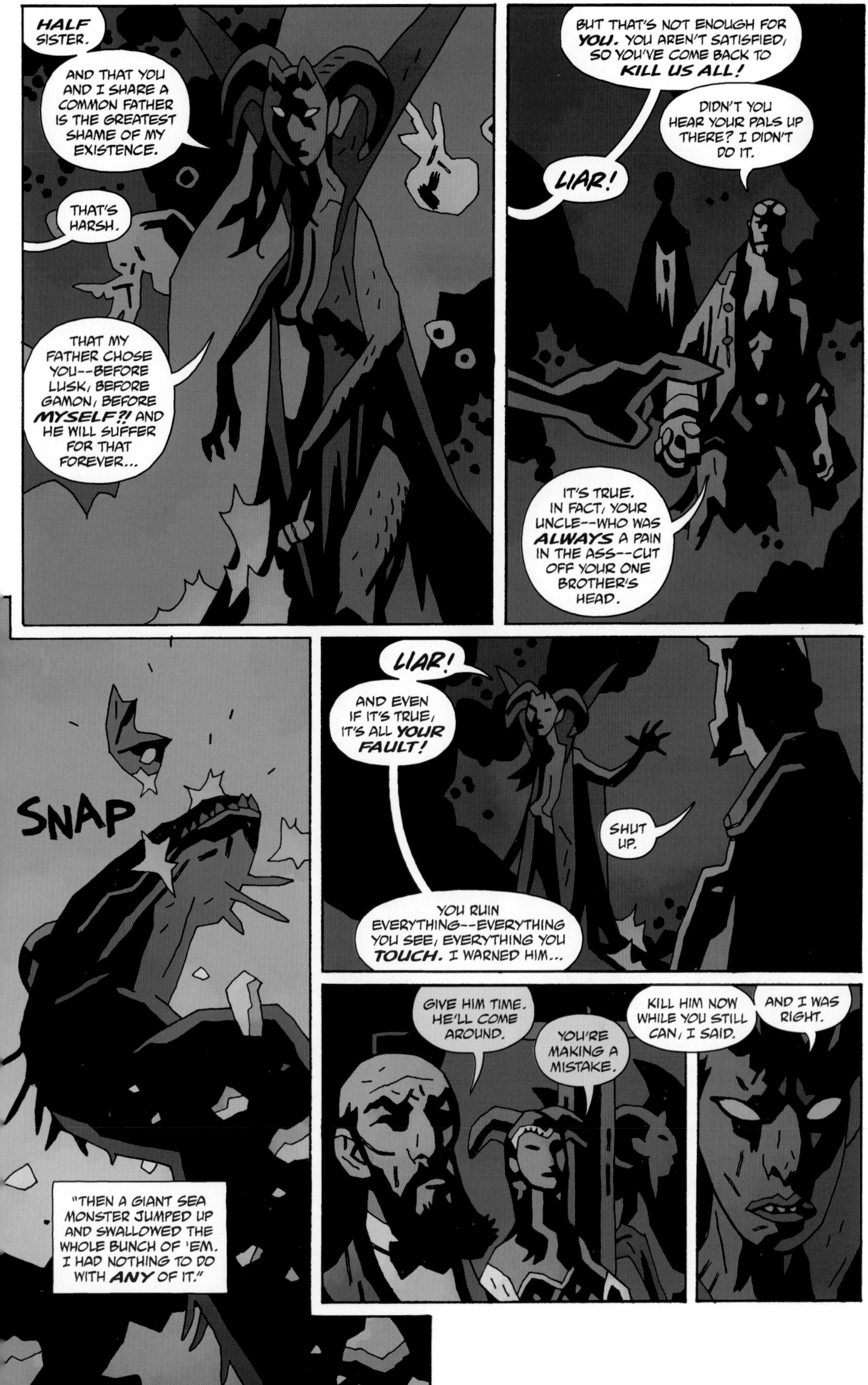
HALF SISTER.
AND THAT YOU AND I SHARE A COMMON FATHER IS THE GREATEST SHAME OF MY EXISTENCE.
THAT'S HARSH.
THAT MY FATHER CHOSE YOU--BEFORE LUSK, BEFORE GAMON, BEFORE MYSELF?! AND HE WILL SUFFER FOR THAT FOREVER...
BUT THAT'S NOT ENOUGH FOR YOU. YOU AREN'T SATISFIED, SO YOU'VE COME BACK TO KILL US ALL!
DIDN'T YOU HEAR YOUR PALS UP THERE? I DIDN'T DO IT.
LIAR!
IT'S TRUE. IN FACT, YOUR UNCLE--WHO WAS ALWAYS A PAIN IN THE ASS--CUT OFF YOUR ONE BROTHER'S HEAD.
SNAP
"THEN A GIANT SEA MONSTER JUMPED UP AND SWALLOWED THE WHOLE BUNCH OF 'EM. I HAD NOTHING TO DO WITH ANY OF IT."
LIAR!
AND EVEN IF IT'S TRUE, IT'S ALL YOUR FAULT!
SHUT UP.
YOU RUIN EVERYTHING--EVERYTHING YOU SEE, EVERYTHING YOU TOUCH. I WARNED HIM...
GIVE HIM TIME. HE'LL COME AROUND.
YOU'RE MAKING A MISTAKE.
KILL HIM NOW WHILE YOU STILL CAN, I SAID.
AND I WAS RIGHT.

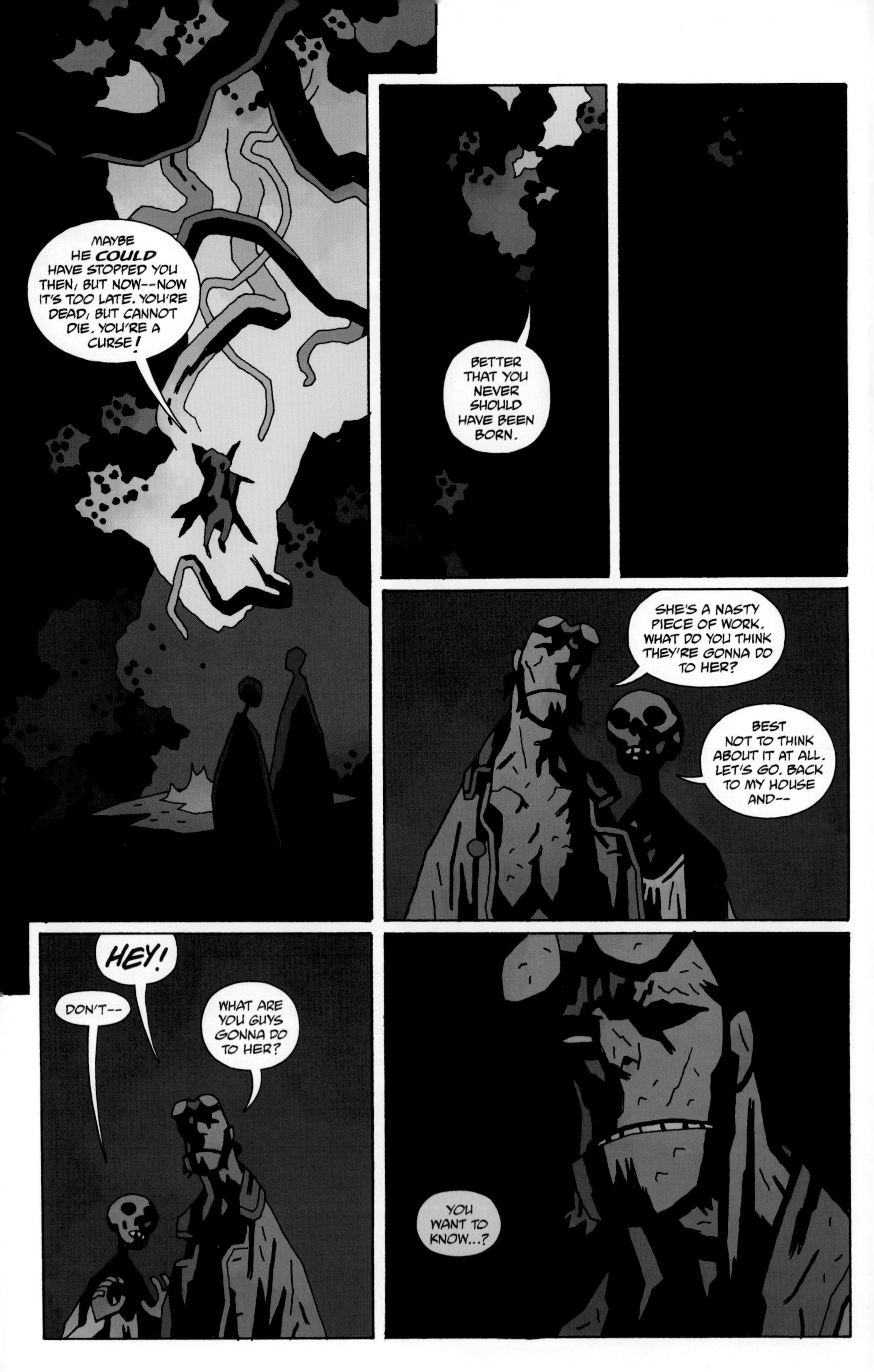
MAYBE HE COULD HAVE STOPPED YOU THEN, BUT NOW--NOW IT'S TOO LATE. YOU'RE DEAD, BUT CANNOT DIE. YOU'RE A CURSE!
BETTER THAT YOU NEVER SHOULD HAVE BEEN BORN.
SHE'S A NASTY PIECE OF WORK. WHAT DO YOU THINK THEY'RE GONNA DO TO HER?
BEST NOT TO THINK ABOUT IT AT ALL. LET'S GO. BACK TO MY HOUSE AND--
HEY!
DON'T--
WHAT ARE YOU GUYS GONNA DO TO HER?
YOU WANT TO KNOW...?

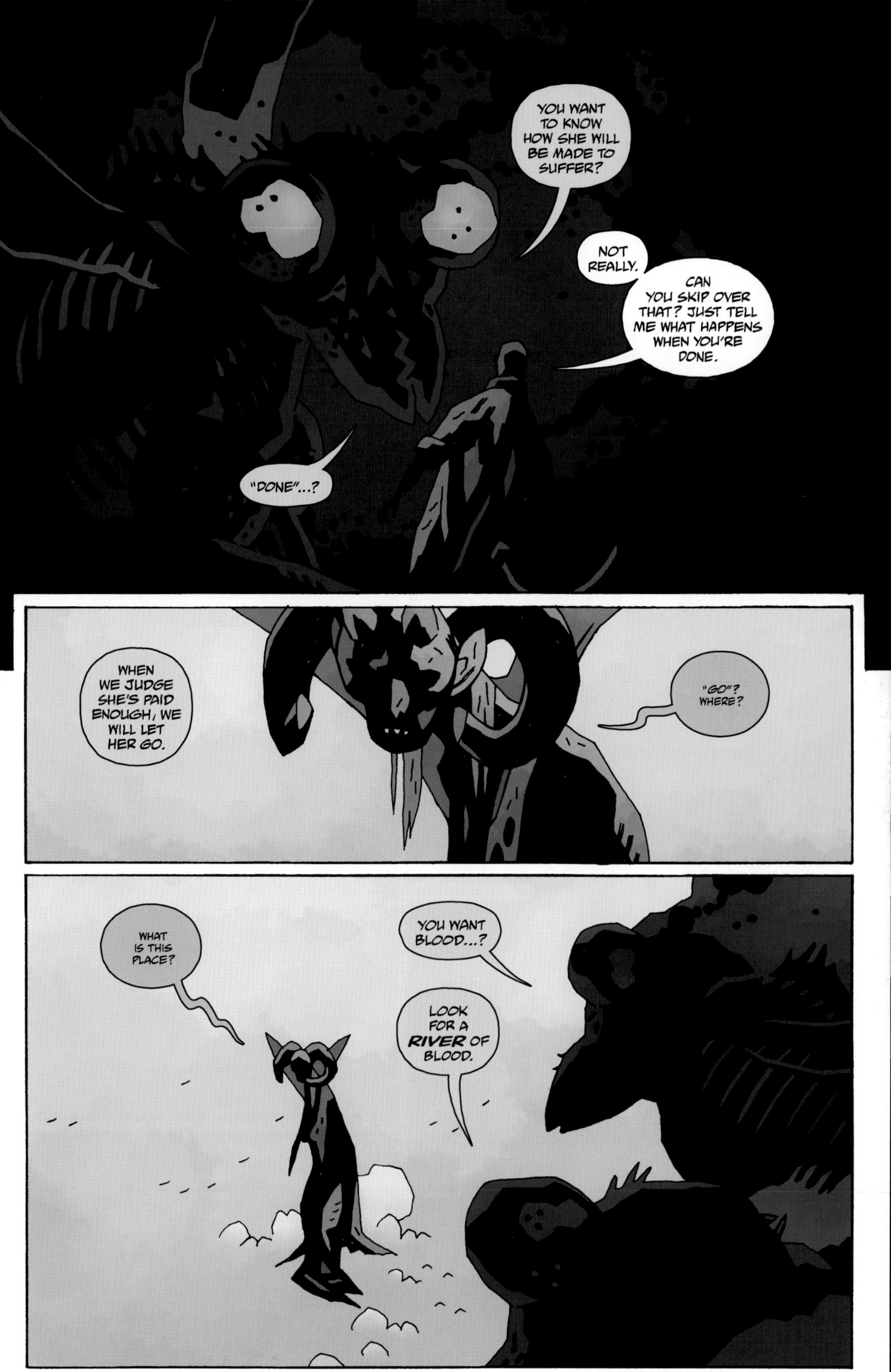
YOU WANT TO KNOW HOW SHE WILL BE MADE TO SUFFER?
NOT REALLY.
CAN YOU SKIP OVER THAT? JUST TELL ME WHAT HAPPENS WHEN YOU'RE DONE.
"DONE"...?
WHEN WE JUDGE SHE'S PAID ENOUGH, WE WILL LET HER GO.
"GO"? WHERE?
WHAT IS THIS PLACE?
YOU WANT BLOOD...?
LOOK FOR A RIVER OF BLOOD.

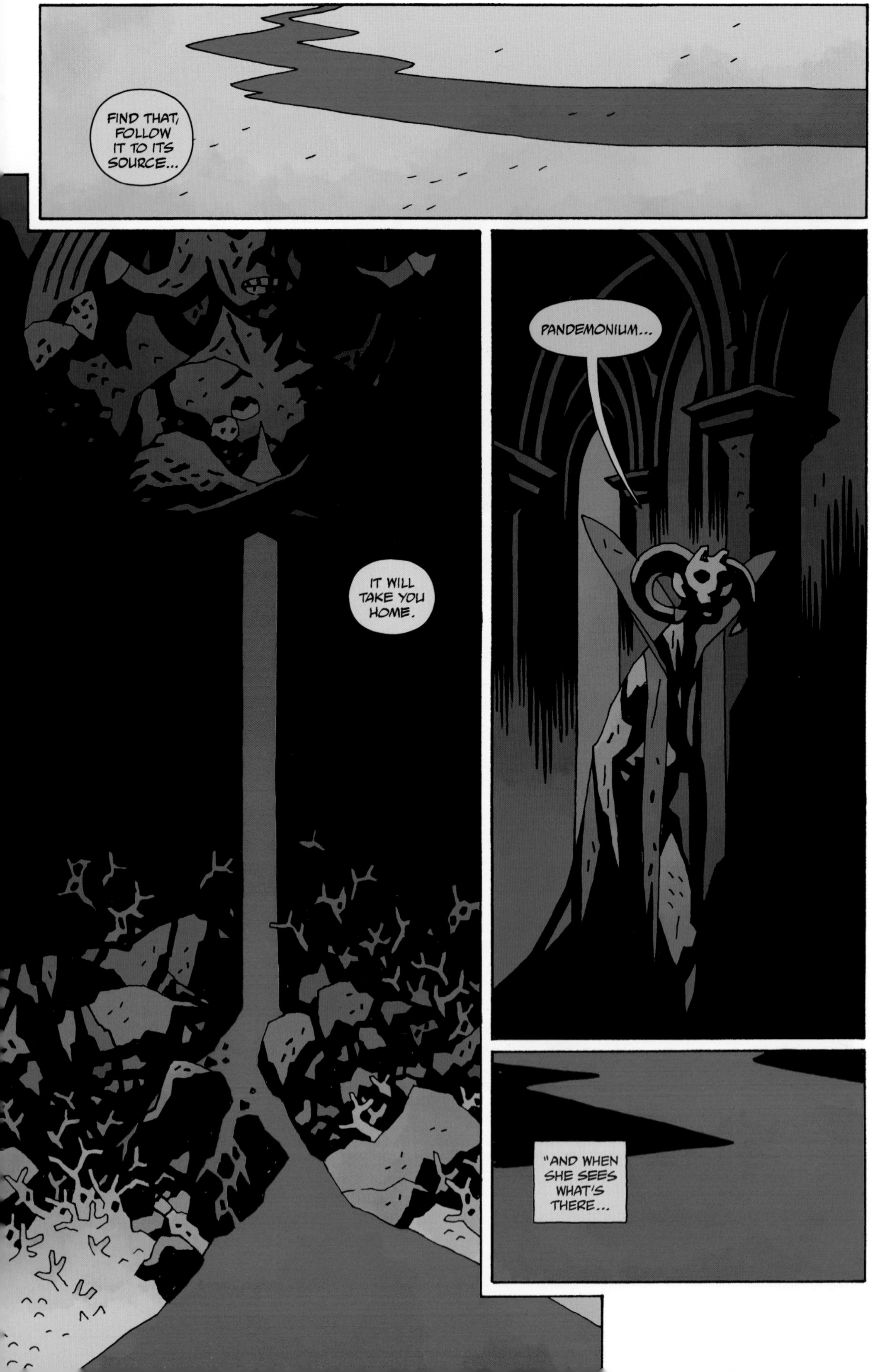
FIND THAT, FOLLOW IT TO ITS SOURCE...
IT WILL TAKE YOU HOME.
PANDEMONIUM...
"AND WHEN SHE SEES WHAT'S THERE...

"THAT THE RIVER RUNS FROM SATAN'S CUT THROAT..."

SHE WILL GO MAD.

AND HER SCREAMING WILL BE SUCH THAT THE WALLS WILL SHATTER AND COME CRASH-ING DOWN AROUND HER...

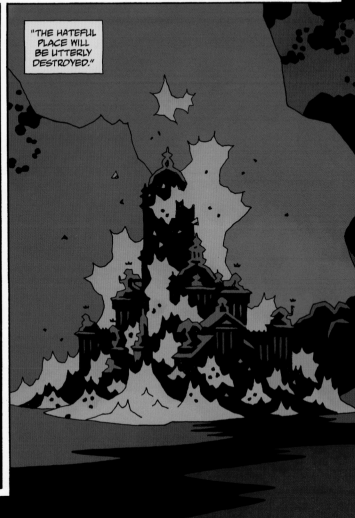

"THE HATEFUL PLACE WILL BE UTTERLY DESTROYED."

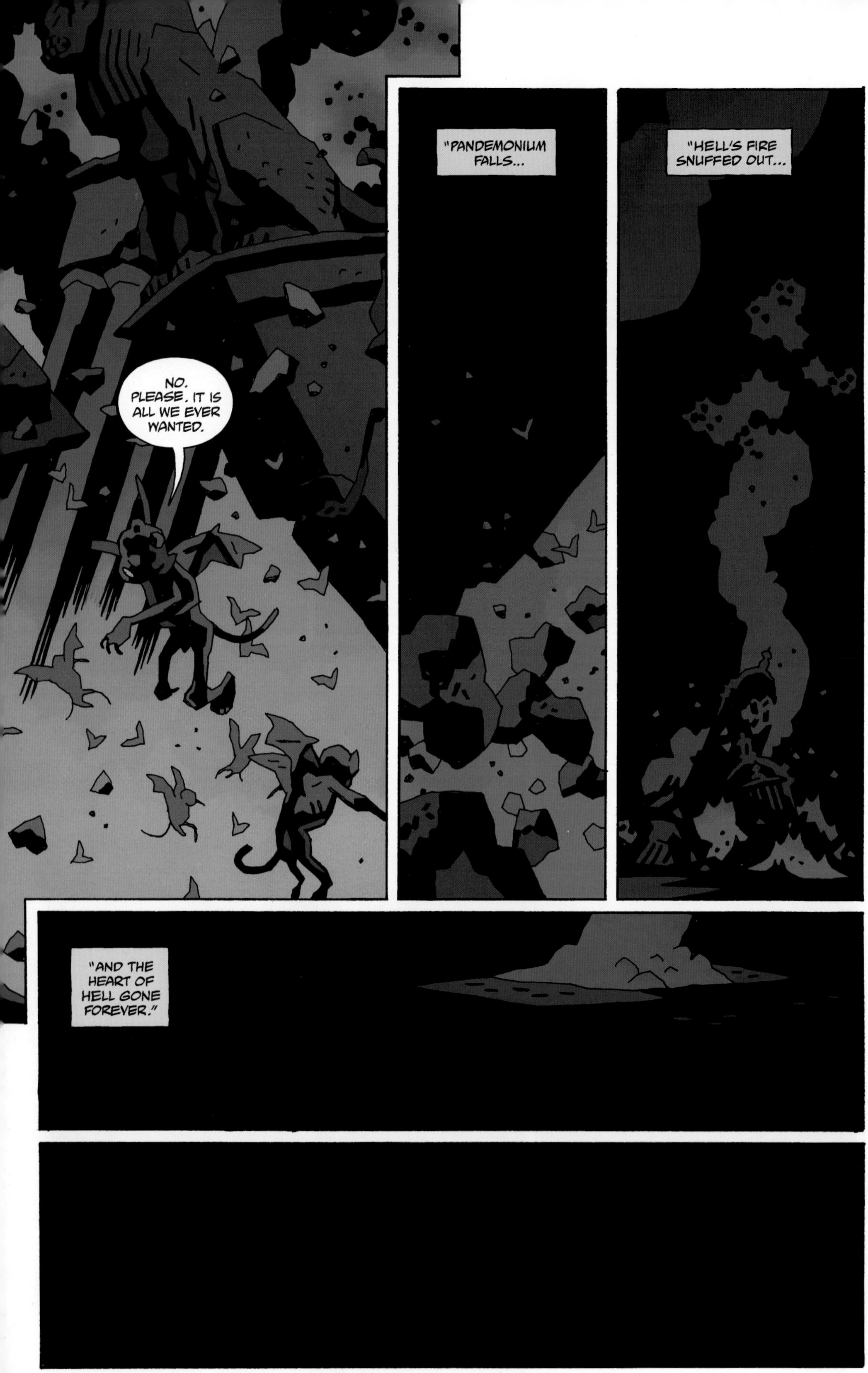
NO. PLEASE. IT IS ALL WE EVER WANTED.
"PANDEMONIUM FALLS...
"HELL'S FIRE SNUFFED OUT...
"AND THE HEART OF HELL GONE FOREVER."

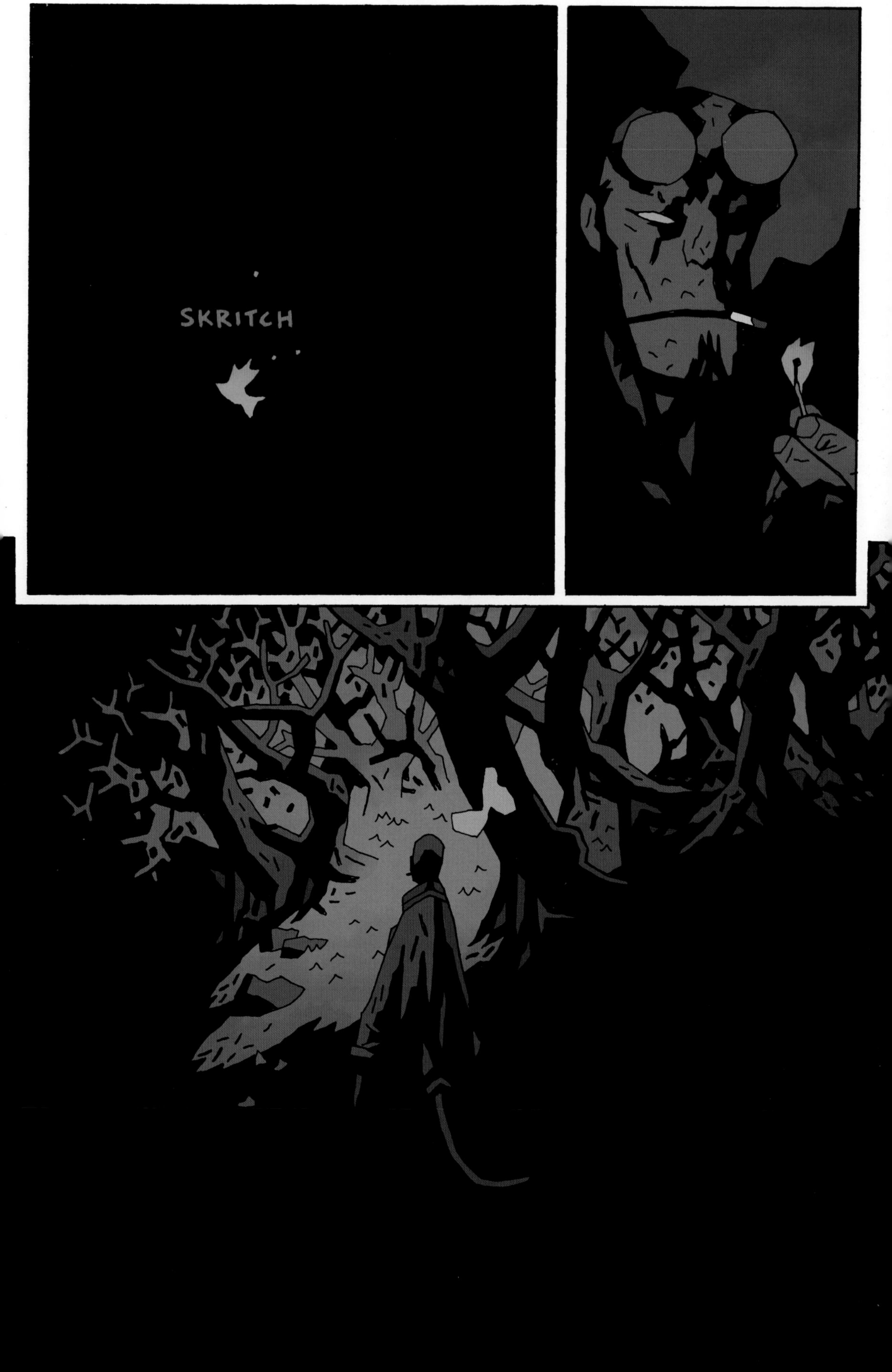
SKRITCH

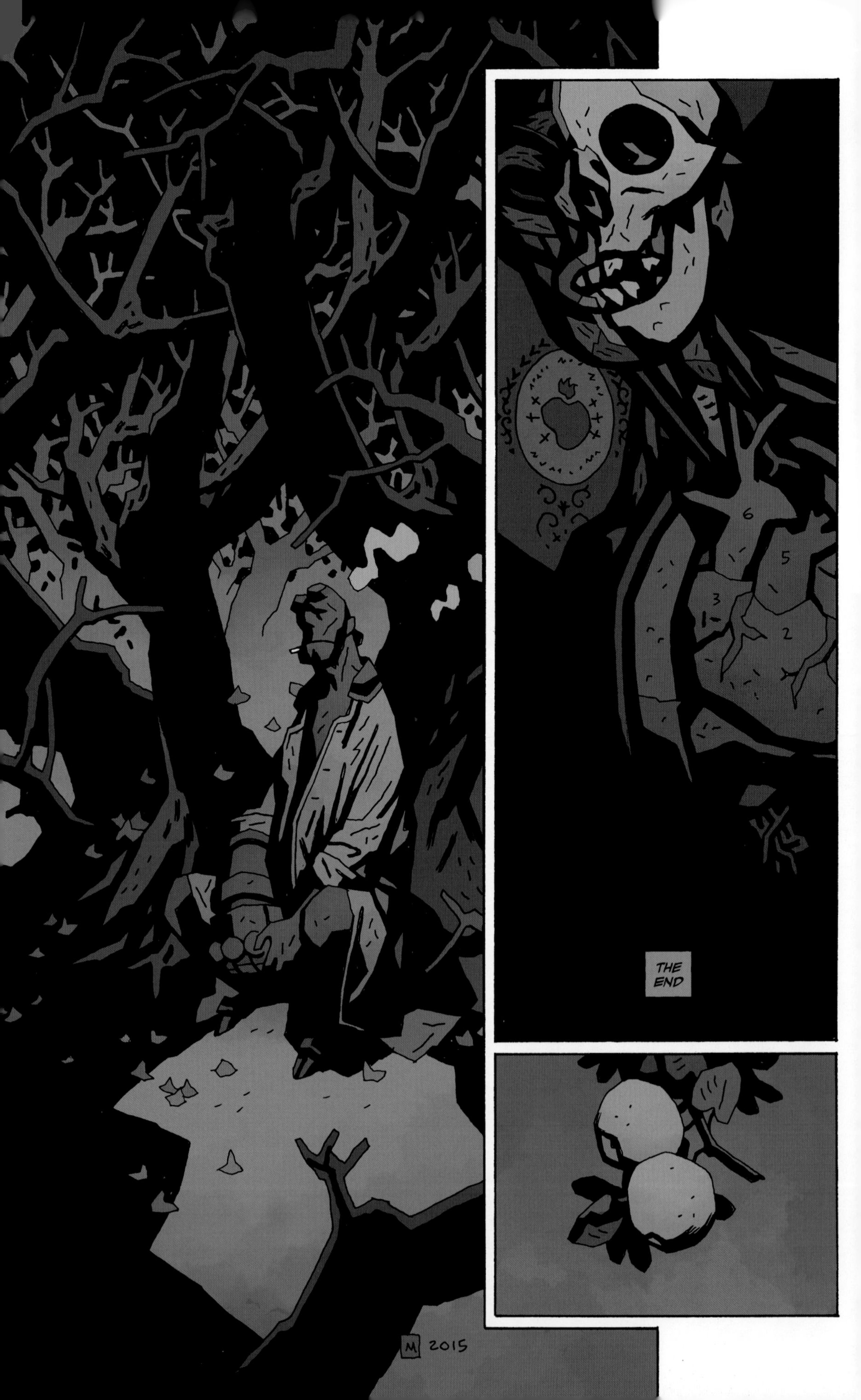

THE END
M 2015

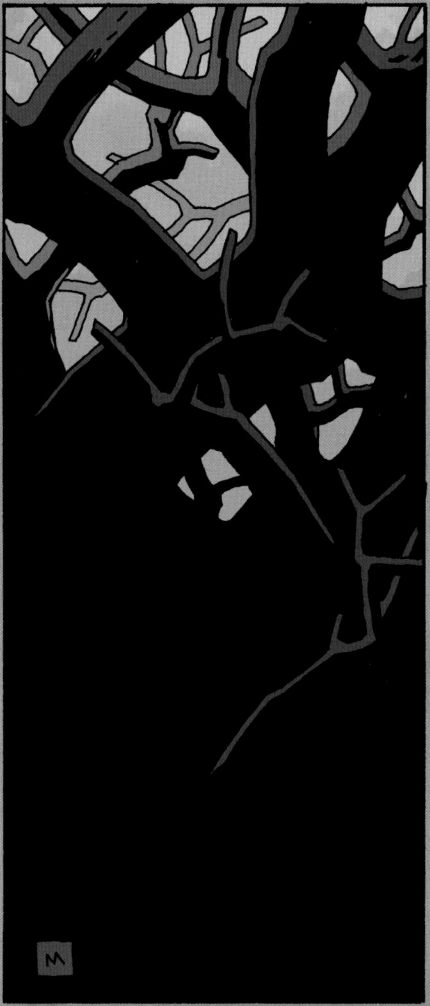

CHAPTER FOUR

THE SPANISH BRIDE

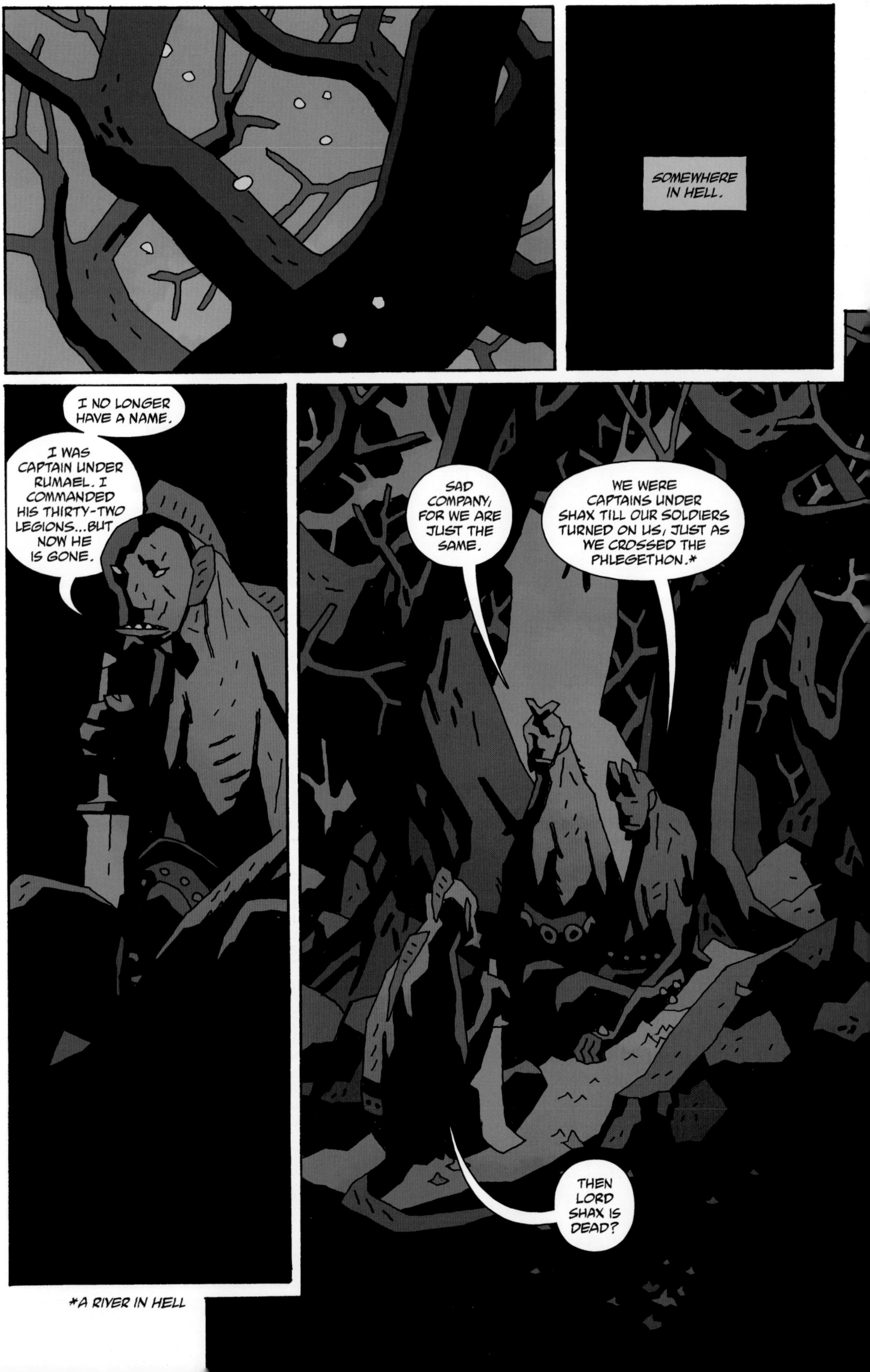
SOMEWHERE IN HELL.
I NO LONGER HAVE A NAME.
I WAS CAPTAIN UNDER RUMAEL. I COMMANDED HIS THIRTY-TWO LEGIONS...BUT NOW HE IS GONE.
SAD COMPANY, FOR WE ARE JUST THE SAME.
WE WERE CAPTAINS UNDER SHAX TILL OUR SOLDIERS TURNED ON US, JUST AS WE CROSSED THE PHLEGETHON.*
THEN LORD SHAX IS DEAD?
*A RIVER IN HELL

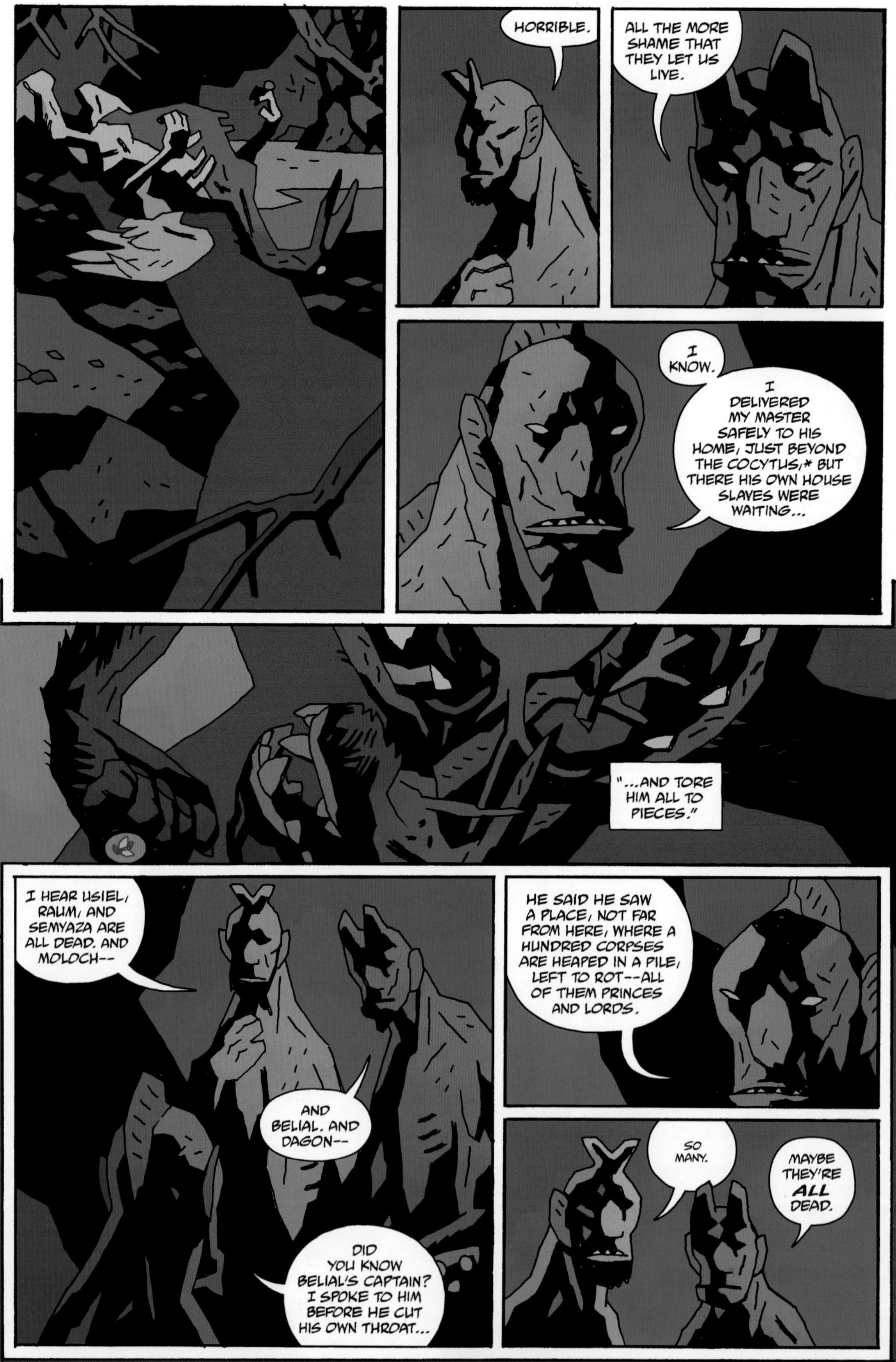

HORRIBLE.
ALL THE MORE SHAME THAT THEY LET US LIVE.
I KNOW.
I DELIVERED MY MASTER SAFELY TO HIS HOME, JUST BEYOND THE COCYTUS,* BUT THERE HIS OWN HOUSE SLAVES WERE WAITING...
"...AND TORE HIM ALL TO PIECES."
I HEAR USIEL, RAUM, AND SEMYAZA ARE ALL DEAD. AND MOLOCH--
AND BELIAL. AND DAGON--
DID YOU KNOW BELIAL'S CAPTAIN? I SPOKE TO HIM BEFORE HE CUT HIS OWN THROAT...
HE SAID HE SAW A PLACE, NOT FAR FROM HERE, WHERE A HUNDRED CORPSES ARE HEAPED IN A PILE, LEFT TO ROT--ALL OF THEM PRINCES AND LORDS.
SO MANY.
MAYBE THEY'RE ***ALL*** DEAD.

*ANOTHER RIVER IN HELL

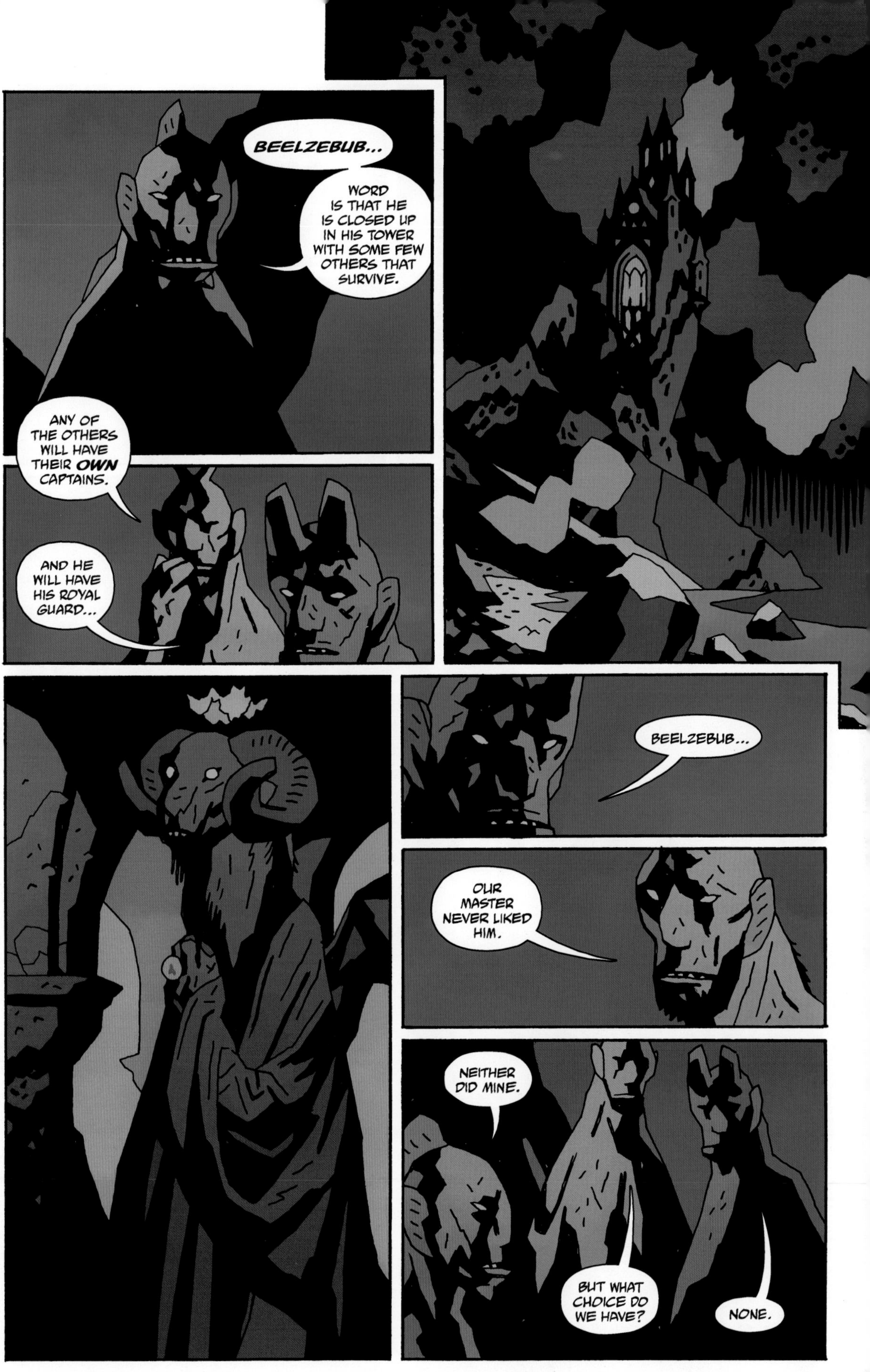
BEELZEBUB...
WORD IS THAT HE IS CLOSED UP IN HIS TOWER WITH SOME FEW OTHERS THAT SURVIVE.
ANY OF THE OTHERS WILL HAVE THEIR OWN CAPTAINS.
AND HE WILL HAVE HIS ROYAL GUARD...
BEELZEBUB...
OUR MASTER NEVER LIKED HIM.
NEITHER DID MINE.
BUT WHAT CHOICE DO WE HAVE?
NONE.

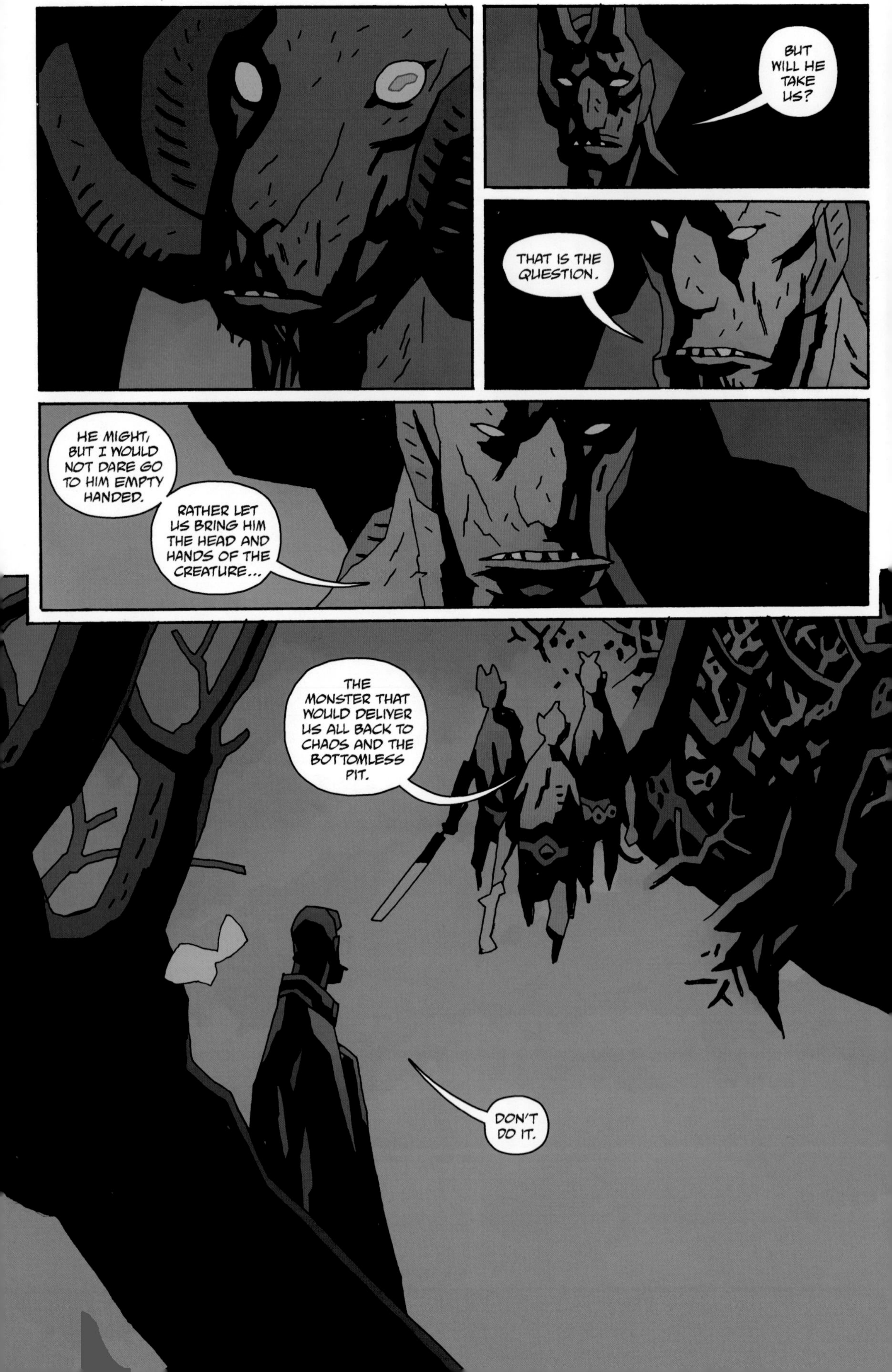
BUT WILL HE TAKE US?
THAT IS THE QUESTION.
HE MIGHT, BUT I WOULD NOT DARE GO TO HIM EMPTY HANDED.
RATHER LET US BRING HIM THE HEAD AND HANDS OF THE CREATURE...
THE MONSTER THAT WOULD DELIVER US ALL BACK TO CHAOS AND THE BOTTOMLESS PIT.
DON'T DO IT.

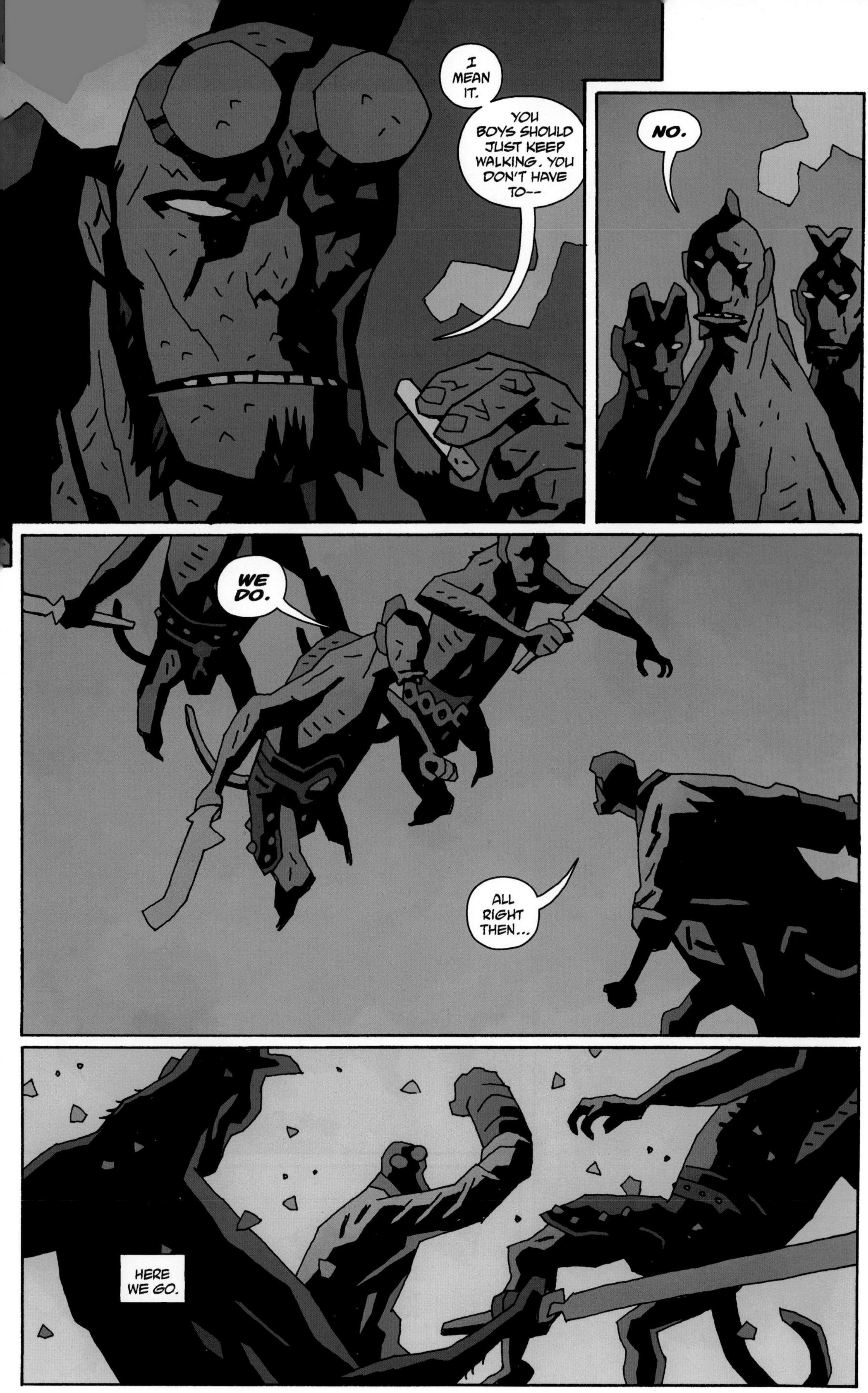
I MEAN IT.
YOU BOYS SHOULD JUST KEEP WALKING. YOU DON'T HAVE TO--
NO.
WE DO.
ALL RIGHT THEN...
HERE WE GO.

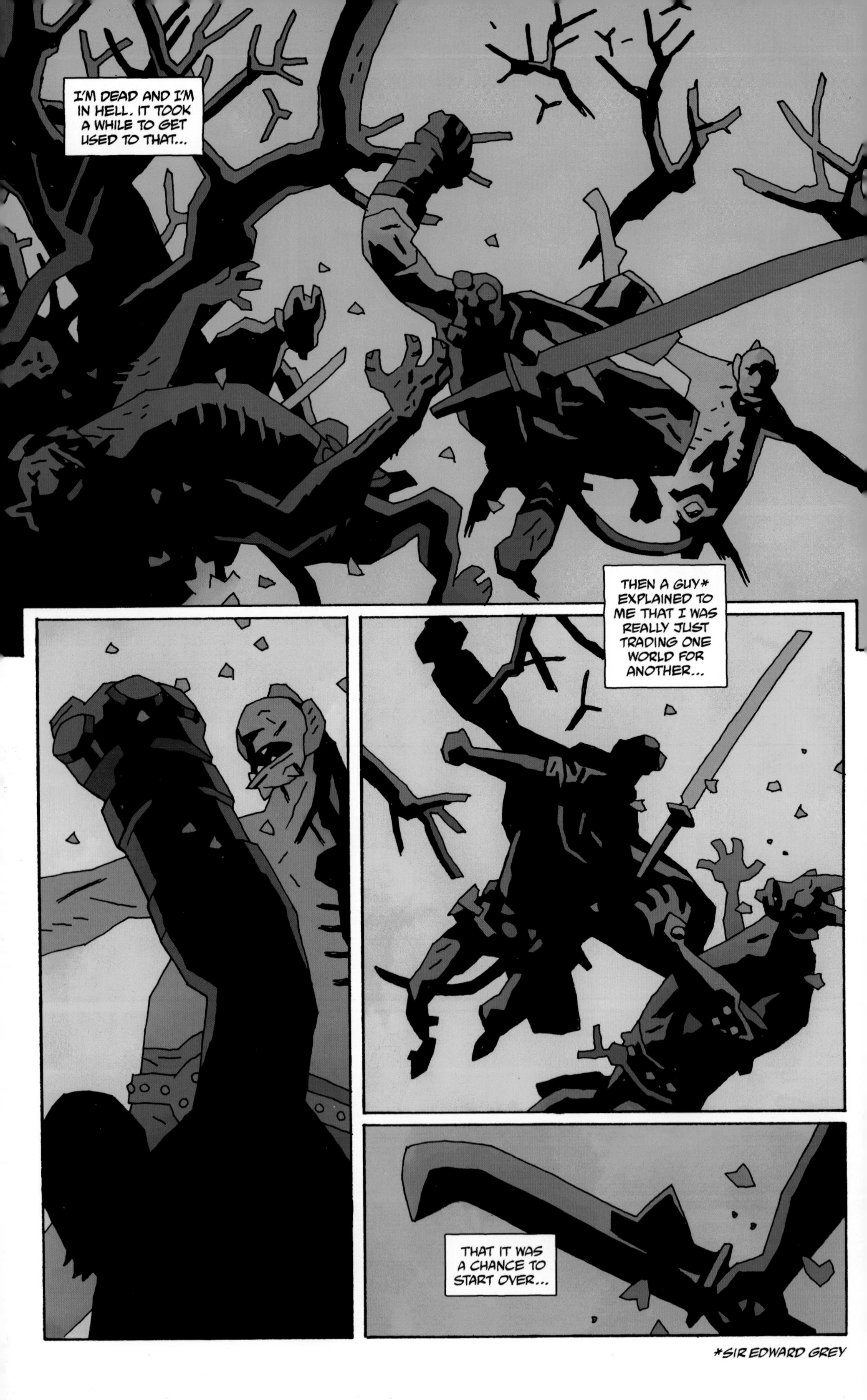
I'M DEAD AND I'M IN HELL. IT TOOK A WHILE TO GET USED TO THAT...
THEN A GUY* EXPLAINED TO ME THAT I WAS REALLY JUST TRADING ONE WORLD FOR ANOTHER...
THAT IT WAS A CHANCE TO START OVER...
*SIR EDWARD GREY

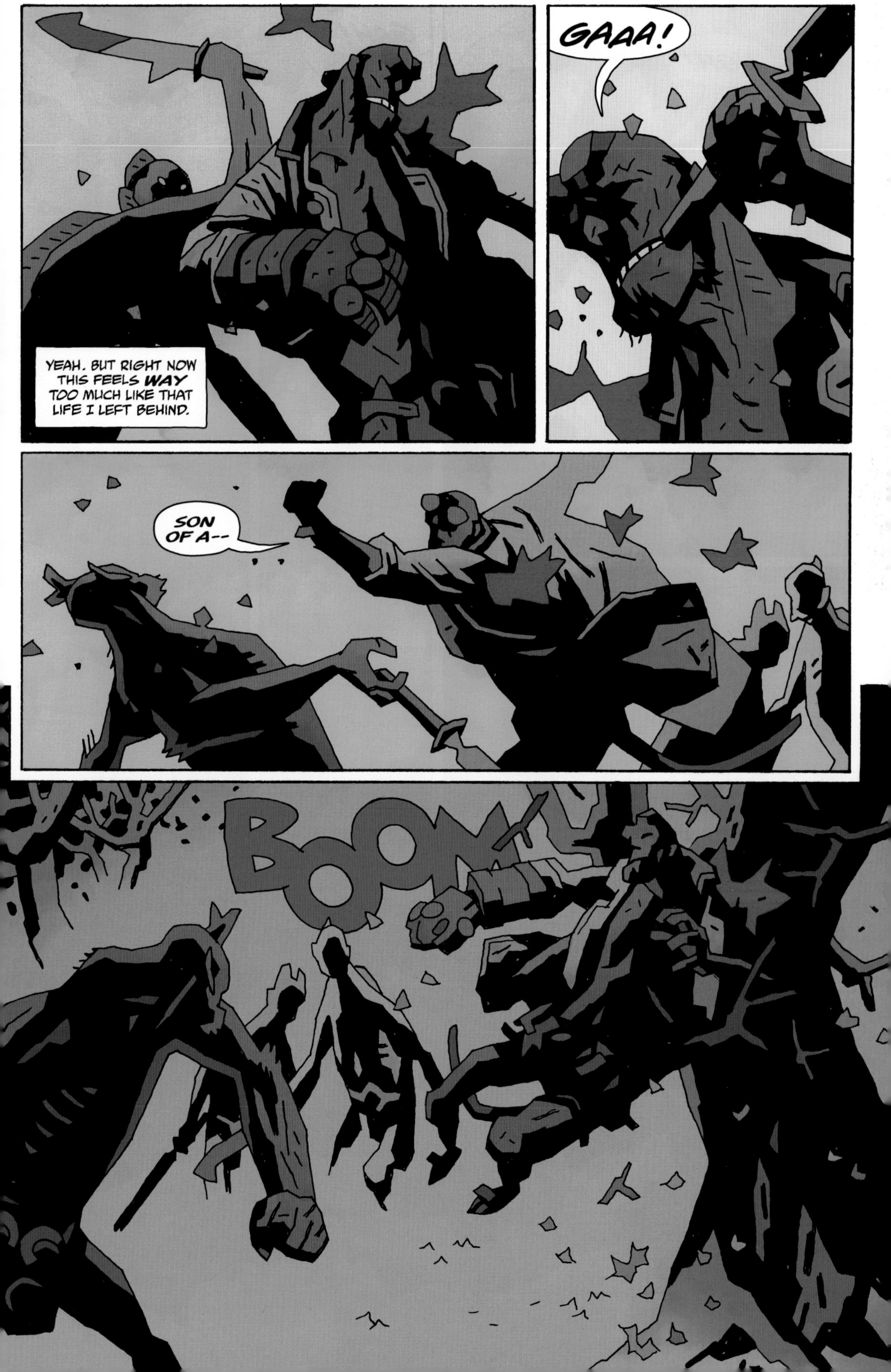
YEAH. BUT RIGHT NOW THIS FEELS WAY TOO MUCH LIKE THAT LIFE I LEFT BEHIND.
GAAA!
SON OF A--
BOOM

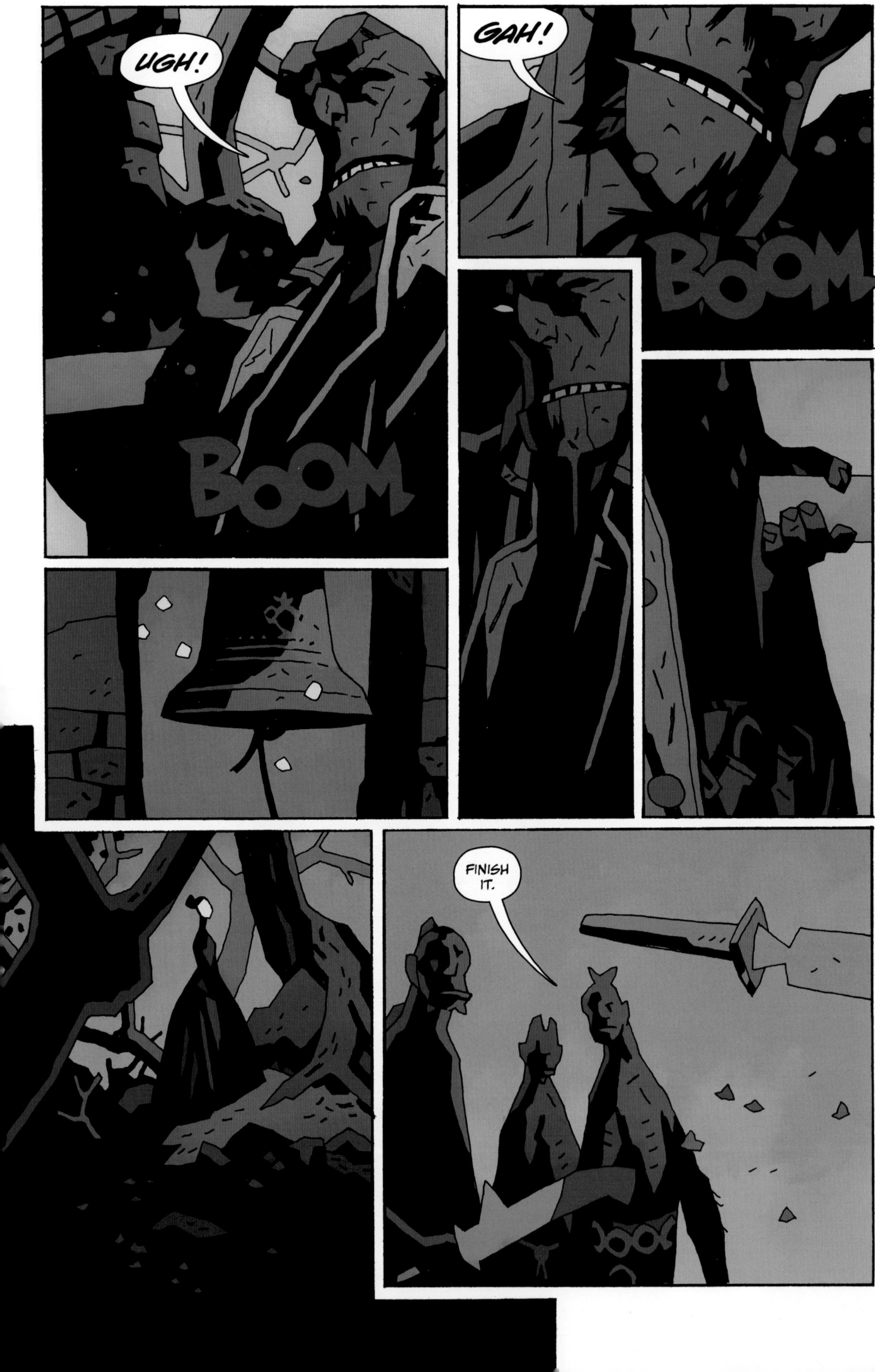
UGH!
BOOM
GAH!
BOOM
FINISH IT.

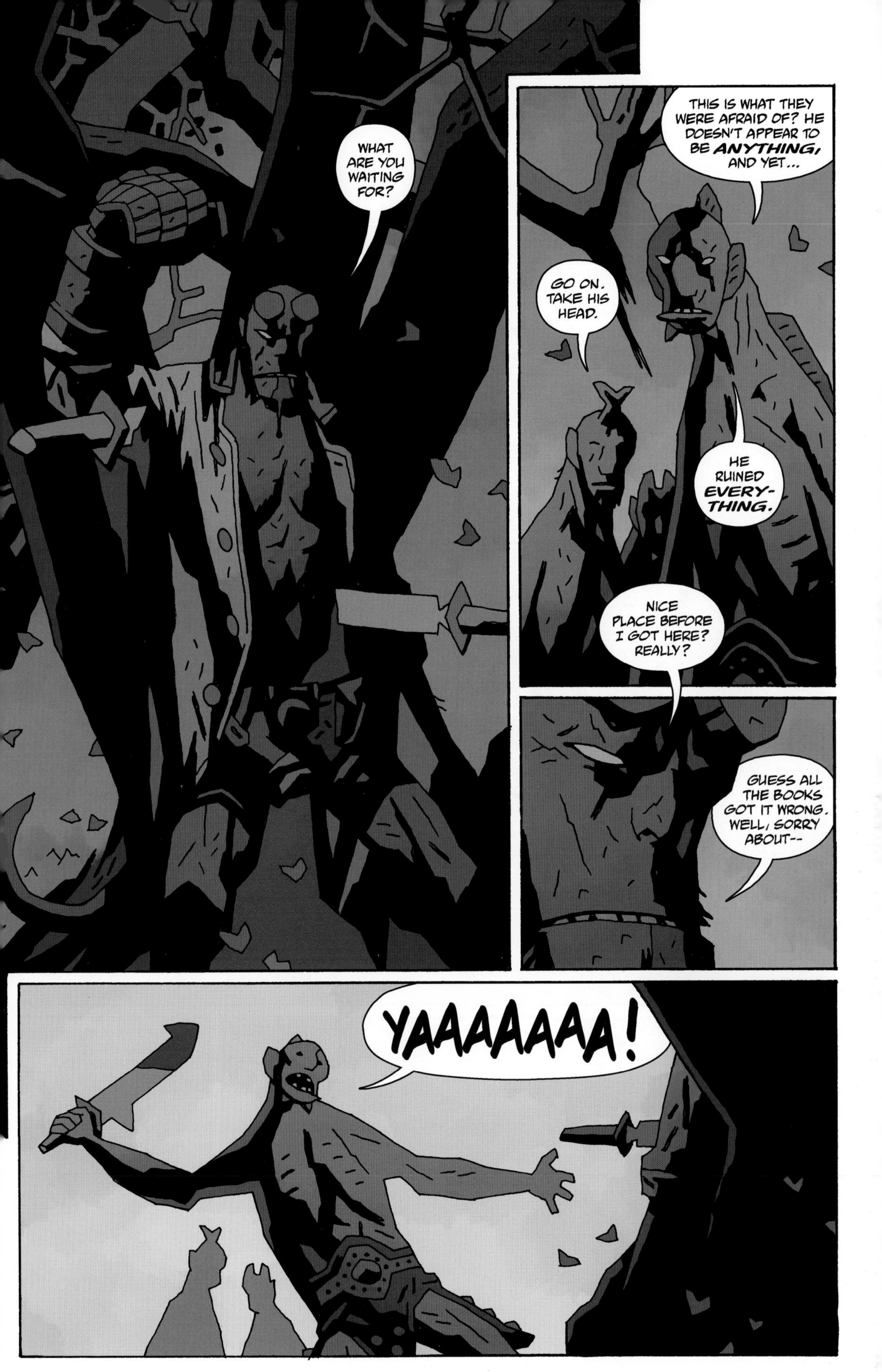
WHAT ARE YOU WAITING FOR?
THIS IS WHAT THEY WERE AFRAID OF? HE DOESN'T APPEAR TO BE ANYTHING, AND YET...
GO ON. TAKE HIS HEAD.
HE RUINED EVERYTHING.
NICE PLACE BEFORE I GOT HERE? REALLY?
GUESS ALL THE BOOKS GOT IT WRONG. WELL, SORRY ABOUT--
YAAAAAAA!

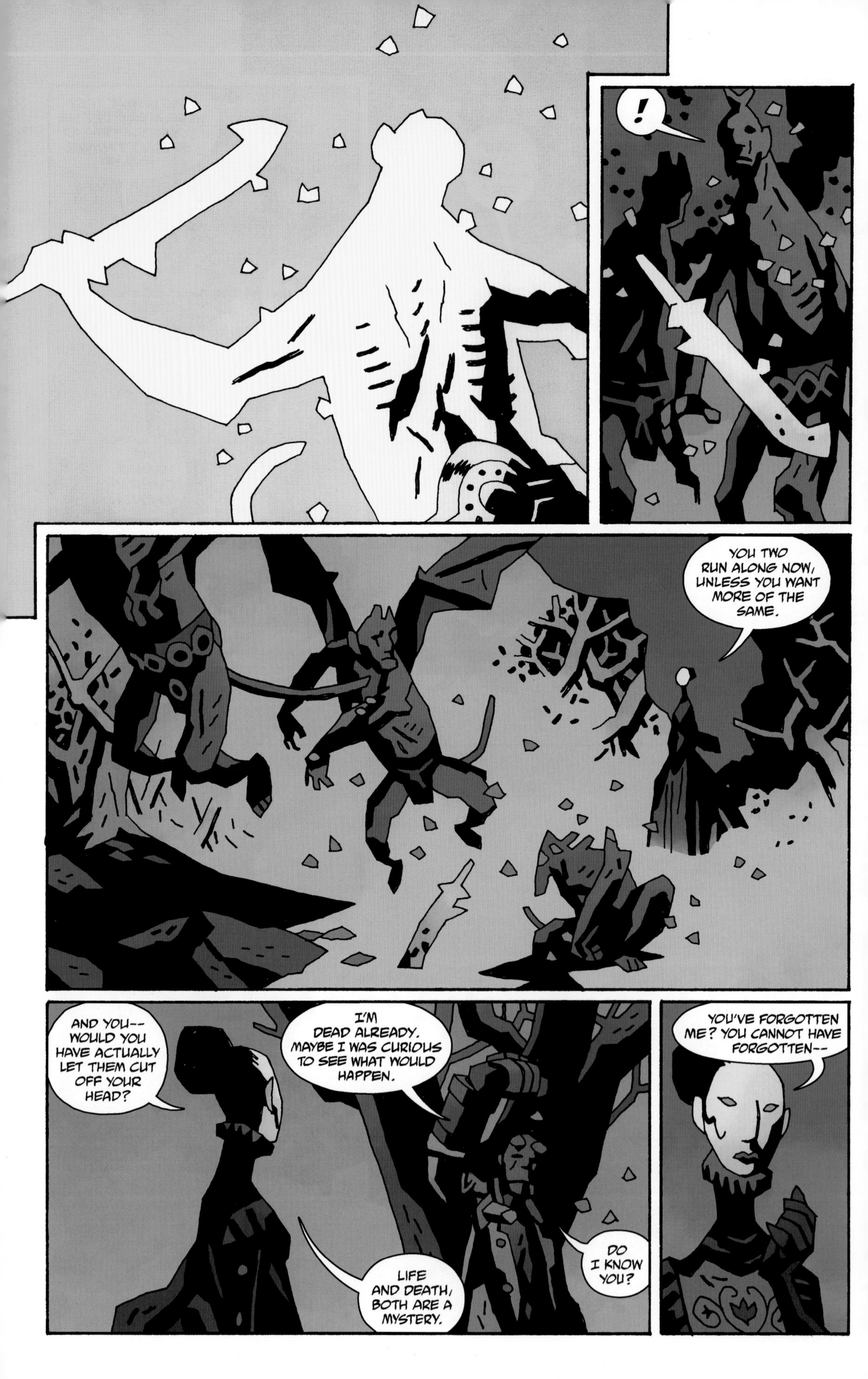
!
YOU TWO RUN ALONG NOW, UNLESS YOU WANT MORE OF THE SAME.
AND YOU-- WOULD YOU HAVE ACTUALLY LET THEM CUT OFF YOUR HEAD?
I'M DEAD ALREADY. MAYBE I WAS CURIOUS TO SEE WHAT WOULD HAPPEN.
LIFE AND DEATH, BOTH ARE A MYSTERY.
DO I KNOW YOU?
YOU'VE FORGOTTEN ME? YOU CANNOT HAVE FORGOTTEN--

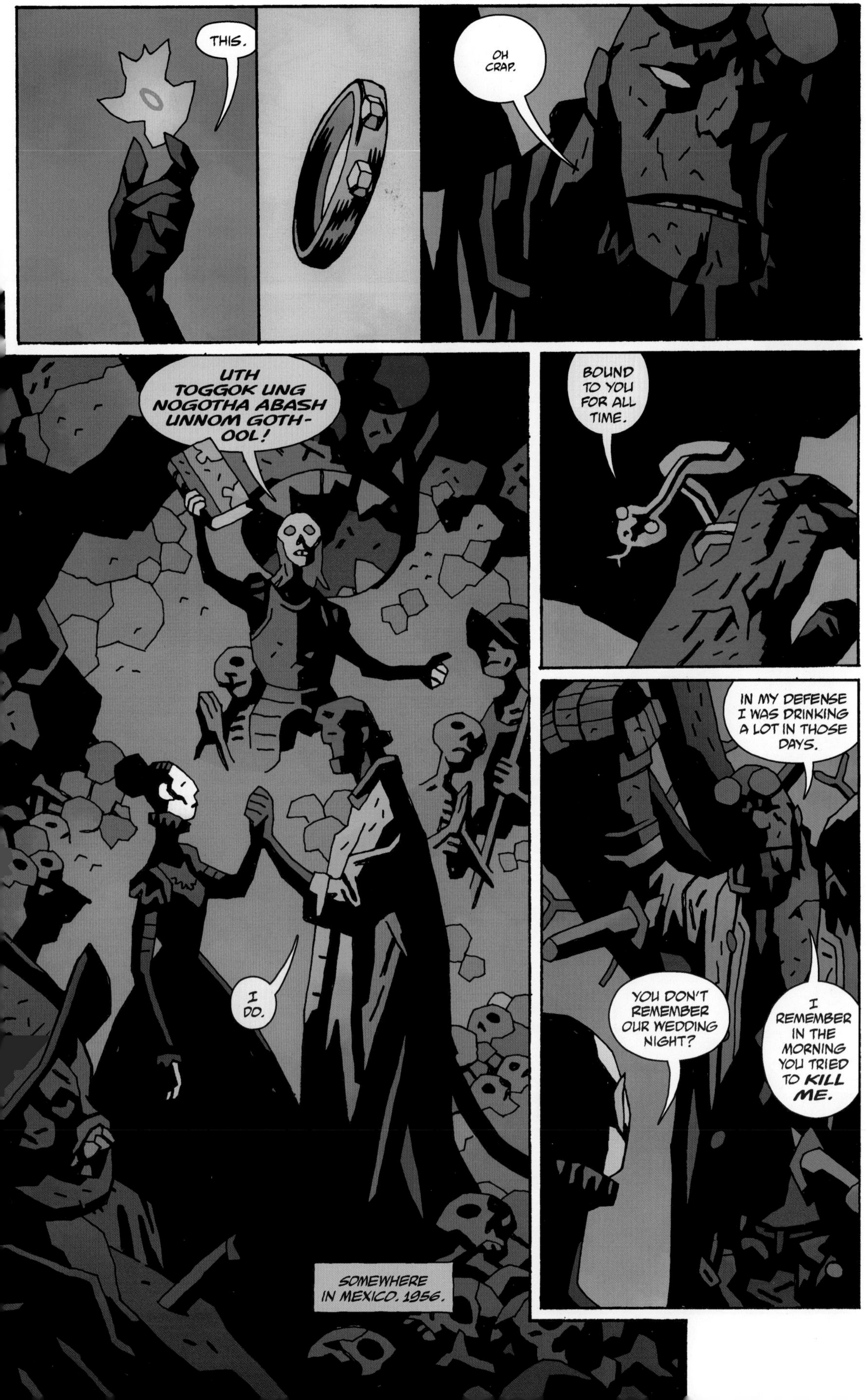
THIS.
OH CRAP.
UTH TOGGOK UNG NOGOTHA ABASH UNNOM GOTH-OOL!
I DO.
SOMEWHERE IN MEXICO. 1956.
BOUND TO YOU FOR ALL TIME.
IN MY DEFENSE I WAS DRINKING A LOT IN THOSE DAYS.
YOU DON'T REMEMBER OUR WEDDING NIGHT?
I REMEMBER IN THE MORNING YOU TRIED TO KILL ME.

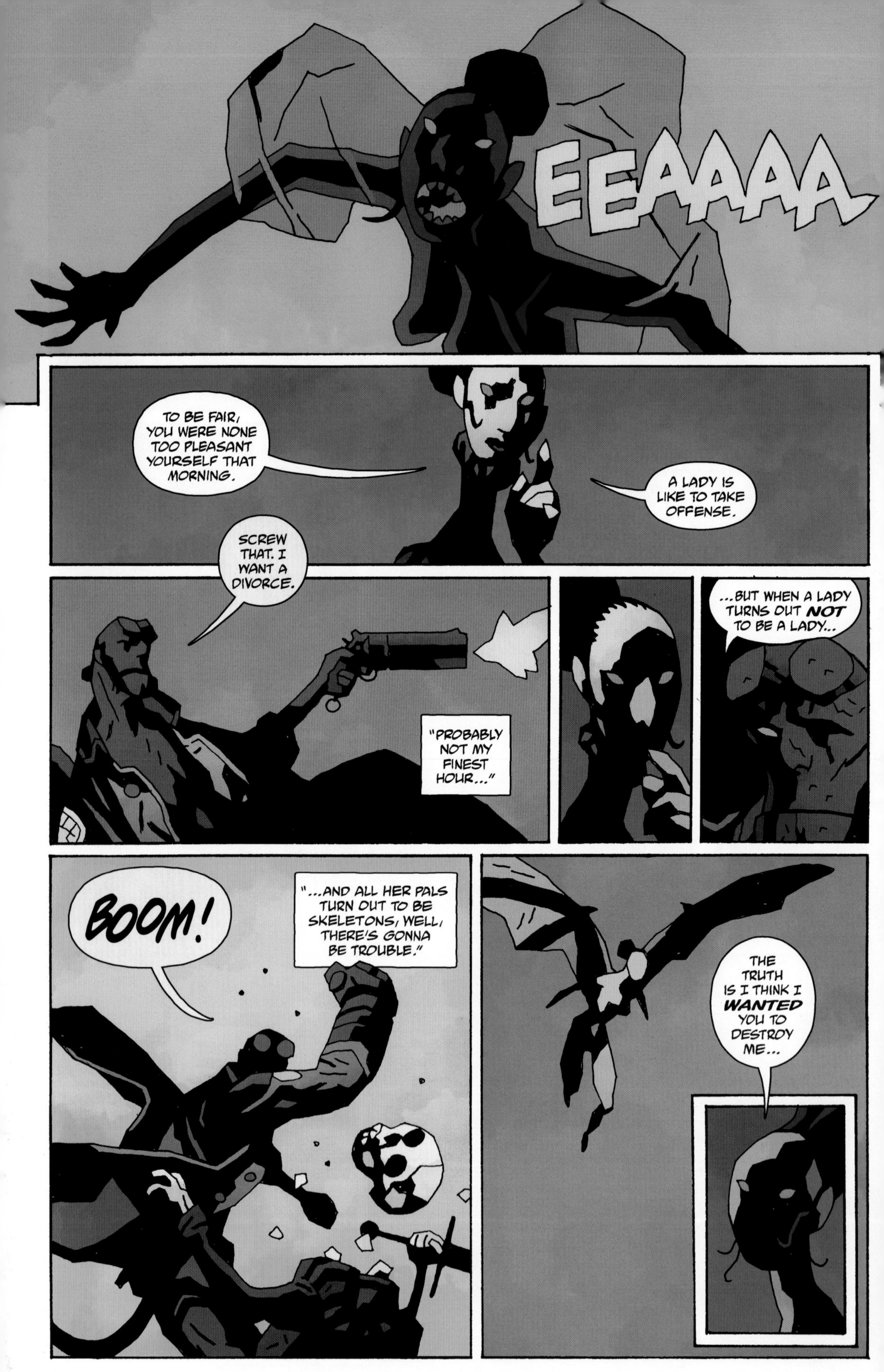
EEAAAA
TO BE FAIR, YOU WERE NONE TOO PLEASANT YOURSELF THAT MORNING.
A LADY IS LIKE TO TAKE OFFENSE.
SCREW THAT. I WANT A DIVORCE.
"PROBABLY NOT MY FINEST HOUR..."
...BUT WHEN A LADY TURNS OUT NOT TO BE A LADY...
BOOM!
"...AND ALL HER PALS TURN OUT TO BE SKELETONS, WELL, THERE'S GONNA BE TROUBLE."
THE TRUTH IS I THINK I WANTED YOU TO DESTROY ME...

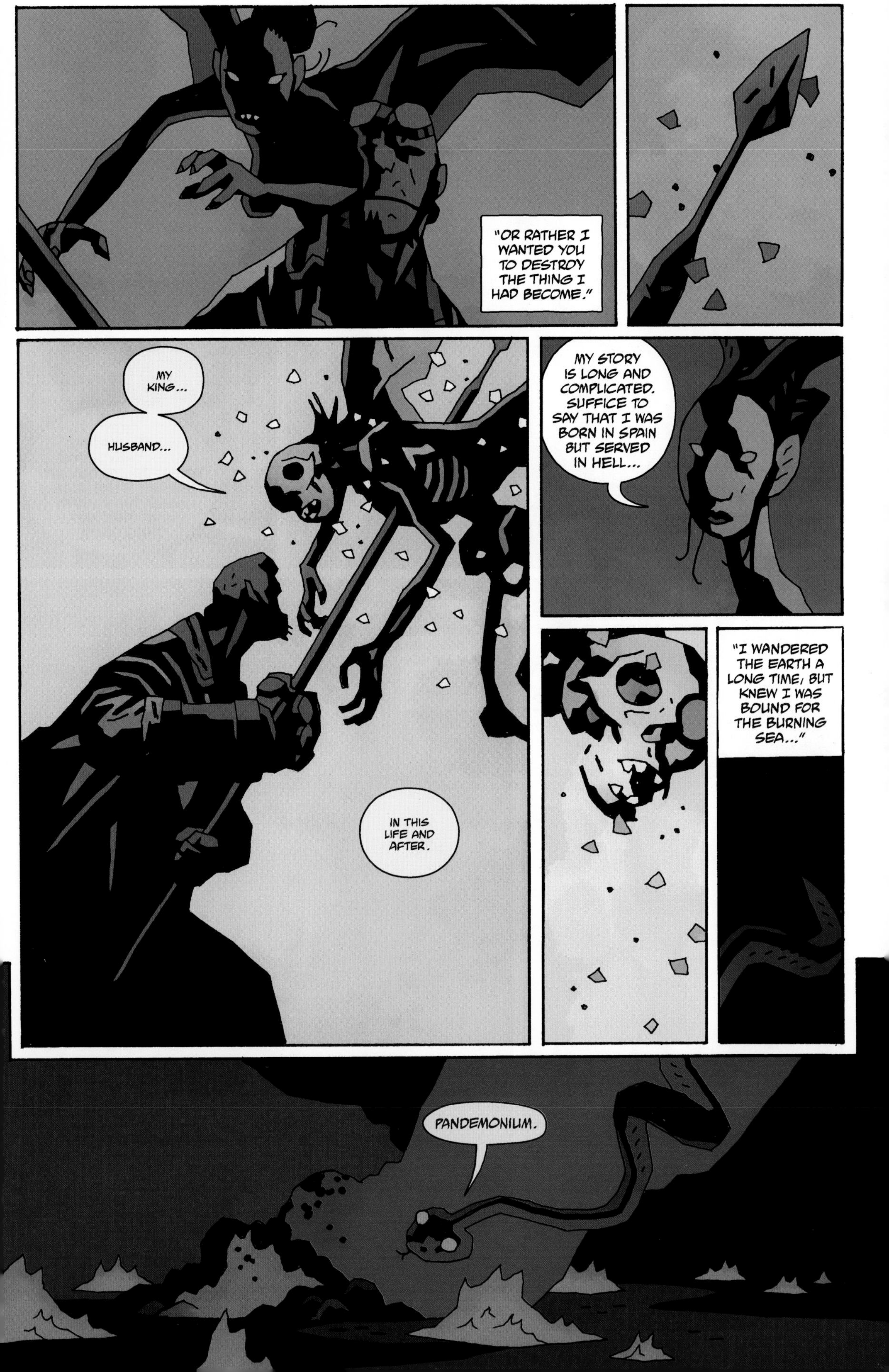
"OR RATHER I WANTED YOU TO DESTROY THE THING I HAD BECOME."
MY KING...
HUSBAND...
IN THIS LIFE AND AFTER.
MY STORY IS LONG AND COMPLICATED. SUFFICE TO SAY THAT I WAS BORN IN SPAIN BUT SERVED IN HELL...
"I WANDERED THE EARTH A LONG TIME, BUT KNEW I WAS BOUND FOR THE BURNING SEA..."
PANDEMONIUM.

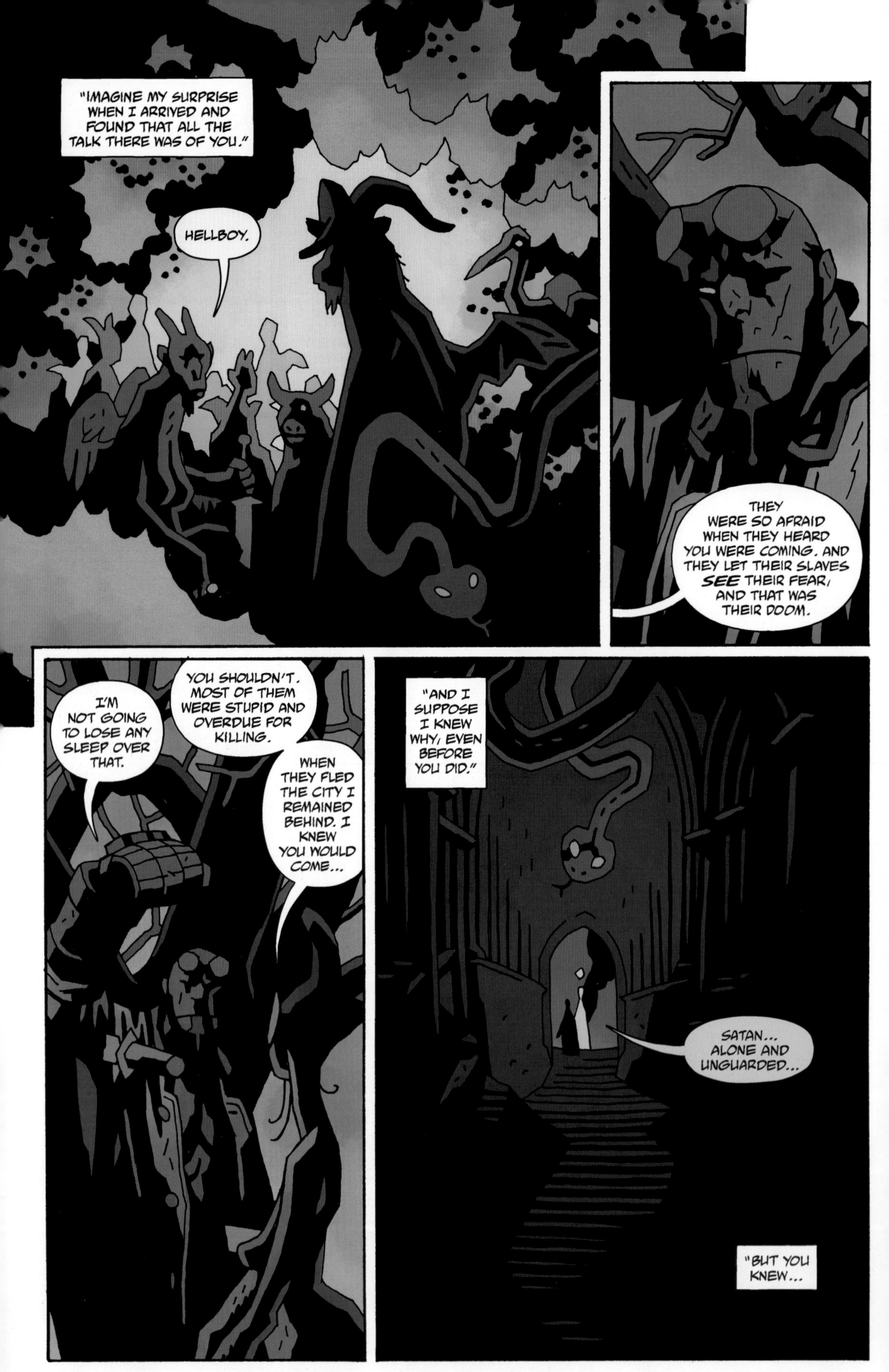
"IMAGINE MY SURPRISE WHEN I ARRIVED AND FOUND THAT ALL THE TALK THERE WAS OF YOU."
HELLBOY.
THEY WERE SO AFRAID WHEN THEY HEARD YOU WERE COMING. AND THEY LET THEIR SLAVES SEE THEIR FEAR, AND THAT WAS THEIR DOOM.
I'M NOT GOING TO LOSE ANY SLEEP OVER THAT.
YOU SHOULDN'T. MOST OF THEM WERE STUPID AND OVERDUE FOR KILLING.
WHEN THEY FLED THE CITY I REMAINED BEHIND. I KNEW YOU WOULD COME...
"AND I SUPPOSE I KNEW WHY, EVEN BEFORE YOU DID."
SATAN... ALONE AND UNGUARDED...
"BUT YOU KNEW...

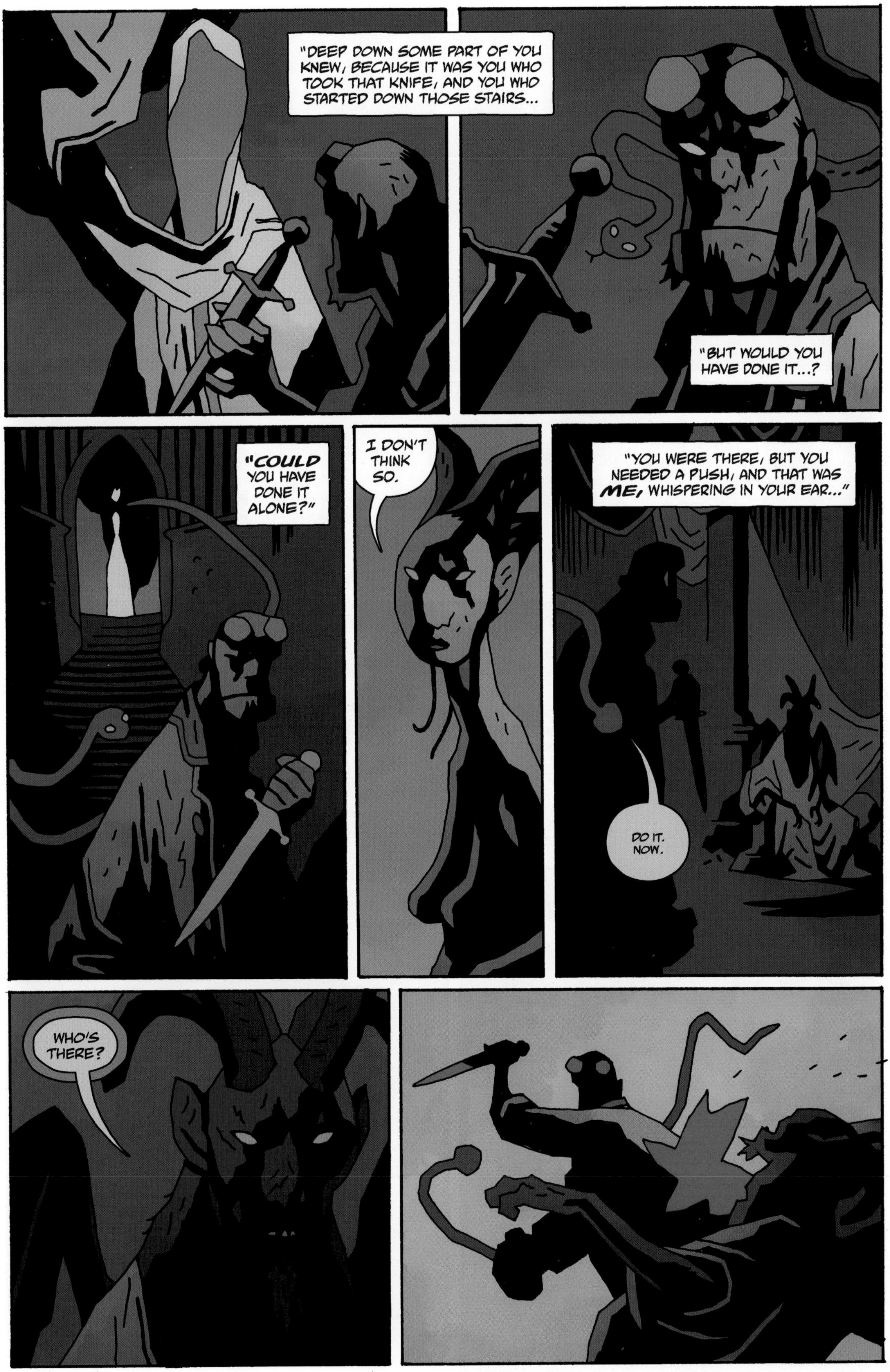
"DEEP DOWN SOME PART OF YOU KNEW, BECAUSE IT WAS YOU WHO TOOK THAT KNIFE, AND YOU WHO STARTED DOWN THOSE STAIRS...
"BUT WOULD YOU HAVE DONE IT...?
"COULD YOU HAVE DONE IT ALONE?"
I DON'T THINK SO.
"YOU WERE THERE, BUT YOU NEEDED A PUSH, AND THAT WAS ME, WHISPERING IN YOUR EAR..."
DO IT. NOW.
WHO'S THERE?

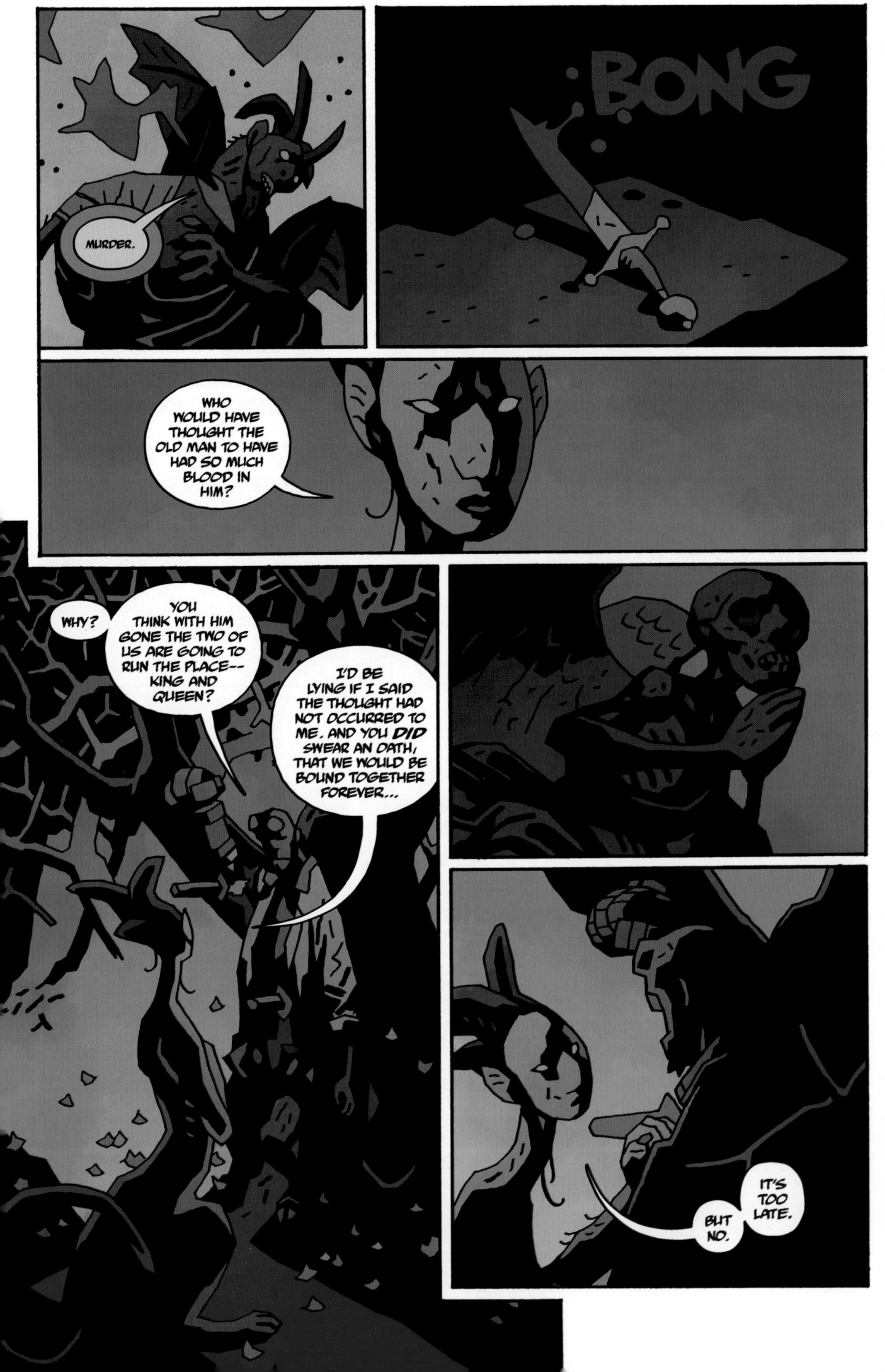
MURDER.
BONG
WHO WOULD HAVE THOUGHT THE OLD MAN TO HAVE HAD SO MUCH BLOOD IN HIM?
WHY?
YOU THINK WITH HIM GONE THE TWO OF US ARE GOING TO RUN THE PLACE-- KING AND QUEEN?
I'D BE LYING IF I SAID THE THOUGHT HAD NOT OCCURRED TO ME. AND YOU *DID* SWEAR AN OATH, THAT WE WOULD BE BOUND TOGETHER FOREVER...
BUT NO.
IT'S TOO LATE.

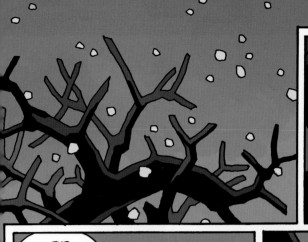

THE WORLD THAT WAS, IT'S NEARLY ALL GONE NOW.

YOU SEE THIS...?

"HELL'S FIRE HAS GONE OUT. PANDEMONIUM HAS FALLEN, COLLAPSED INTO THE SEA, AND ALL HER TREASURES DROWNED...

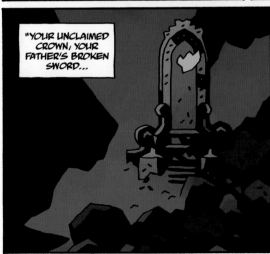

"YOUR UNCLAIMED CROWN, YOUR FATHER'S BROKEN SWORD...

"HIS RING..."

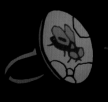

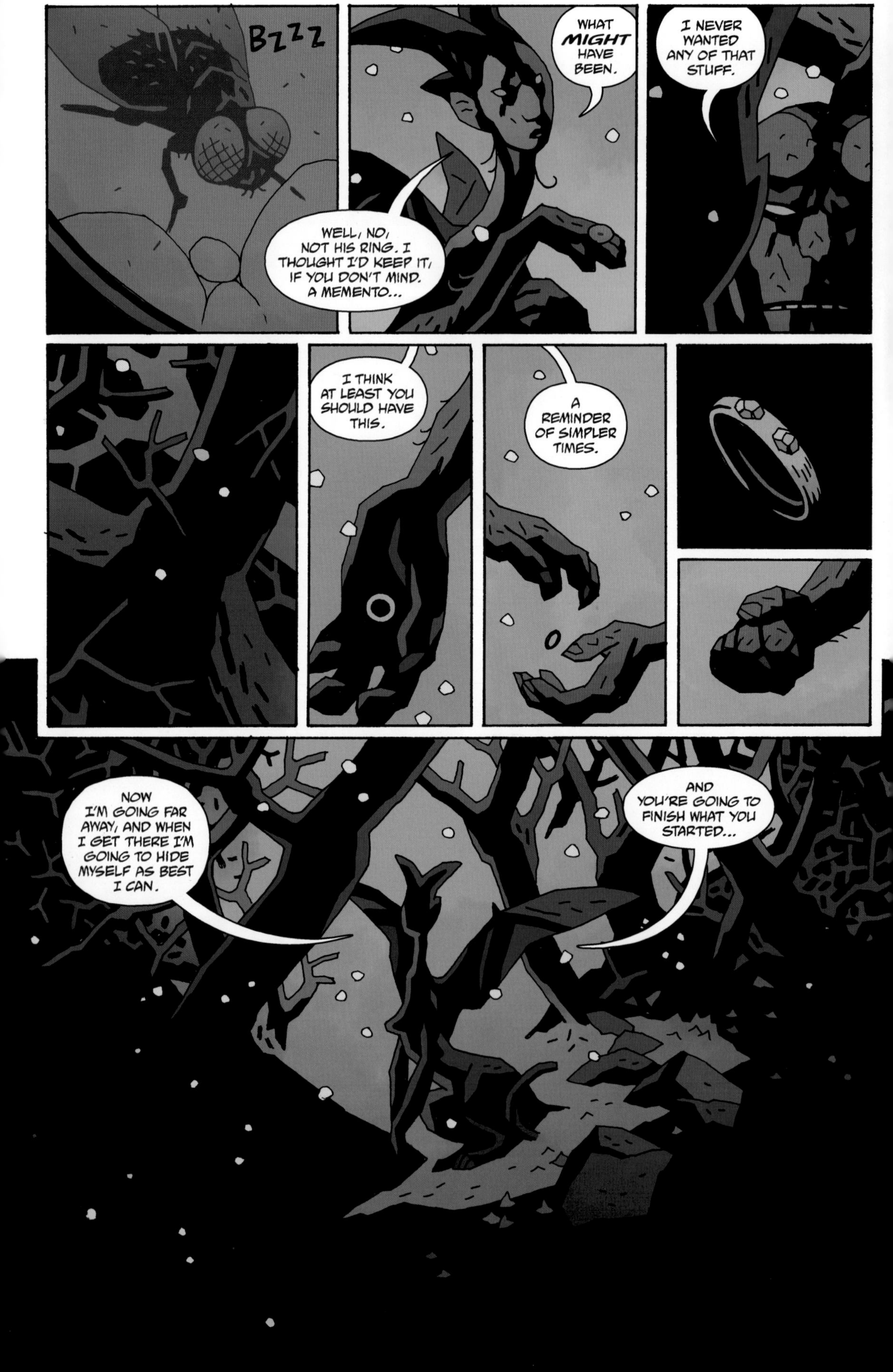
BZZZ
WHAT *MIGHT* HAVE BEEN.
WELL, NO, NOT HIS RING. I THOUGHT I'D KEEP IT, IF YOU DON'T MIND. A MEMENTO...
I NEVER WANTED ANY OF THAT STUFF.
I THINK AT LEAST YOU SHOULD HAVE THIS.
A REMINDER OF SIMPLER TIMES.
NOW I'M GOING FAR AWAY, AND WHEN I GET THERE I'M GOING TO HIDE MYSELF AS BEST I CAN.
AND YOU'RE GOING TO FINISH WHAT YOU STARTED...

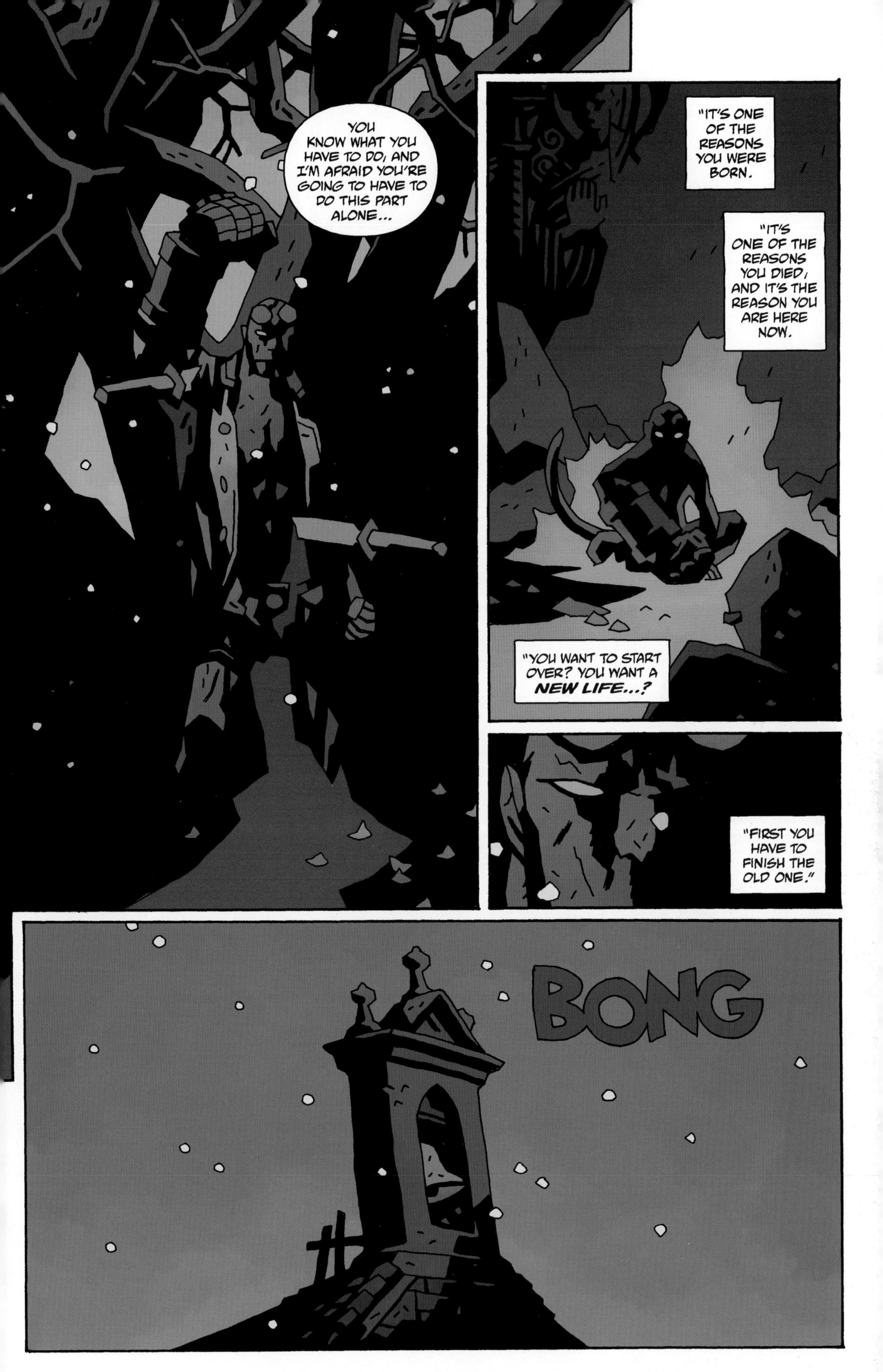
YOU KNOW WHAT YOU HAVE TO DO, AND I'M AFRAID YOU'RE GOING TO HAVE TO DO THIS PART ALONE...
"IT'S ONE OF THE REASONS YOU WERE BORN.
"IT'S ONE OF THE REASONS YOU DIED, AND IT'S THE REASON YOU ARE HERE NOW.
"YOU WANT TO START OVER? YOU WANT A NEW LIFE...?
"FIRST YOU HAVE TO FINISH THE OLD ONE."
BONG

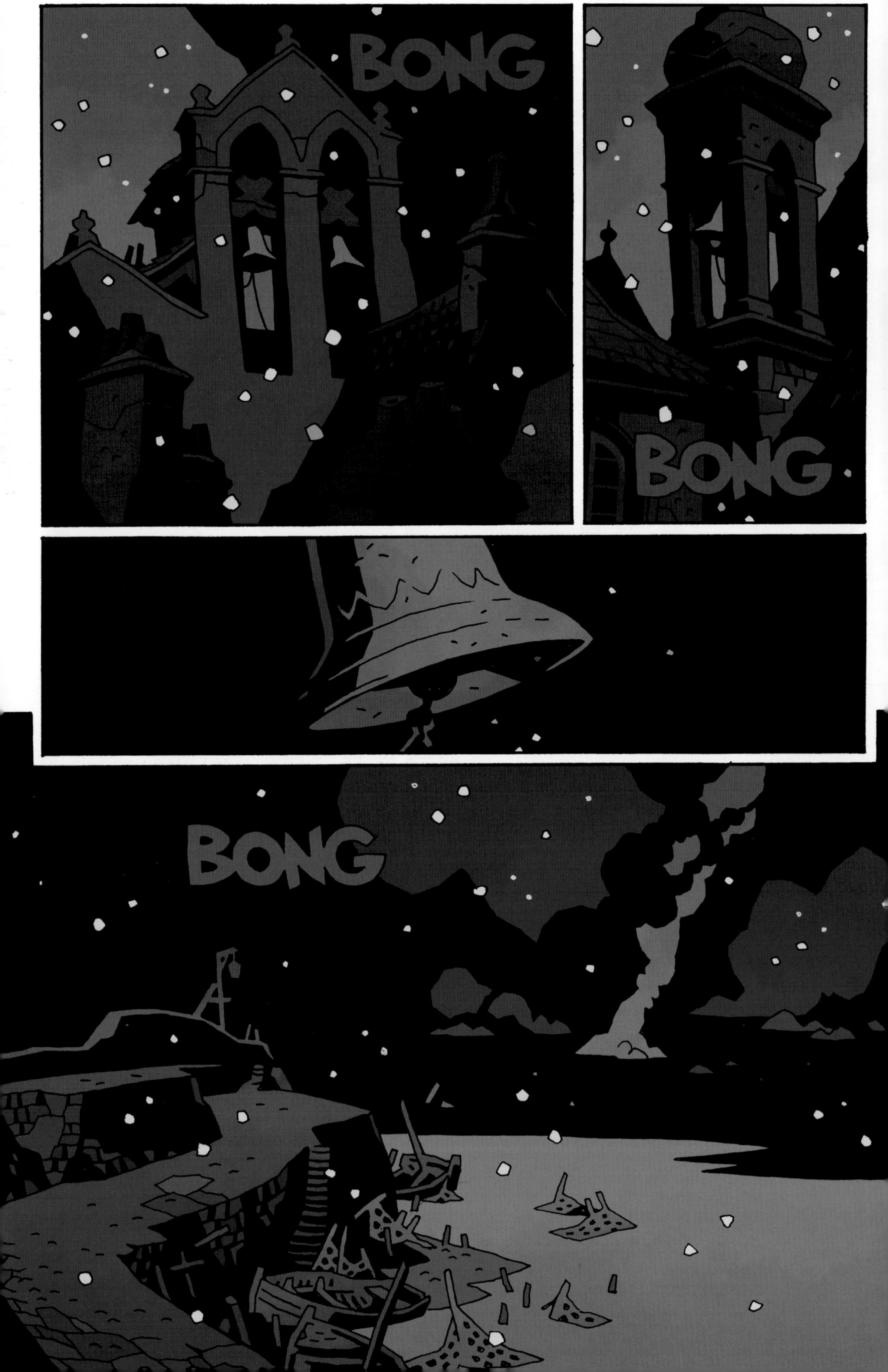
BONG
BONG
BONG

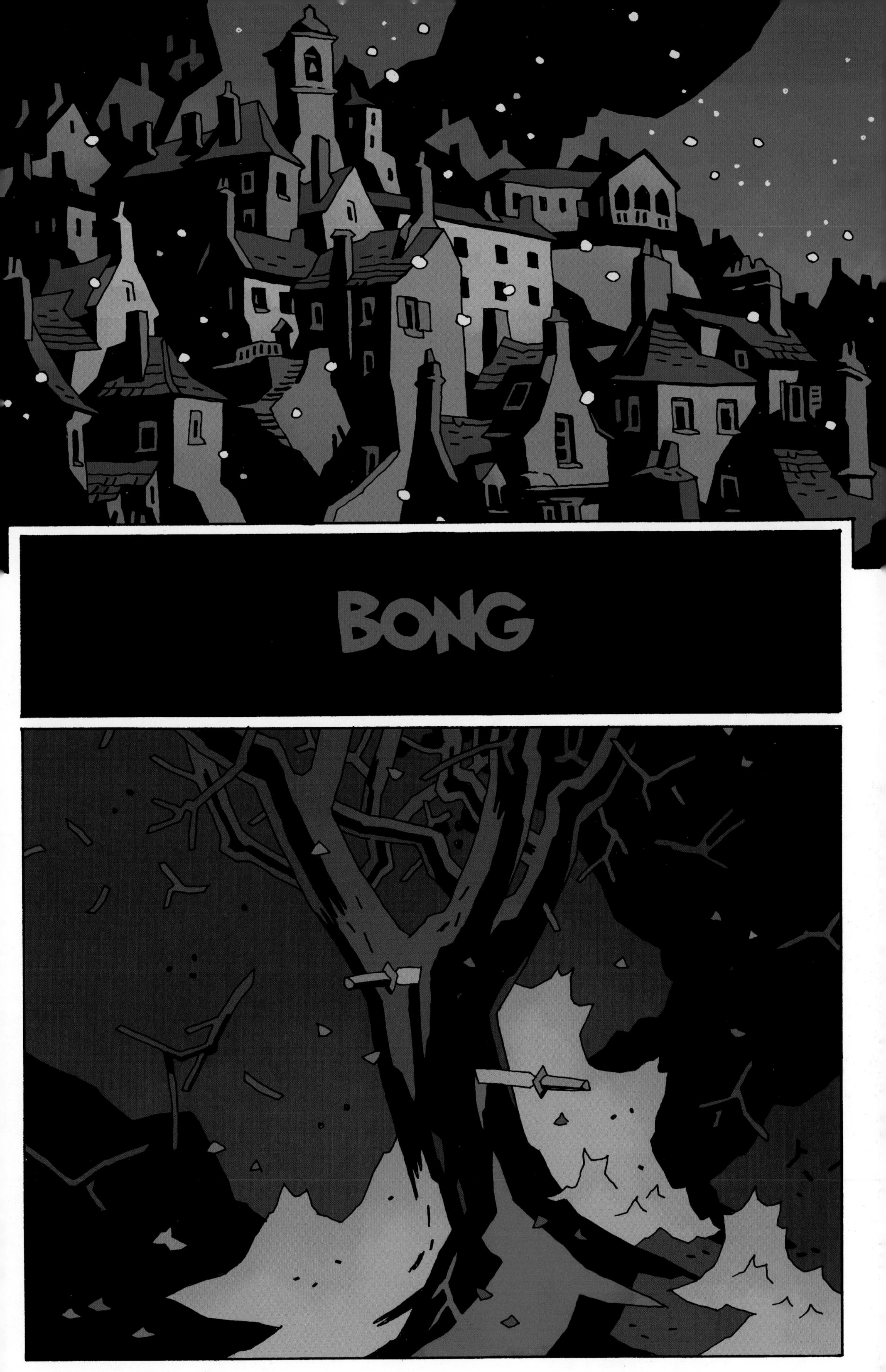
BONG

CHAPTER FIVE

FOR WHOM THE BELL TOLLS

NO MAN IS AN ISLAND...

EACH MAN'S DEATH DIMINISHES ME, FOR I AM INVOLVED IN MANKIND.

THEREFORE, SEND NOT TO KNOW FOR WHOM THE BELL TOLLS...

IT TOLLS FOR THEE.*

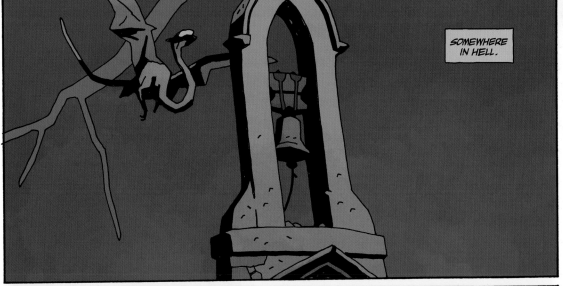

SOMEWHERE IN HELL.

*DEVOTIONS UPON EMERGENT OCCASIONS (1624) BY JOHN DONNE

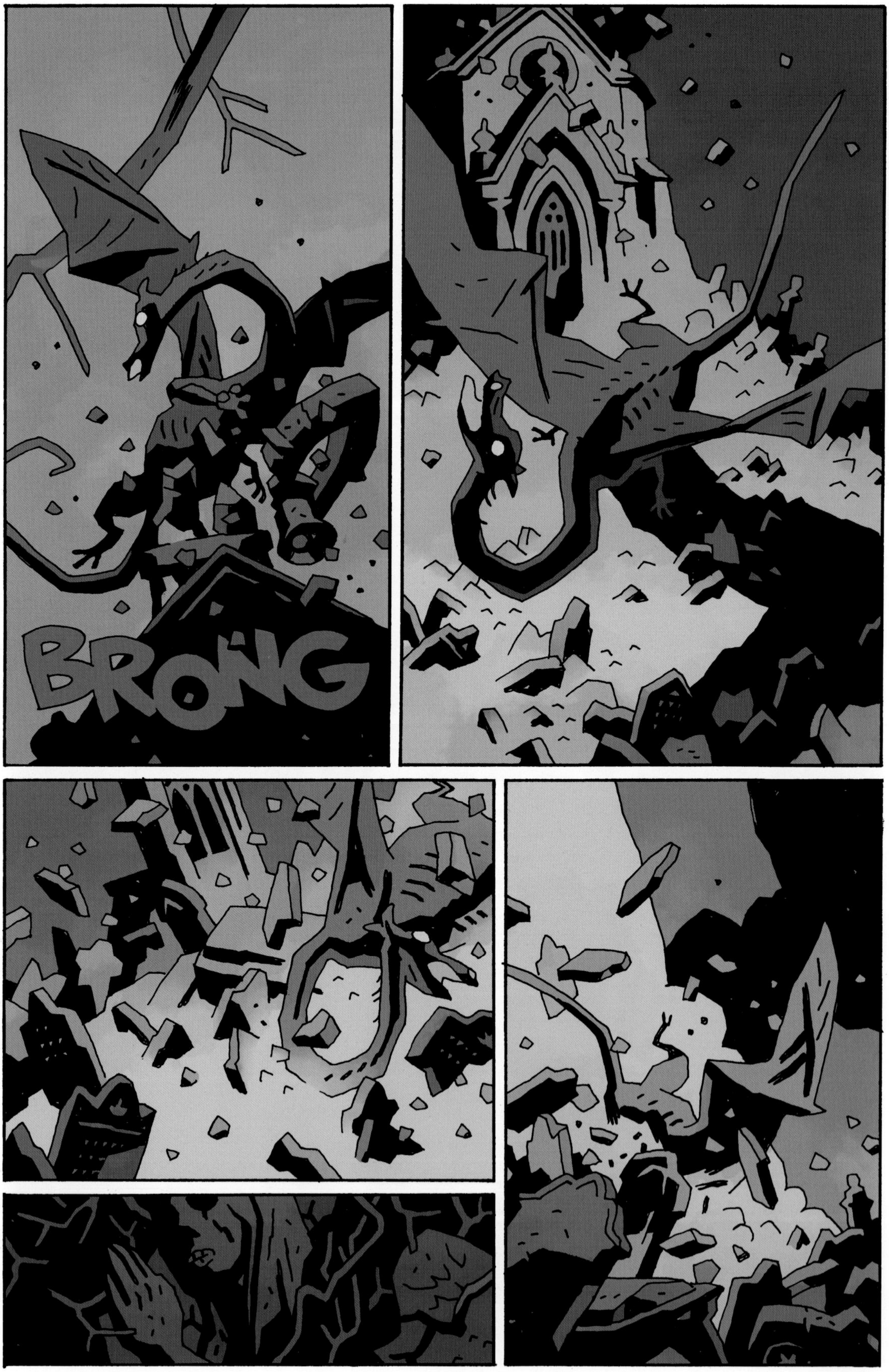
BRONG

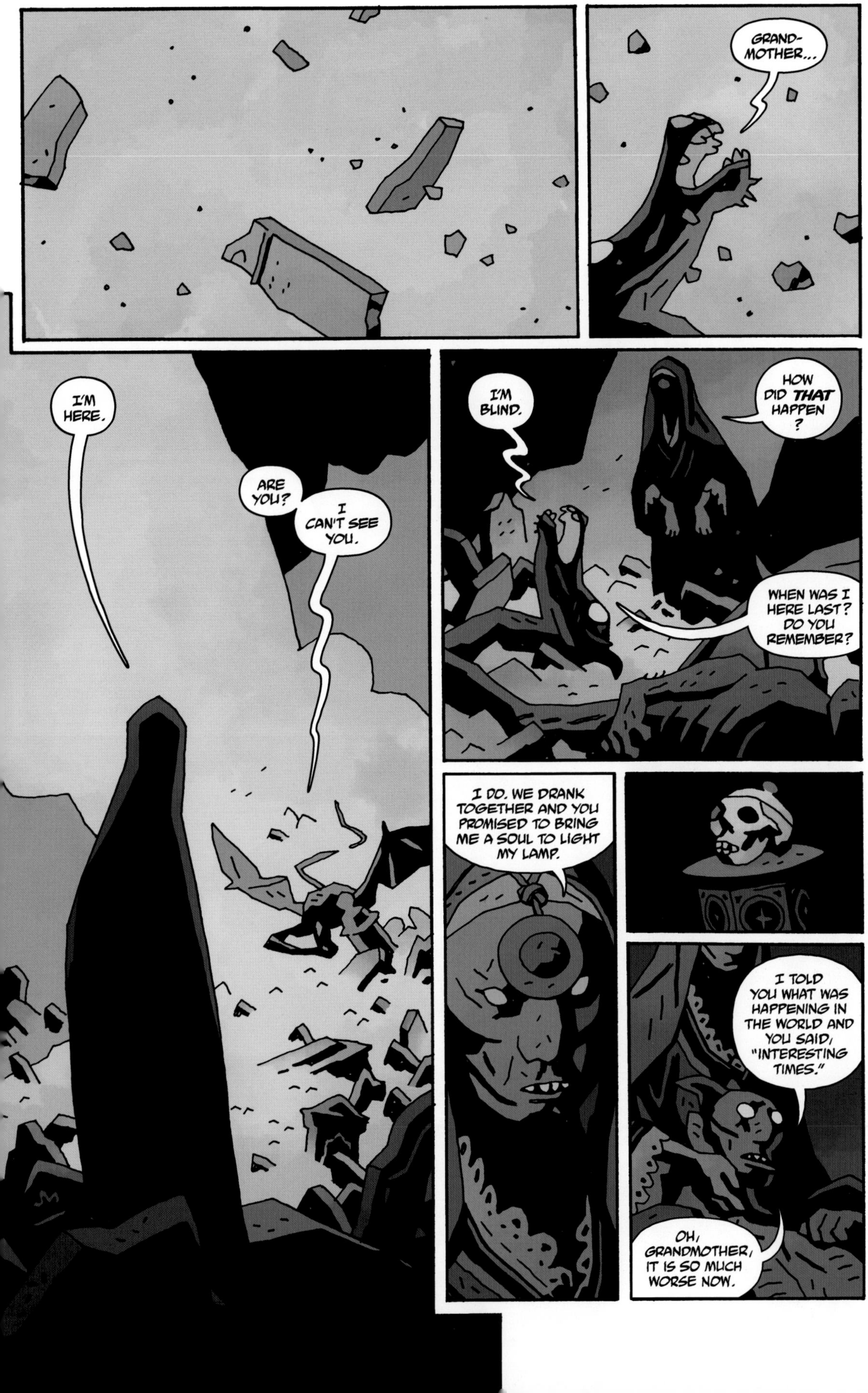
GRAND-MOTHER...
I'M HERE.
ARE YOU?
I CAN'T SEE YOU.
I'M BLIND.
HOW DID THAT HAPPEN?
WHEN WAS I HERE LAST? DO YOU REMEMBER?
I DO. WE DRANK TOGETHER AND YOU PROMISED TO BRING ME A SOUL TO LIGHT MY LAMP.
I TOLD YOU WHAT WAS HAPPENING IN THE WORLD AND YOU SAID, "INTERESTING TIMES."
OH, GRANDMOTHER, IT IS SO MUCH WORSE NOW.

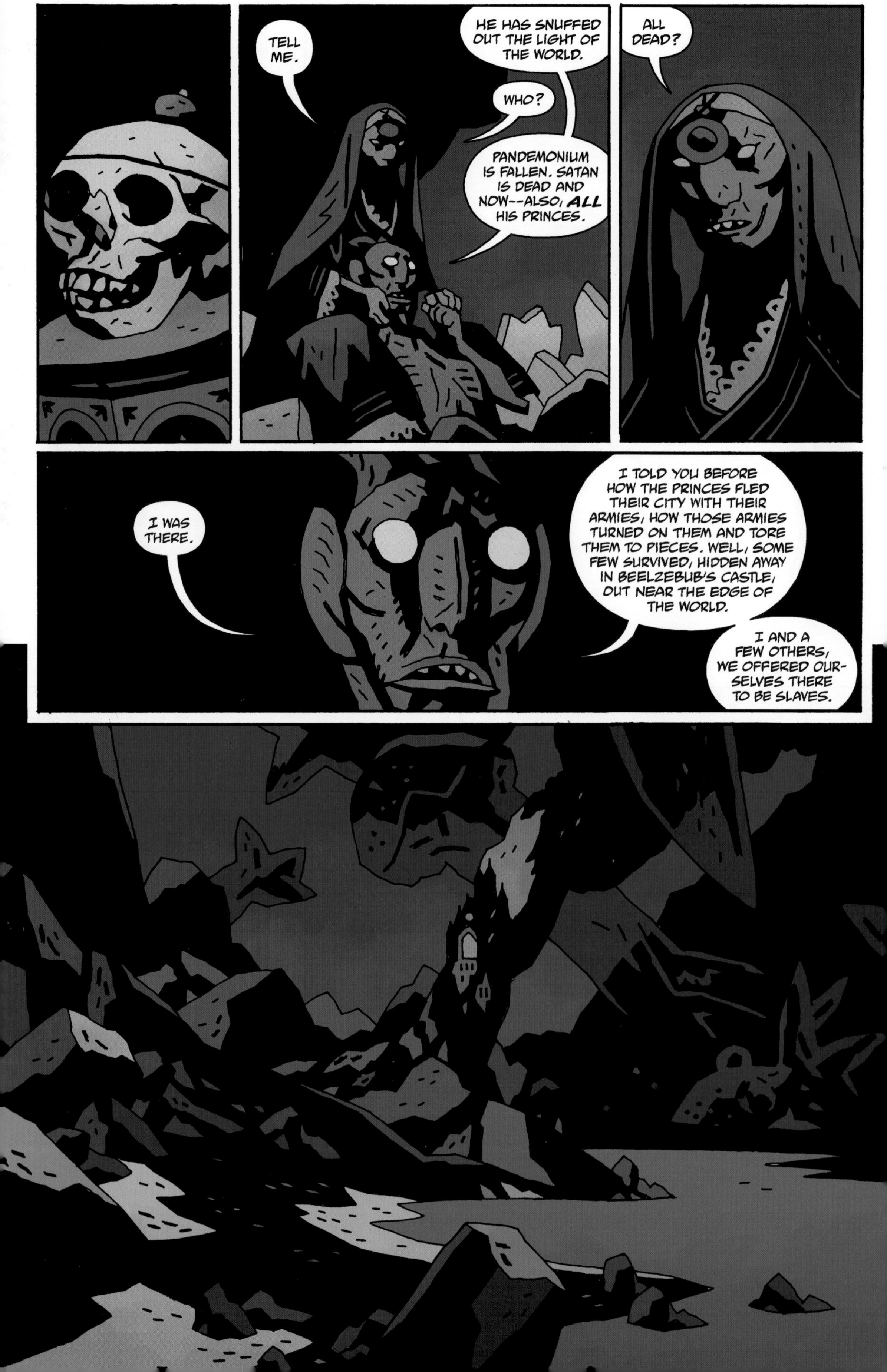
TELL ME.
HE HAS SNUFFED OUT THE LIGHT OF THE WORLD.
WHO?
PANDEMONIUM IS FALLEN. SATAN IS DEAD AND NOW--ALSO, ALL HIS PRINCES.
ALL DEAD?
I WAS THERE.
I TOLD YOU BEFORE HOW THE PRINCES FLED THEIR CITY WITH THEIR ARMIES, HOW THOSE ARMIES TURNED ON THEM AND TORE THEM TO PIECES. WELL, SOME FEW SURVIVED, HIDDEN AWAY IN BEELZEBUB'S CASTLE, OUT NEAR THE EDGE OF THE WORLD.
I AND A FEW OTHERS, WE OFFERED OURSELVES THERE TO BE SLAVES.

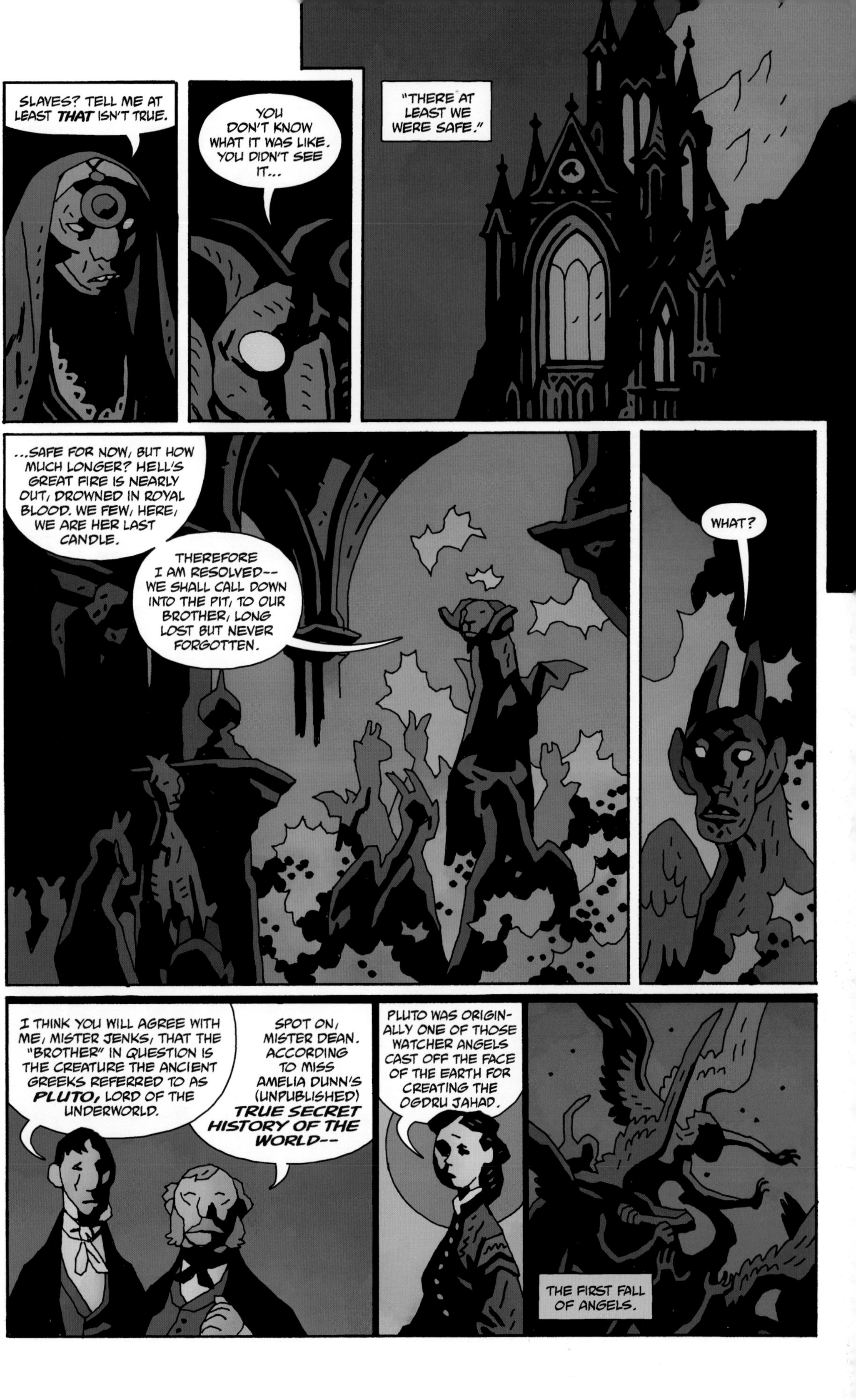

SLAVES? TELL ME AT LEAST THAT ISN'T TRUE.
YOU DON'T KNOW WHAT IT WAS LIKE. YOU DIDN'T SEE IT...
"THERE AT LEAST WE WERE SAFE."
...SAFE FOR NOW, BUT HOW MUCH LONGER? HELL'S GREAT FIRE IS NEARLY OUT, DROWNED IN ROYAL BLOOD. WE FEW, HERE, WE ARE HER LAST CANDLE.
THEREFORE I AM RESOLVED-- WE SHALL CALL DOWN INTO THE PIT, TO OUR BROTHER, LONG LOST BUT NEVER FORGOTTEN.
WHAT?
I THINK YOU WILL AGREE WITH ME, MISTER JENKS, THAT THE "BROTHER" IN QUESTION IS THE CREATURE THE ANCIENT GREEKS REFERRED TO AS PLUTO, LORD OF THE UNDERWORLD.
SPOT ON, MISTER DEAN. ACCORDING TO MISS AMELIA DUNN'S (UNPUBLISHED) TRUE SECRET HISTORY OF THE WORLD--
PLUTO WAS ORIGINALLY ONE OF THOSE WATCHER ANGELS CAST OFF THE FACE OF THE EARTH FOR CREATING THE OGDRU JAHAD.
THE FIRST FALL OF ANGELS.

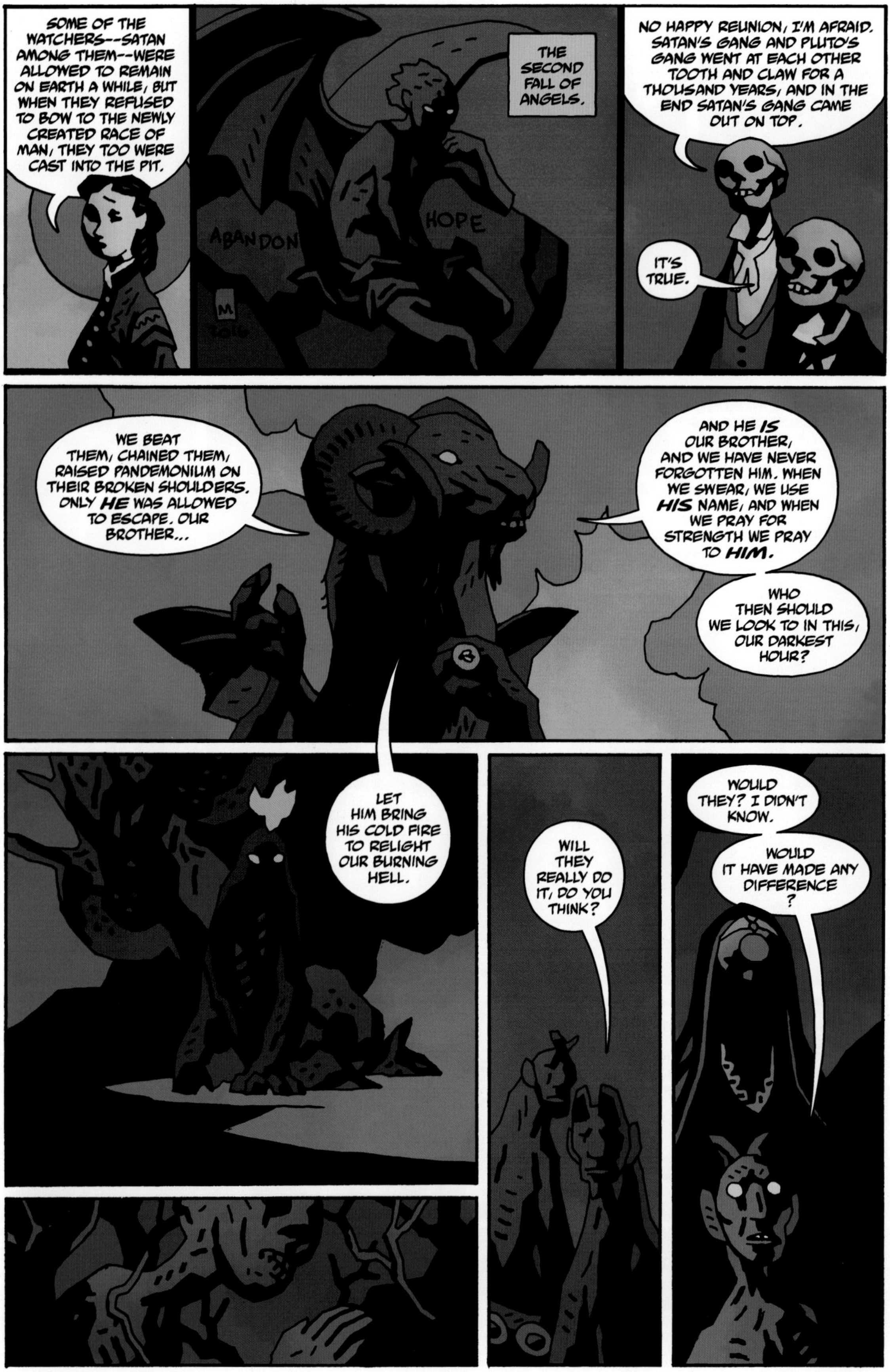
SOME OF THE WATCHERS--SATAN AMONG THEM--WERE ALLOWED TO REMAIN ON EARTH A WHILE, BUT WHEN THEY REFUSED TO BOW TO THE NEWLY CREATED RACE OF MAN, THEY TOO WERE CAST INTO THE PIT.
THE SECOND FALL OF ANGELS.
ABANDON
HOPE
NO HAPPY REUNION, I'M AFRAID. SATAN'S GANG AND PLUTO'S GANG WENT AT EACH OTHER TOOTH AND CLAW FOR A THOUSAND YEARS, AND IN THE END SATAN'S GANG CAME OUT ON TOP.
IT'S TRUE.
WE BEAT THEM, CHAINED THEM, RAISED PANDEMONIUM ON THEIR BROKEN SHOULDERS. ONLY HE WAS ALLOWED TO ESCAPE. OUR BROTHER...
AND HE IS OUR BROTHER, AND WE HAVE NEVER FORGOTTEN HIM. WHEN WE SWEAR, WE USE HIS NAME, AND WHEN WE PRAY FOR STRENGTH WE PRAY TO HIM.
WHO THEN SHOULD WE LOOK TO IN THIS, OUR DARKEST HOUR?
LET HIM BRING HIS COLD FIRE TO RELIGHT OUR BURNING HELL.
WILL THEY REALLY DO IT, DO YOU THINK?
WOULD THEY? I DIDN'T KNOW.
WOULD IT HAVE MADE ANY DIFFERENCE?

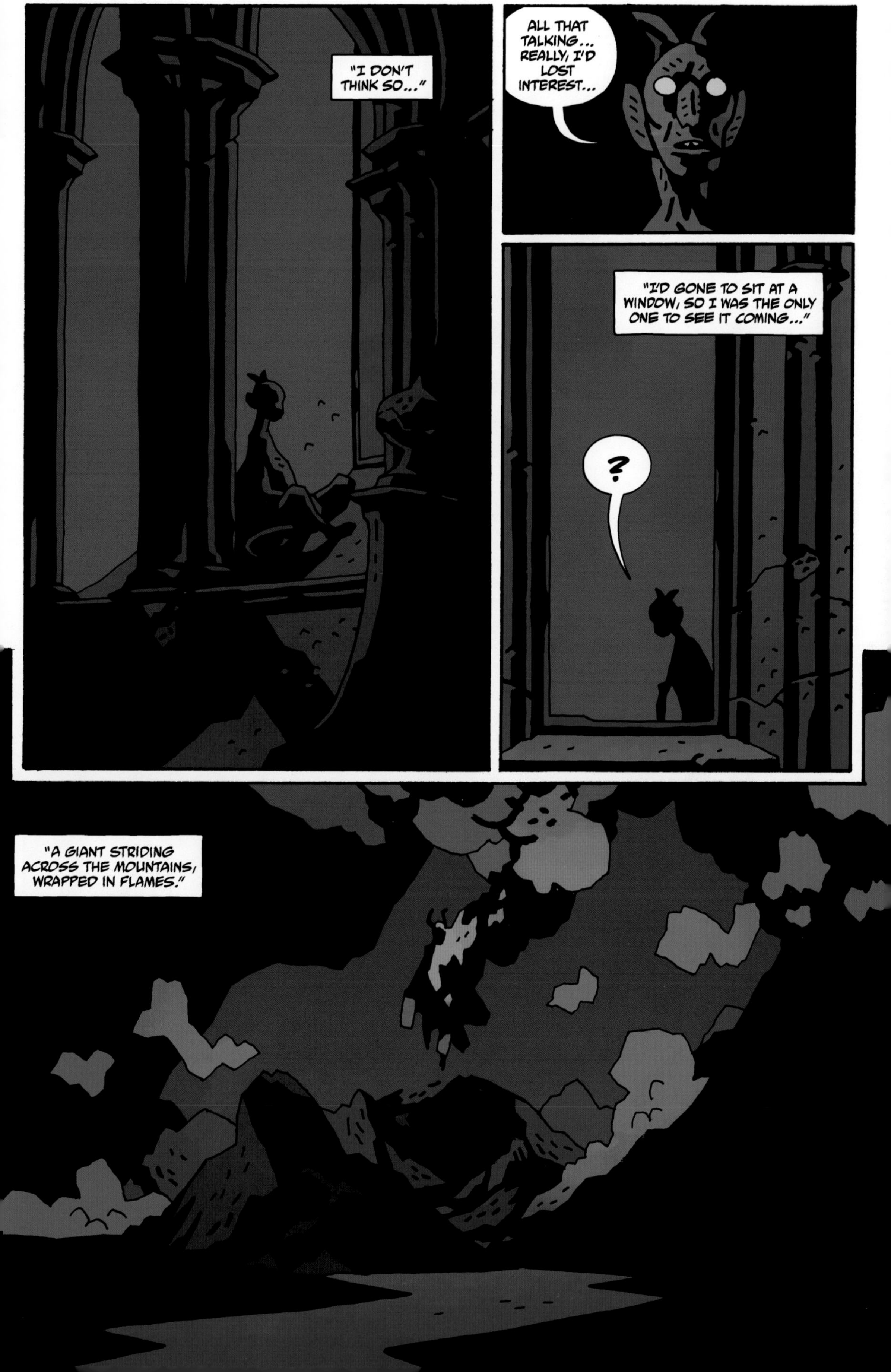
"I DON'T THINK SO..."
ALL THAT TALKING... REALLY, I'D LOST INTEREST...
"I'D GONE TO SIT AT A WINDOW, SO I WAS THE ONLY ONE TO SEE IT COMING..."
?
"A GIANT STRIDING ACROSS THE MOUNTAINS, WRAPPED IN FLAMES."

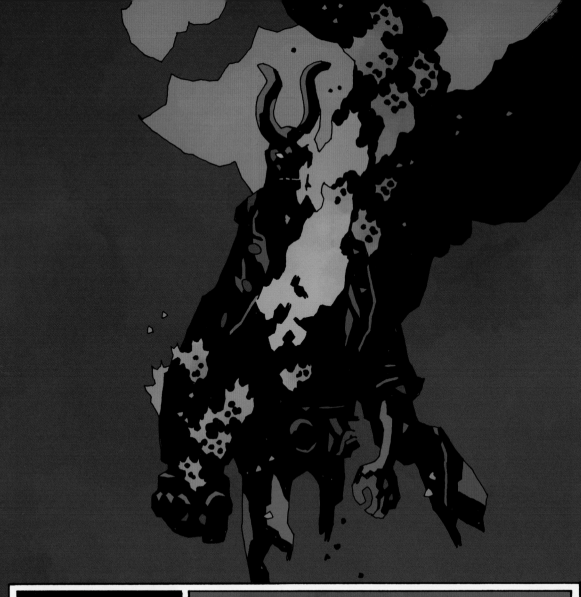

THEN I SAW LEVIATHAN RISE UP OUT OF THE SEA...

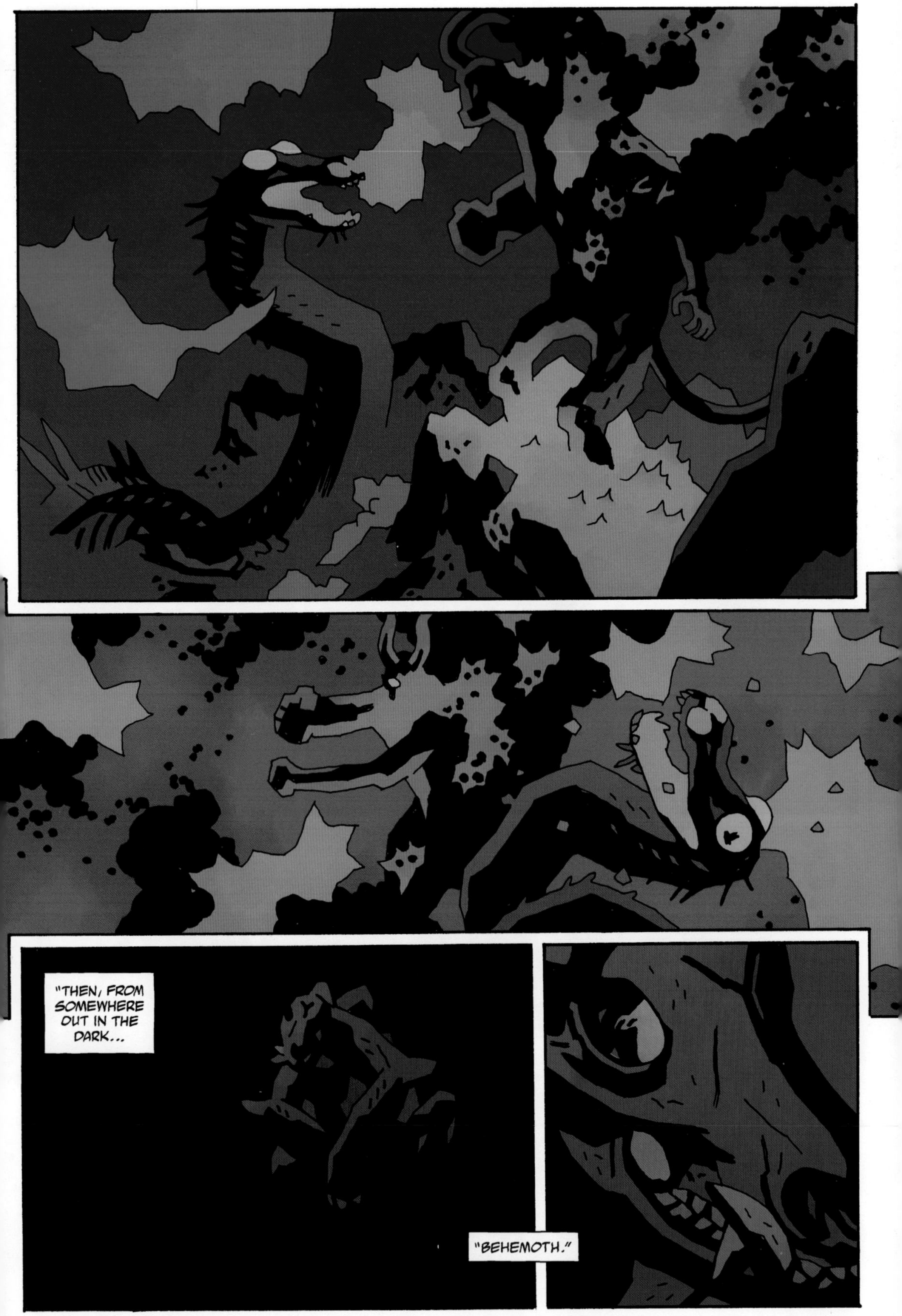
"THEN, FROM SOMEWHERE OUT IN THE DARK...
"BEHEMOTH."

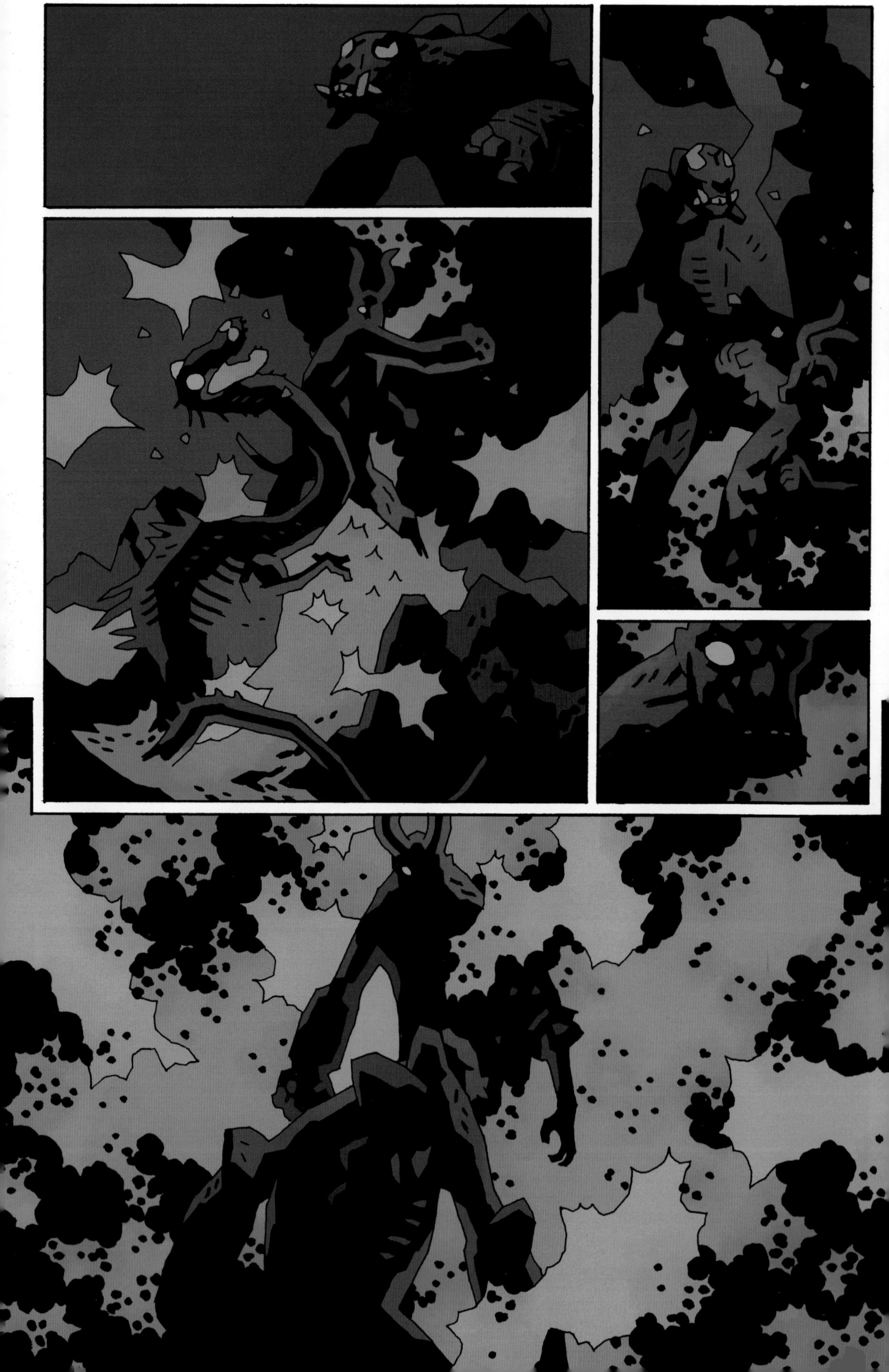

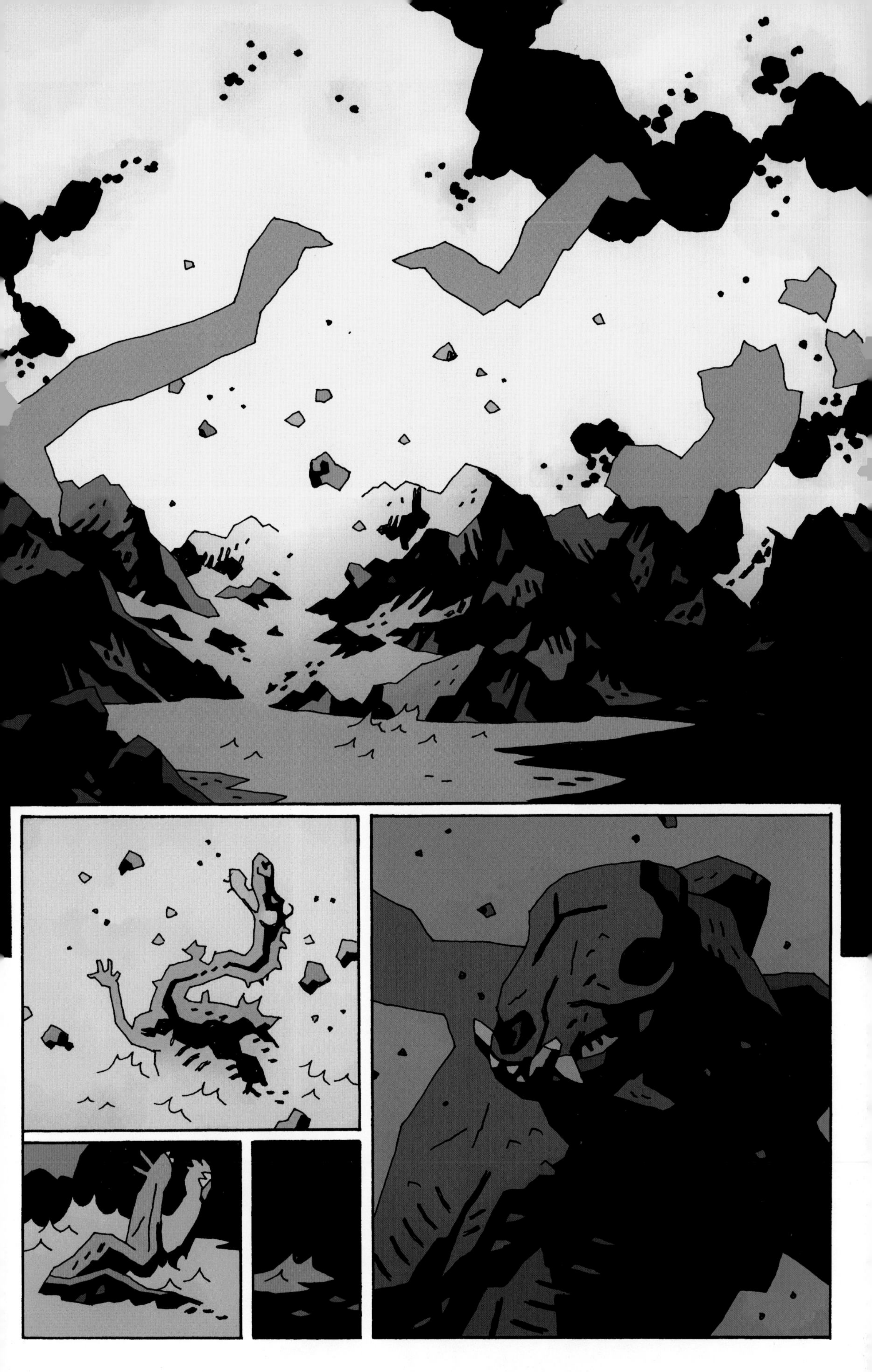

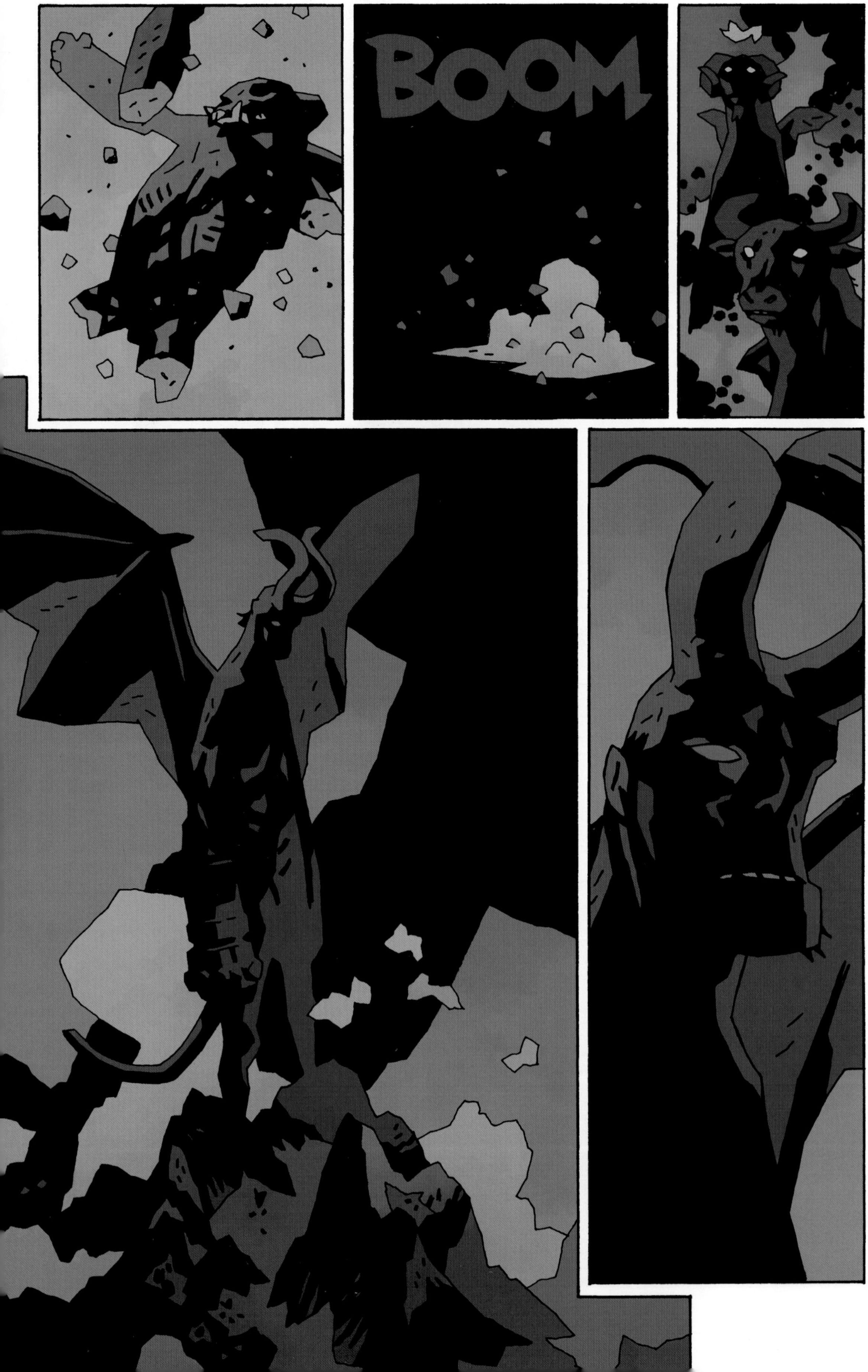
BOOM

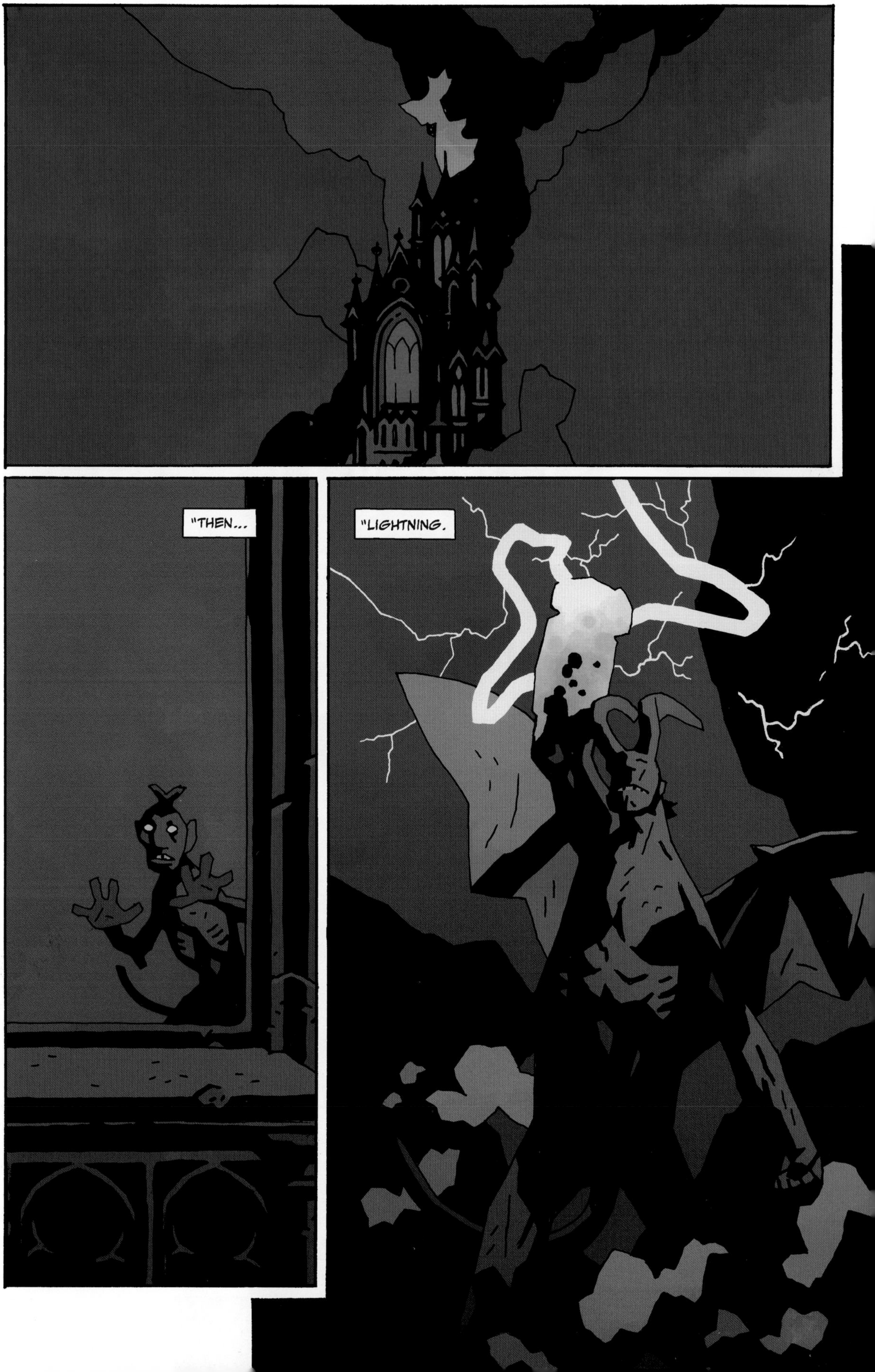
"THEN...
"LIGHTNING.

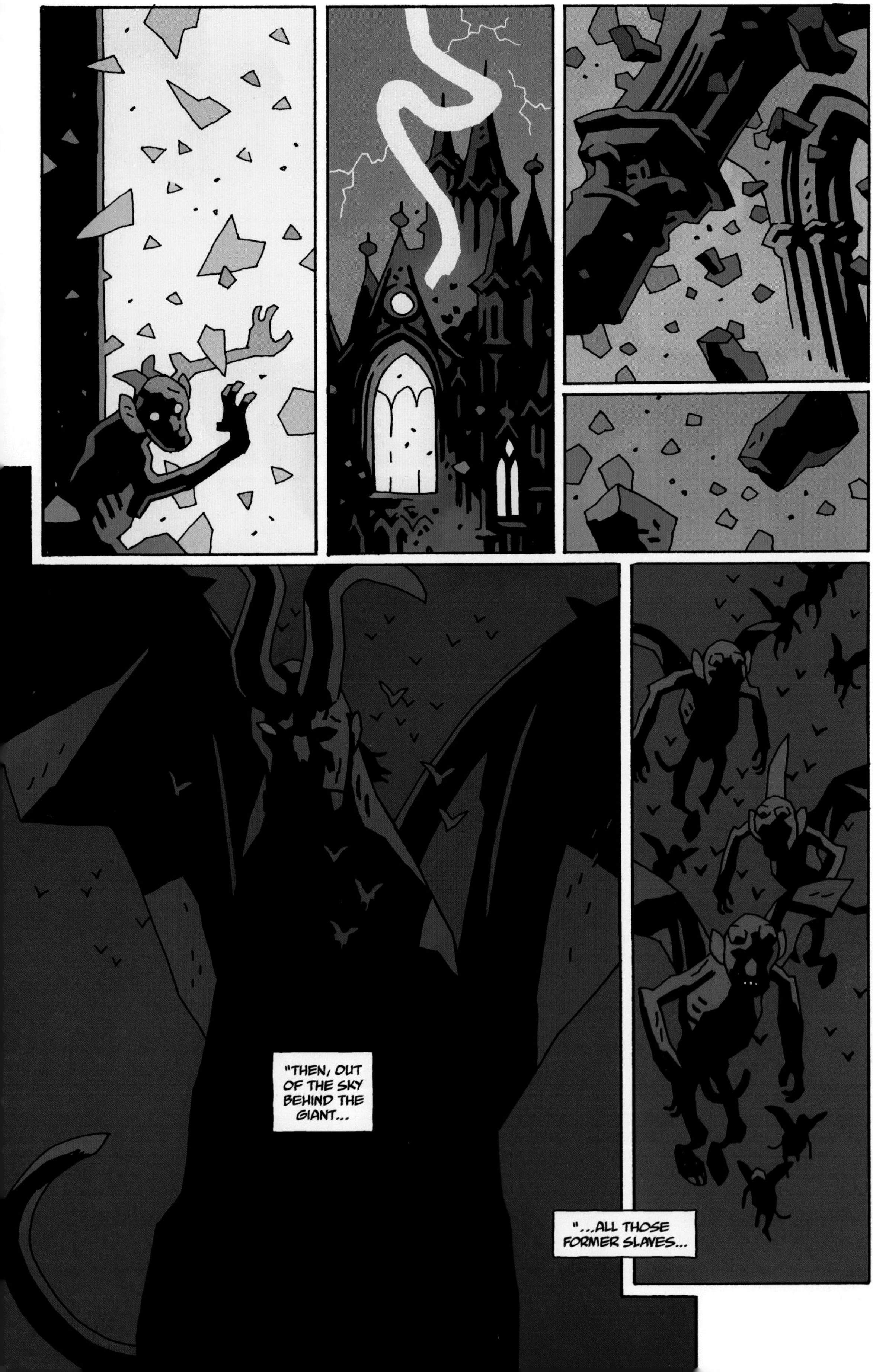
"THEN, OUT OF THE SKY BEHIND THE GIANT...
"...ALL THOSE FORMER SLAVES...

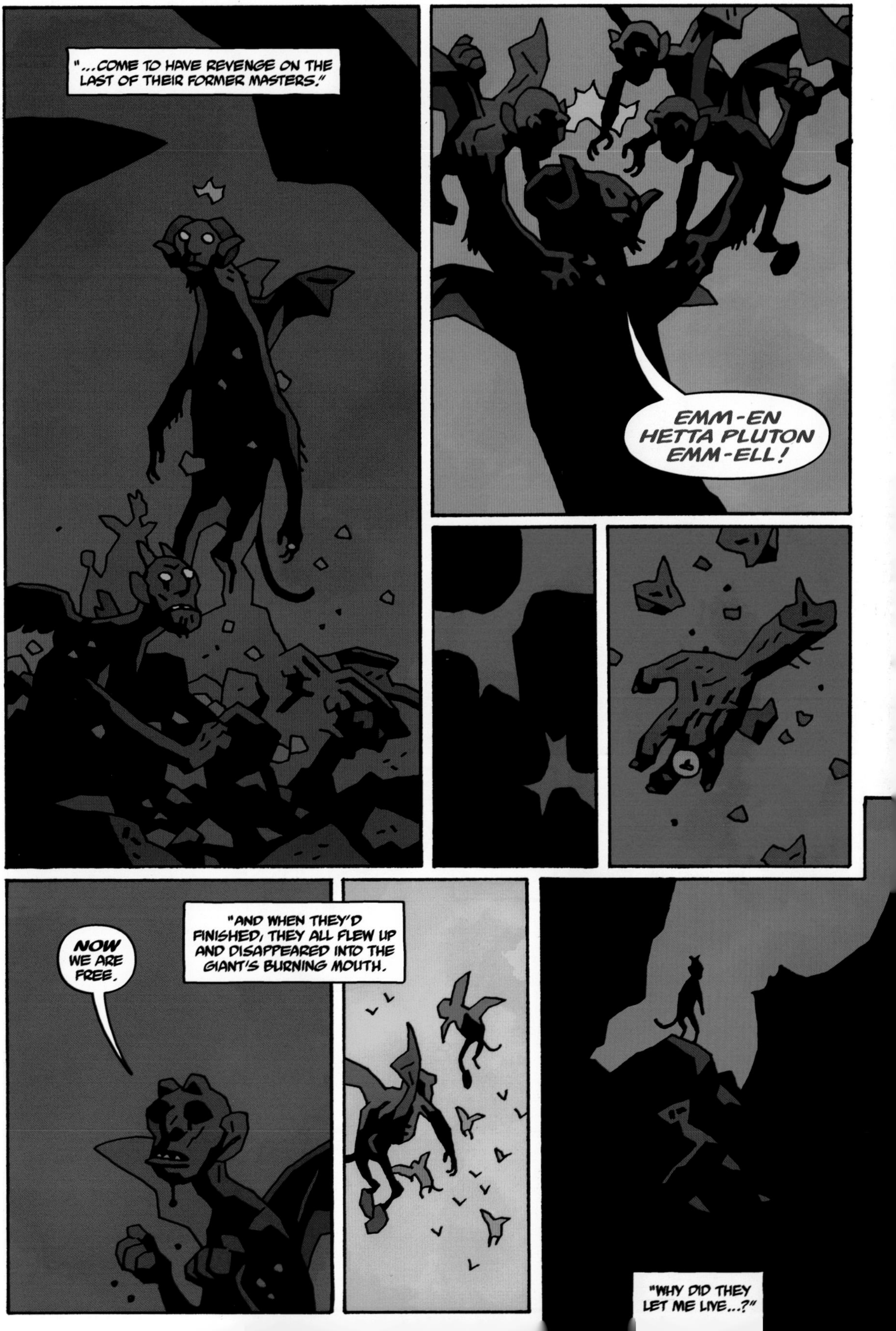
"...COME TO HAVE REVENGE ON THE LAST OF THEIR FORMER MASTERS."
EMM-EN HETTA PLUTON EMM-ELL!
NOW WE ARE FREE.
"AND WHEN THEY'D FINISHED, THEY ALL FLEW UP AND DISAPPEARED INTO THE GIANT'S BURNING MOUTH.
"WHY DID THEY LET ME LIVE...?"

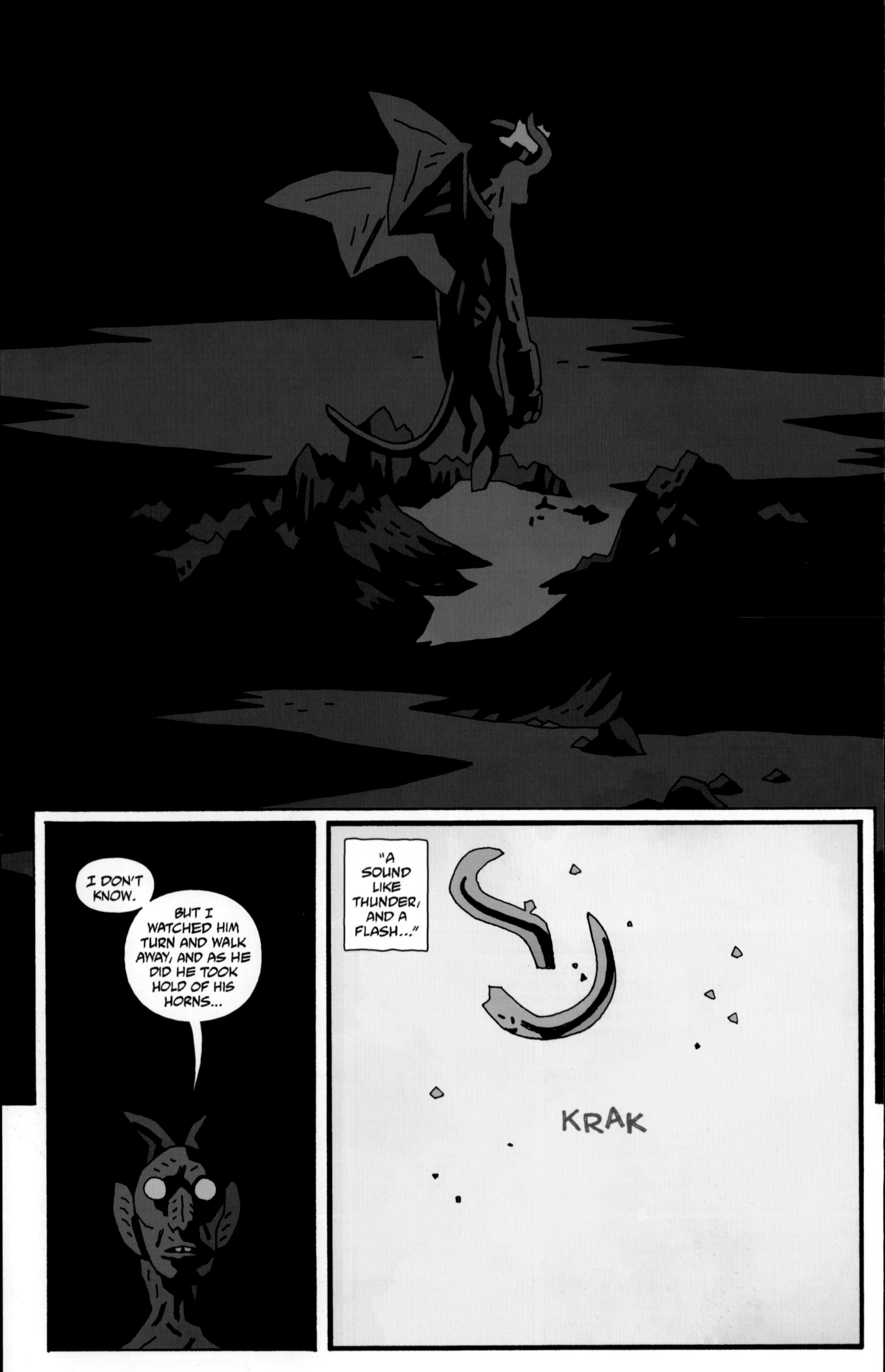
I DON'T KNOW.
BUT I WATCHED HIM TURN AND WALK AWAY, AND AS HE DID HE TOOK HOLD OF HIS HORNS...
"A SOUND LIKE THUNDER, AND A FLASH..."
KRAK

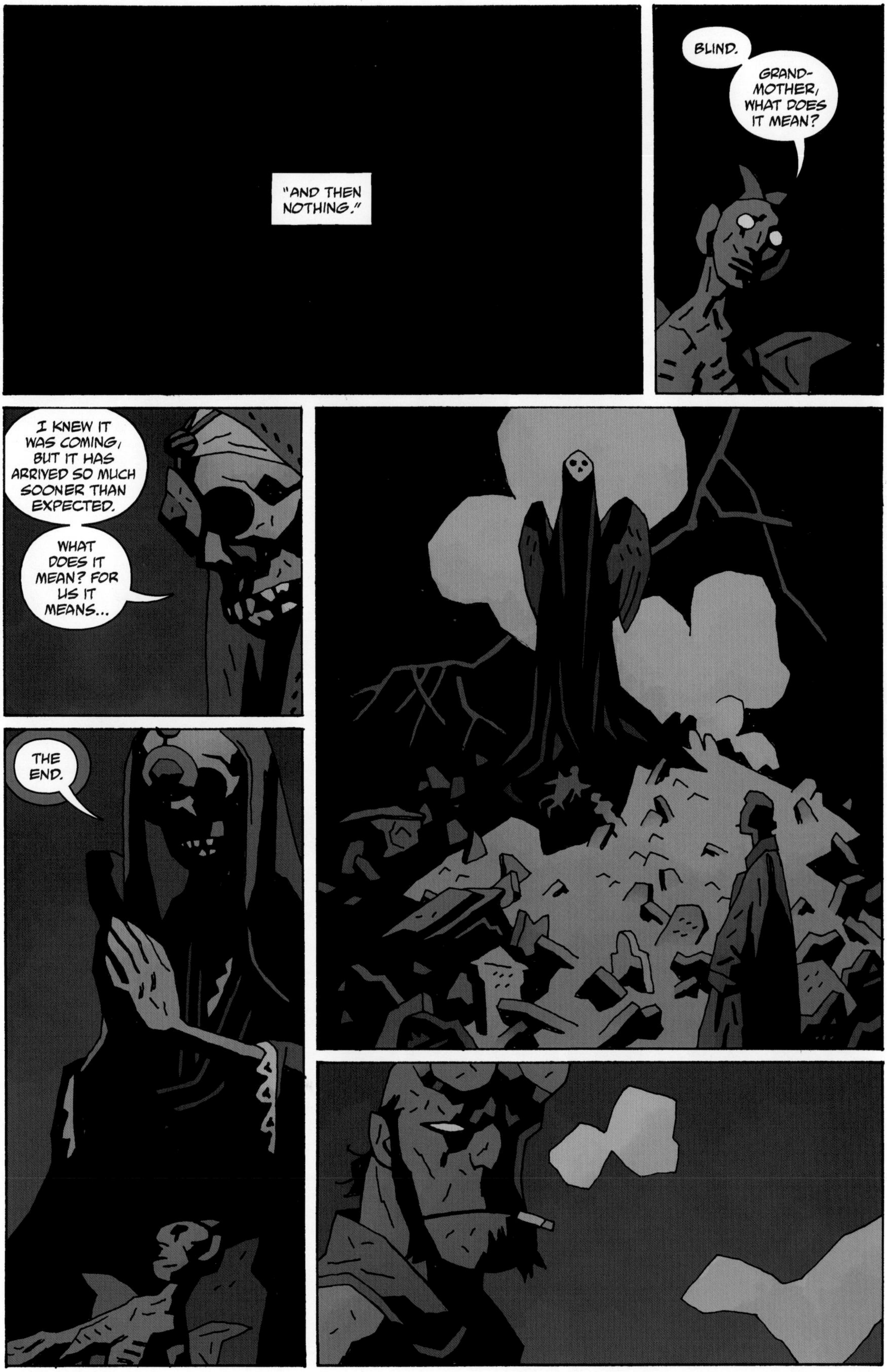
"AND THEN NOTHING."
BLIND.
GRAND-MOTHER, WHAT DOES IT MEAN?
I KNEW IT WAS COMING, BUT IT HAS ARRIVED SO MUCH SOONER THAN EXPECTED.
WHAT DOES IT MEAN? FOR US IT MEANS...
THE END.

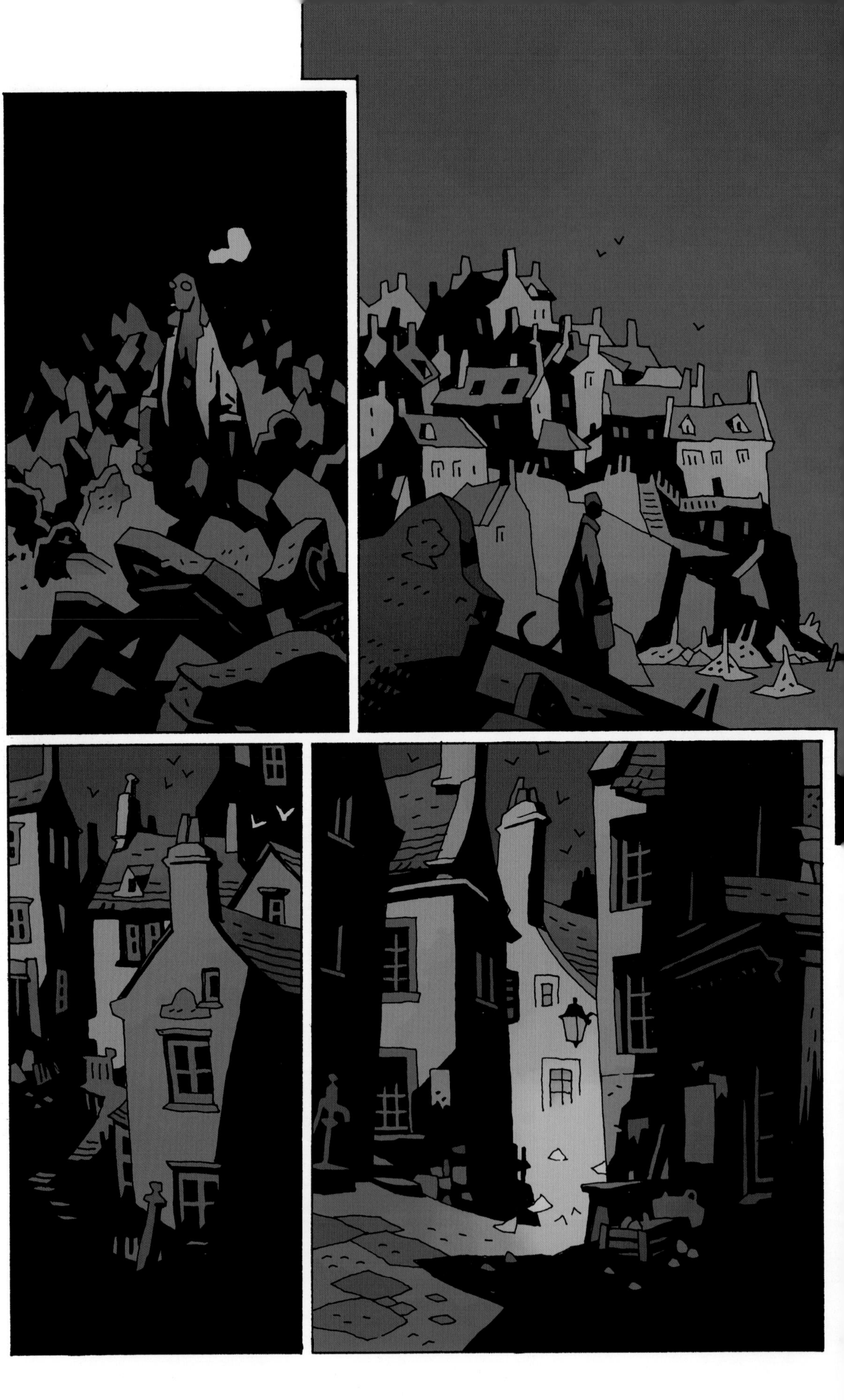

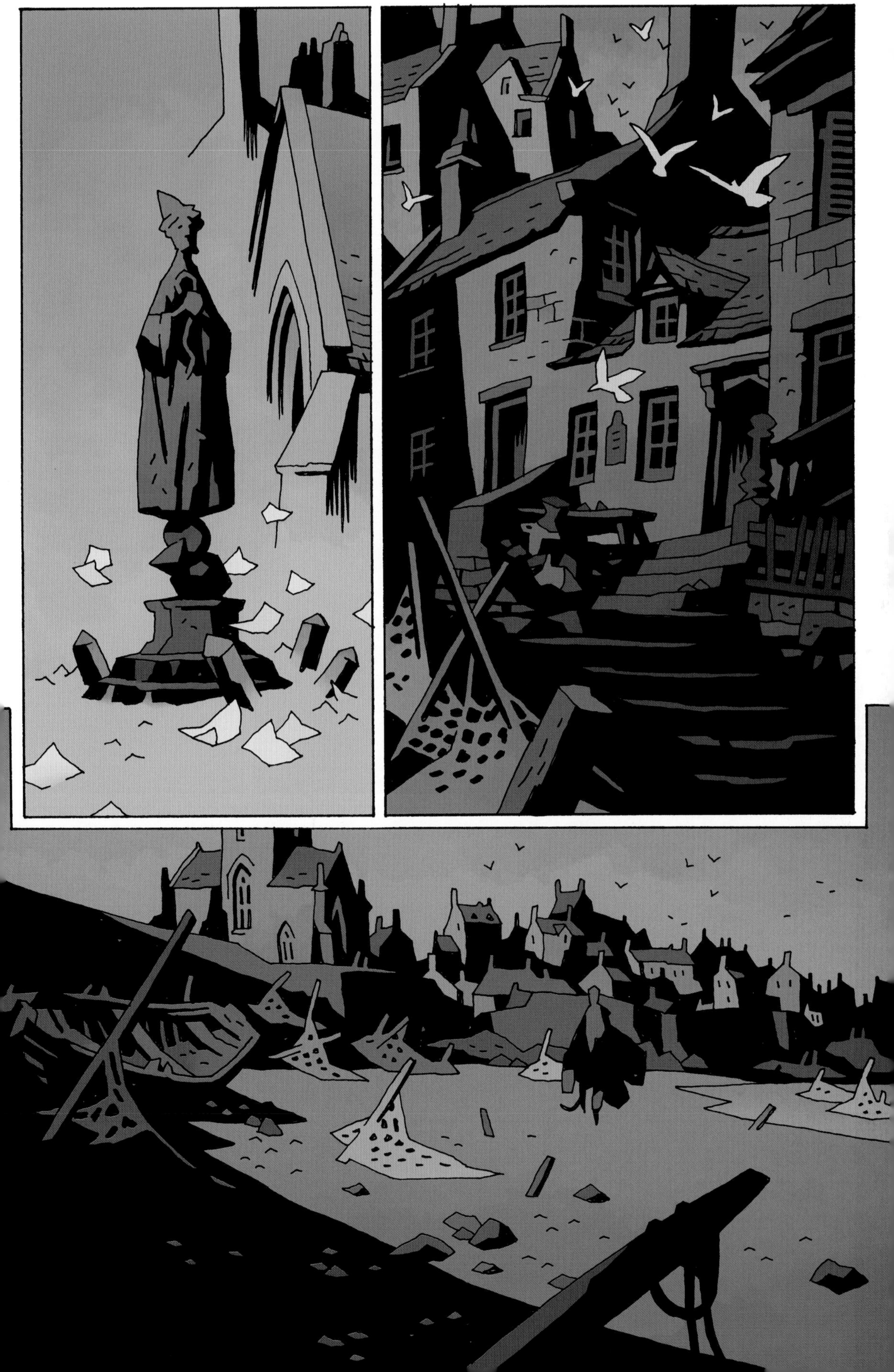

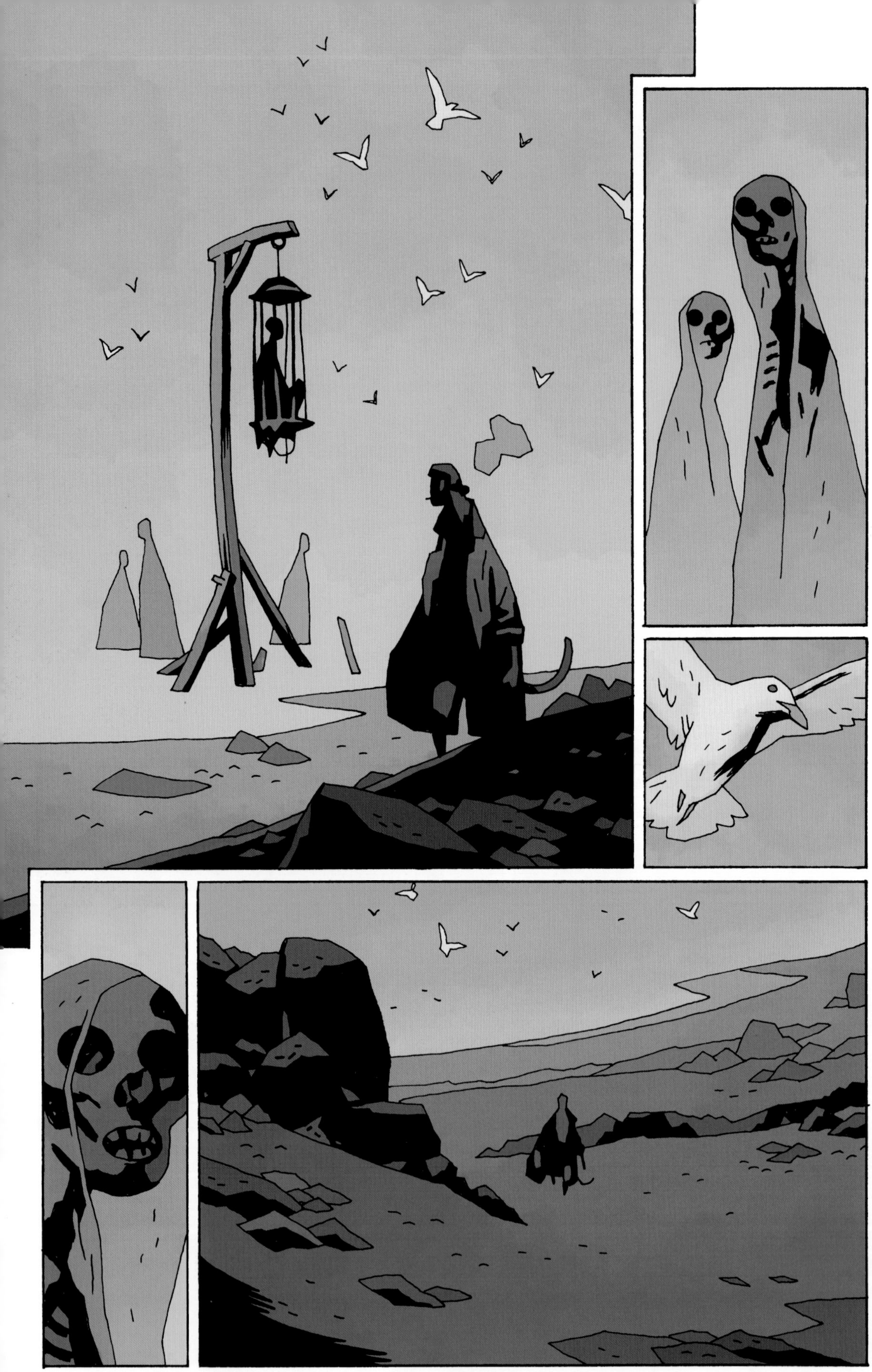

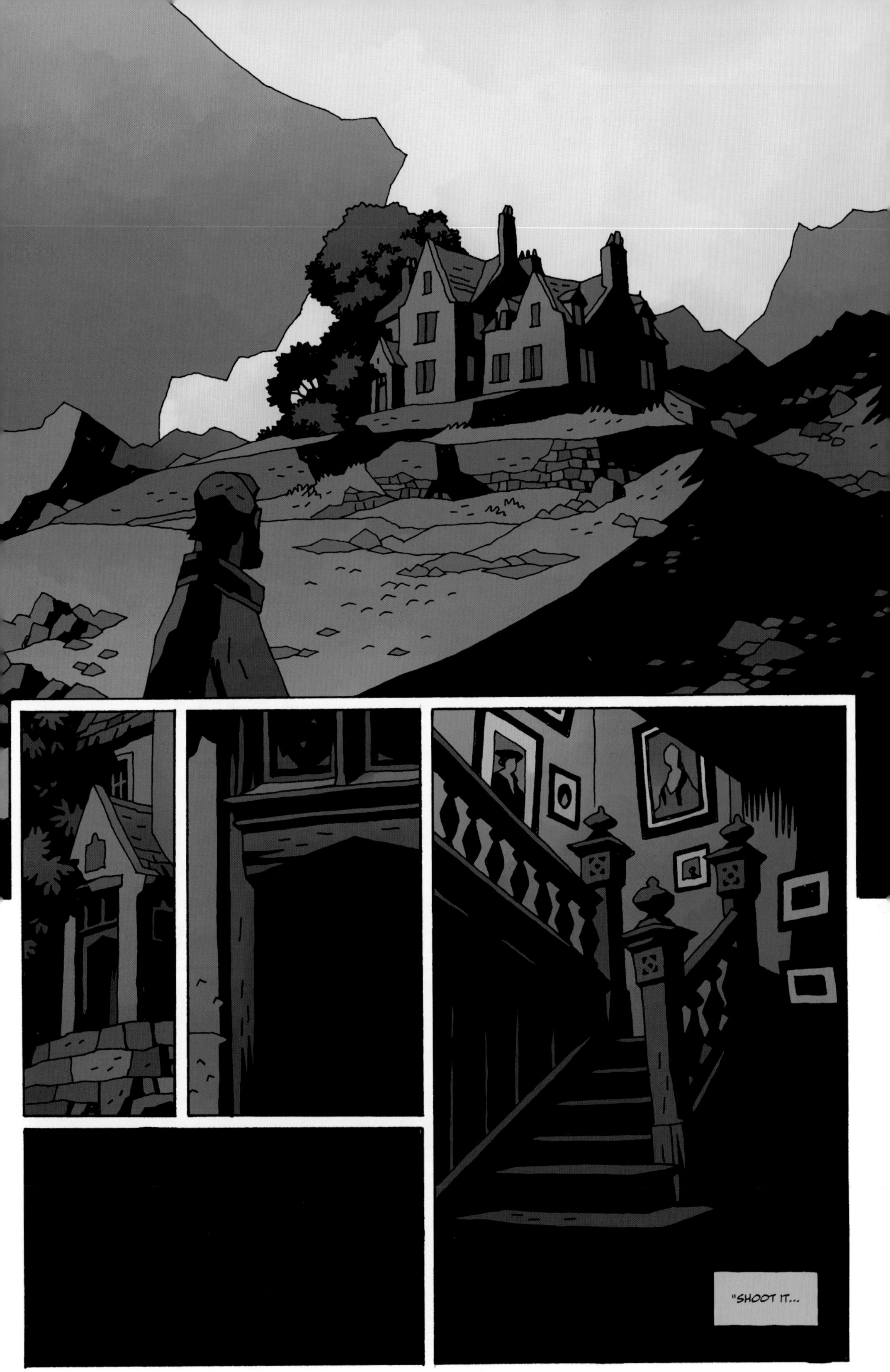
"SHOOT IT...

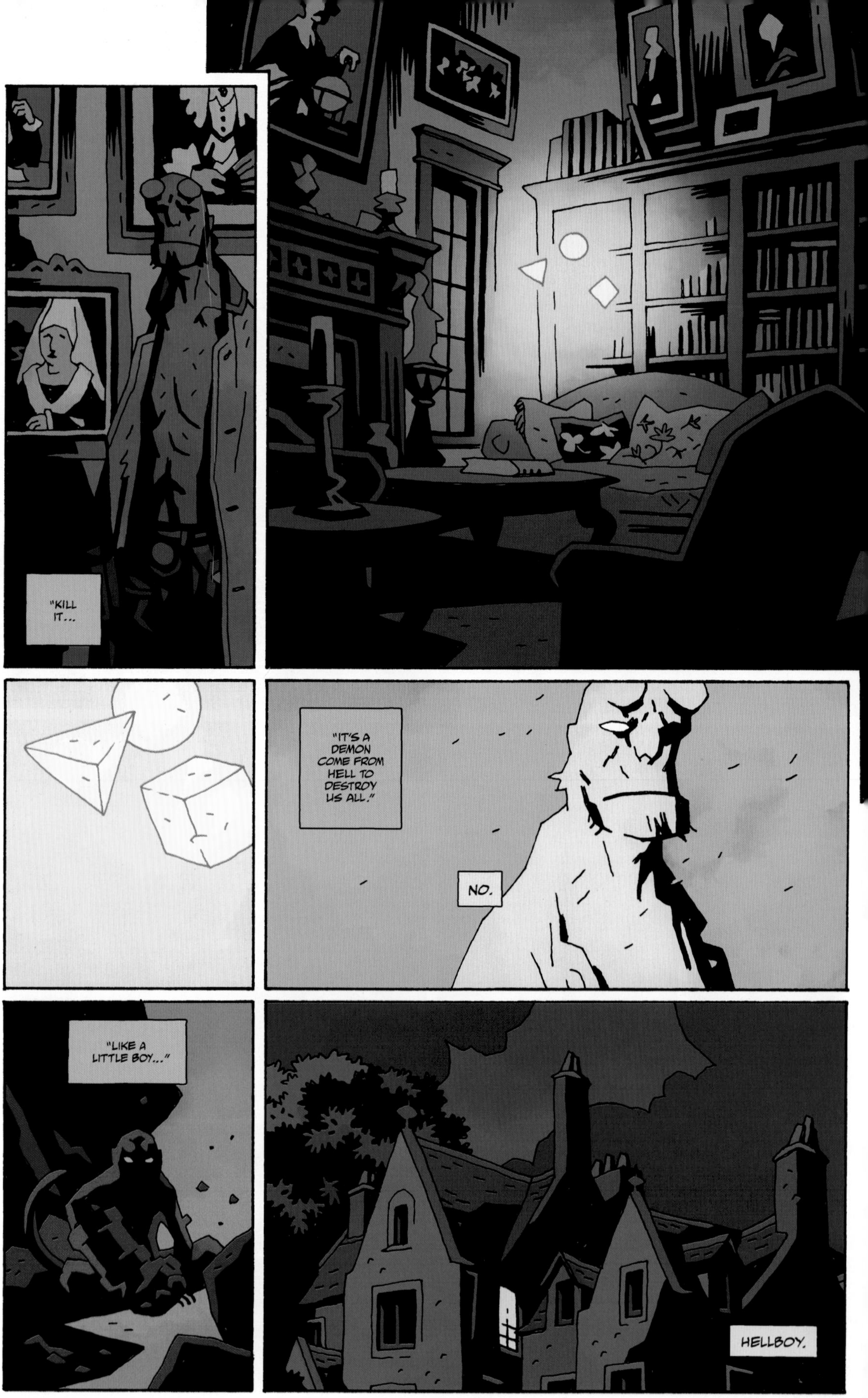
"KILL IT...
"IT'S A DEMON COME FROM HELL TO DESTROY US ALL."
NO.
"LIKE A LITTLE BOY..."
HELLBOY.

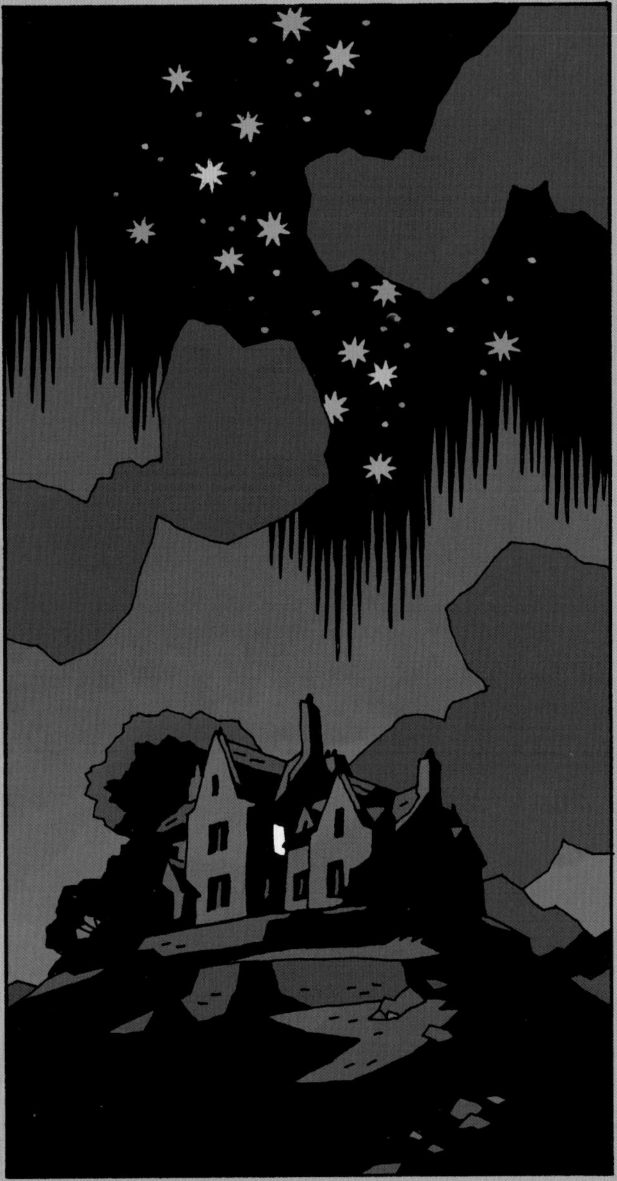

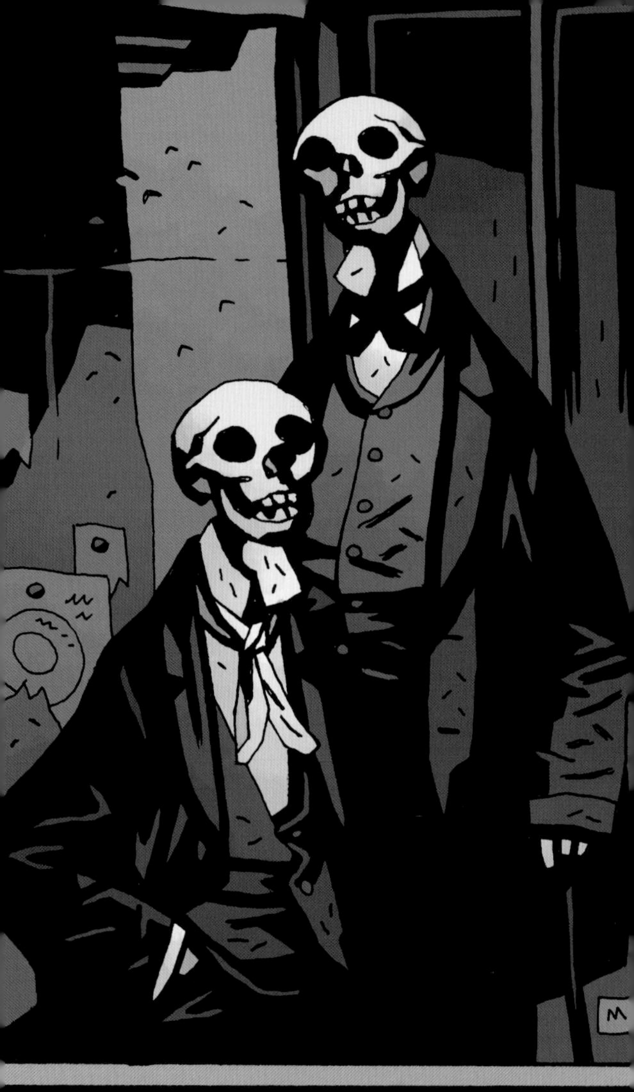
M

JENKS AND DEAN

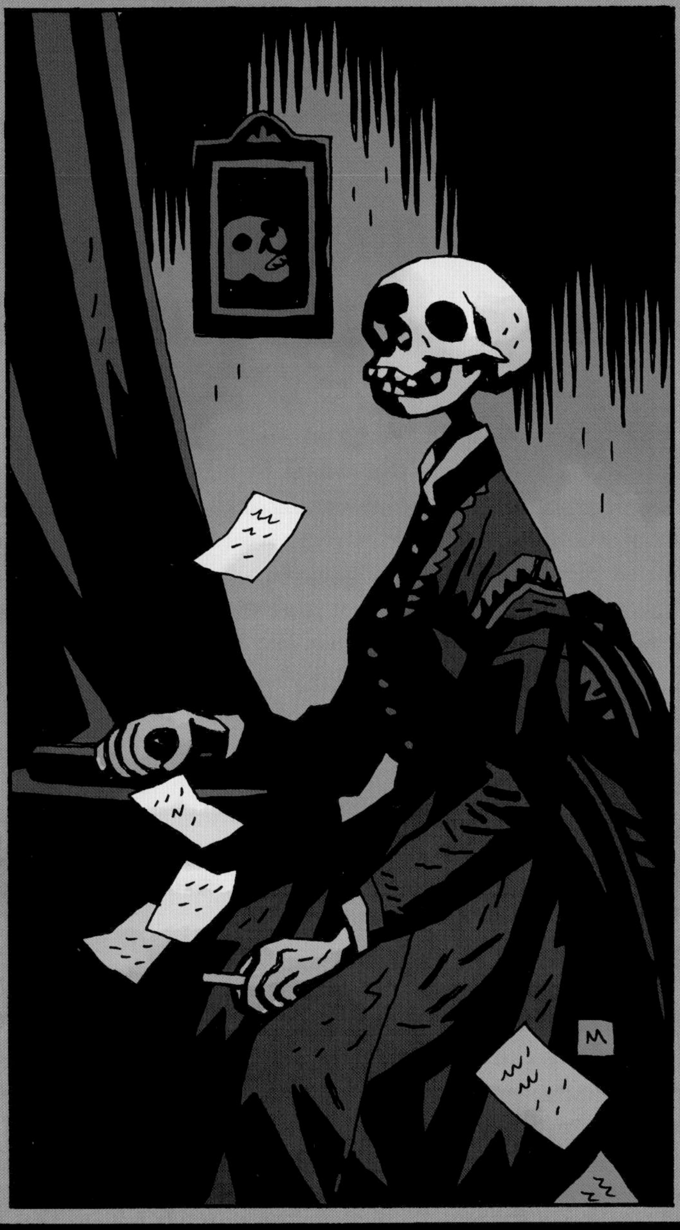

AMELIA DUNN

lowing the murder of her parents in 1902, forty-five-year-old s
Amelia Dunn became known as the "Rhode Island Lizzy Bord
ugh (like Lizzy Borden) she was eventually found not guilty of
ne, she would spend the rest of her life as a near recluse. She devo
self to Spiritualism and, according to a neighbor, "descended
iet sort of madness." In 1911 she claimed to be in regular con
h a spirit she called William. Over the next two years he wo
tate *The True Secret History of the World* to her, and she wo
nd the rest of her life trying, unsuccessfully, to have it publis
died a broken woman on September 13, 1928, and is believe

AFTERWORD

THE NICE OLD LADY in the cemetery said, "I knew it was coming, but it has arrived so much sooner than expected." Exactly. When I started this series, the plan was that it would go on forever, a rambling parade of standalone stories. Well, that didn't happen. I guess it was that bit where Hellboy killed Satan. That became a much bigger deal than I originally intended (how did I *not* think that would be a big deal?), and that pretty much changed everything. I started looking at the thing as one big story. It looked like it would be four books, twenty issues of the comic. Then, when things started moving faster than expected, it sort of condensed itself to three. Then, when I got to the end of issue eight (chapter three here), the whole thing sort of stopped cold. That last page just looked (and really felt) like the end of the series. I can't explain that other than to say these things tend to take on a life of their own, and sometimes they just tell you when they're done. Note we kept "The End" on the last page of that chapter, though we removed it from others.

Chapter four—I'd planned to do something much different with Hellboy's ex-wife, but when I realized the series was wrapping up, I scrapped a lot of things, moved a lot of things around, and, trust me, this is much better.

Chapter five—this is always how it was going to end.

And is it the end? As I write this people are already asking, and I keep pointing out that Hellboy is already dead, has been for years now. How can you ever really end something if your character dies and just keeps wandering around?

On the following pages you'll find "The Exorcist of Vorsk," cowritten with my brother Todd and loosely based on a Russian folktale. This was originally published in *Dark Horse Presents* #16. It takes place (if it takes place) somewhere between chapters three and four of this book. At one point I was going to insert it there for this collection, but, really, it would not have worked there. It's just a bit too odd. Maybe if I hadn't decided to draw most of the characters as puppets . . .

MIKE MIGNOLA

The Exorcist of Vorsk

A puppet story told in Hell
by Todd and Mike Mignola

Colors by Dave Stewart Letters by Clem Robins

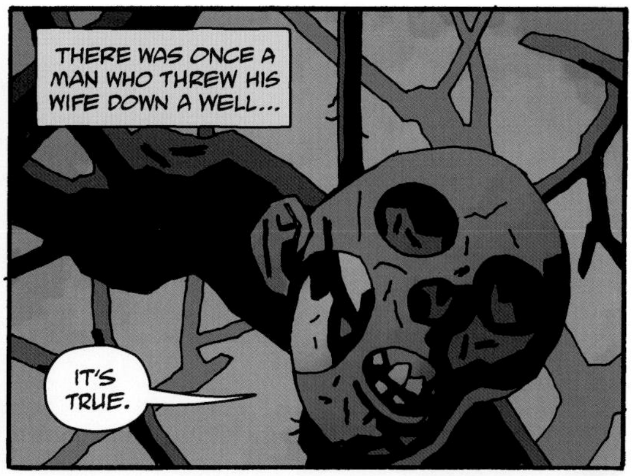

THERE WAS ONCE A MAN WHO THREW HIS WIFE DOWN A WELL...
IT'S TRUE.

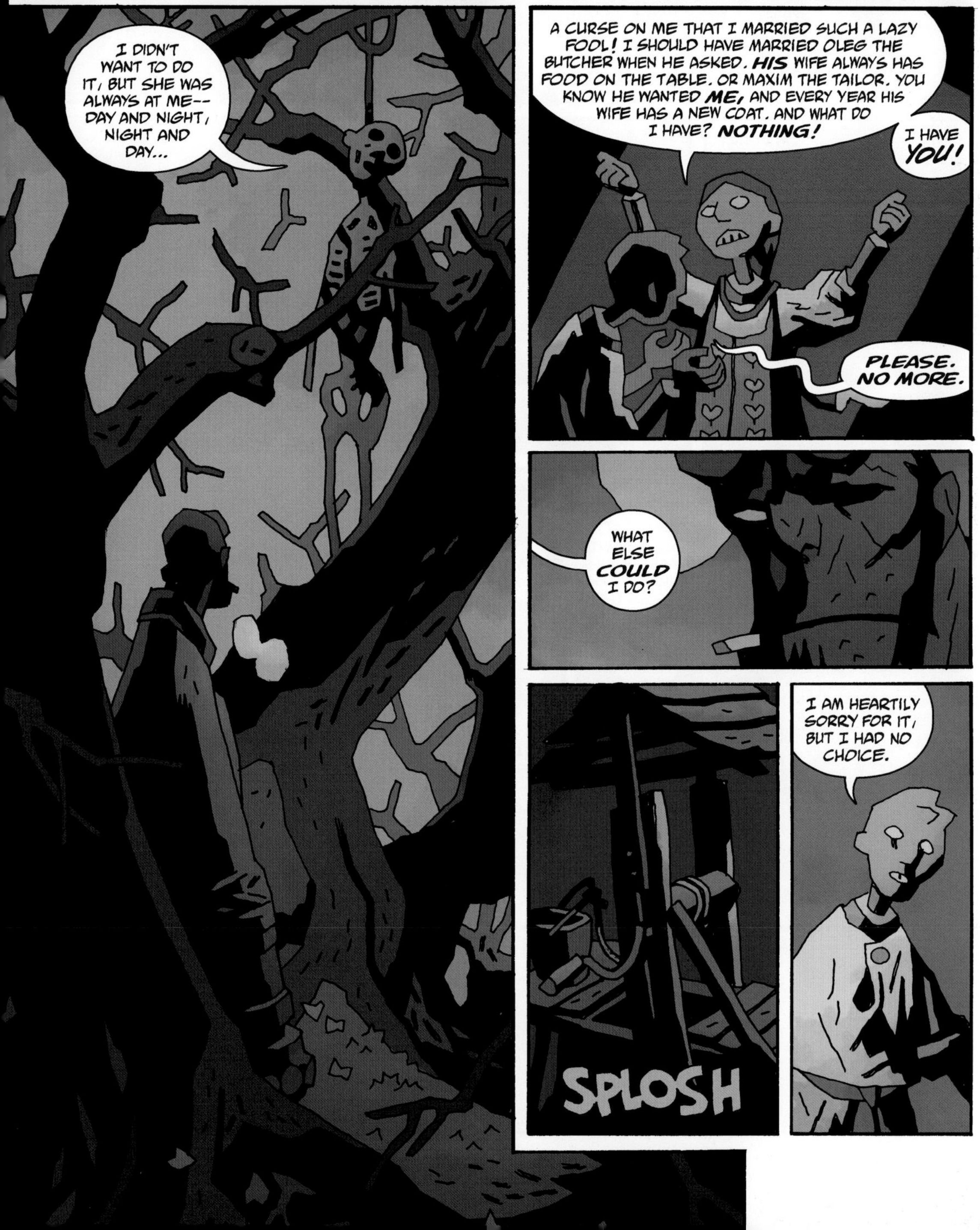

I DIDN'T WANT TO DO IT, BUT SHE WAS ALWAYS AT ME-- DAY AND NIGHT, NIGHT AND DAY...
A CURSE ON ME THAT I MARRIED SUCH A LAZY FOOL! I SHOULD HAVE MARRIED OLEG THE BUTCHER WHEN HE ASKED. HIS WIFE ALWAYS HAS FOOD ON THE TABLE. OR MAXIM THE TAILOR. YOU KNOW HE WANTED ME, AND EVERY YEAR HIS WIFE HAS A NEW COAT. AND WHAT DO I HAVE? NOTHING!
I HAVE YOU!
PLEASE. NO MORE.
WHAT ELSE COULD I DO?
SPLOSH
I AM HEARTILY SORRY FOR IT, BUT I HAD NO CHOICE.

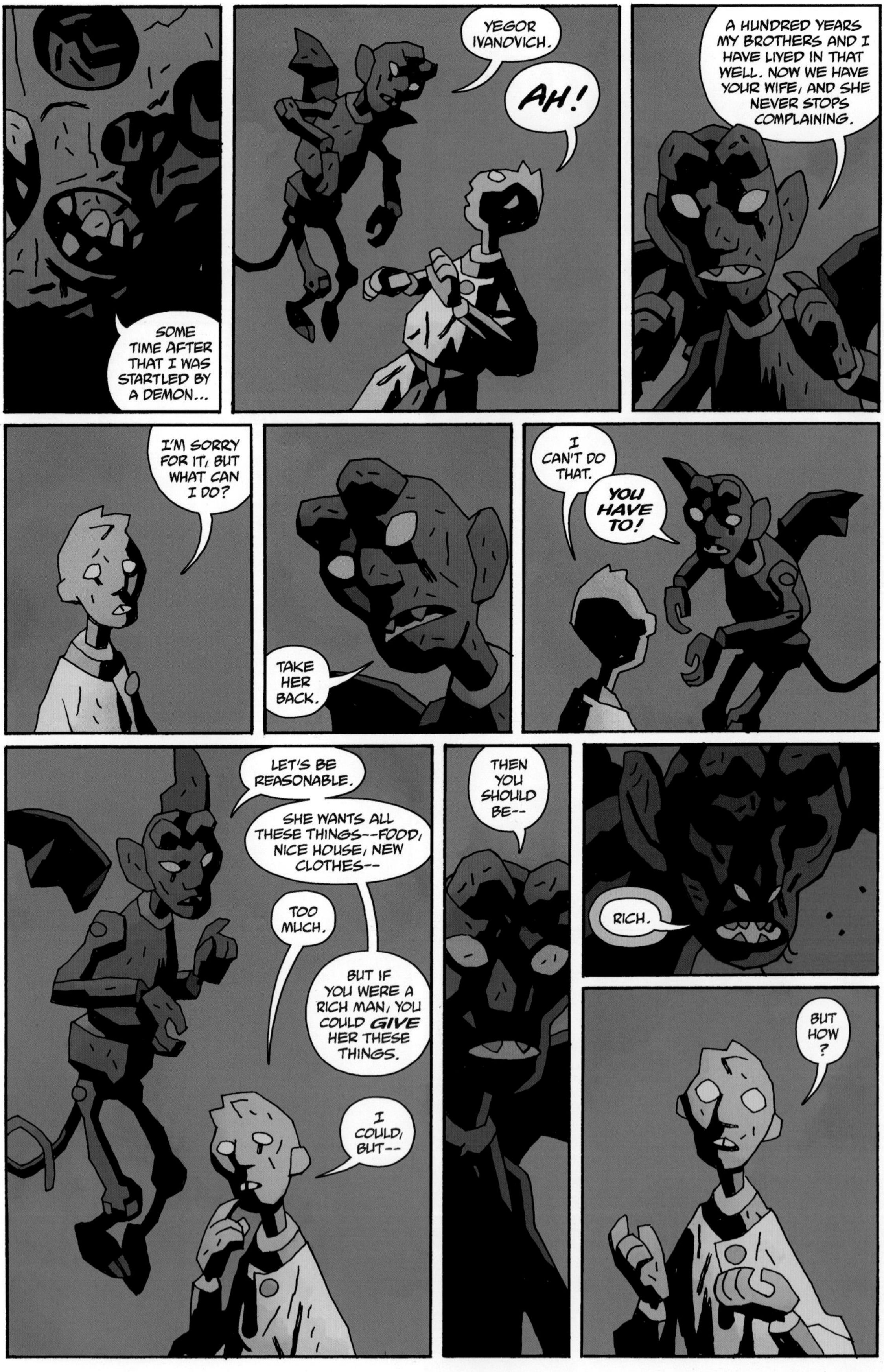
SOME TIME AFTER THAT I WAS STARTLED BY A DEMON...
YEGOR IVANOVICH.
AH!
A HUNDRED YEARS MY BROTHERS AND I HAVE LIVED IN THAT WELL. NOW WE HAVE YOUR WIFE, AND SHE NEVER STOPS COMPLAINING.
I'M SORRY FOR IT, BUT WHAT CAN I DO?
TAKE HER BACK.
I CAN'T DO THAT.
YOU HAVE TO!
LET'S BE REASONABLE.
SHE WANTS ALL THESE THINGS--FOOD, NICE HOUSE, NEW CLOTHES--
TOO MUCH.
BUT IF YOU WERE A RICH MAN, YOU COULD GIVE HER THESE THINGS.
I COULD, BUT--
THEN YOU SHOULD BE--
RICH.
BUT HOW?

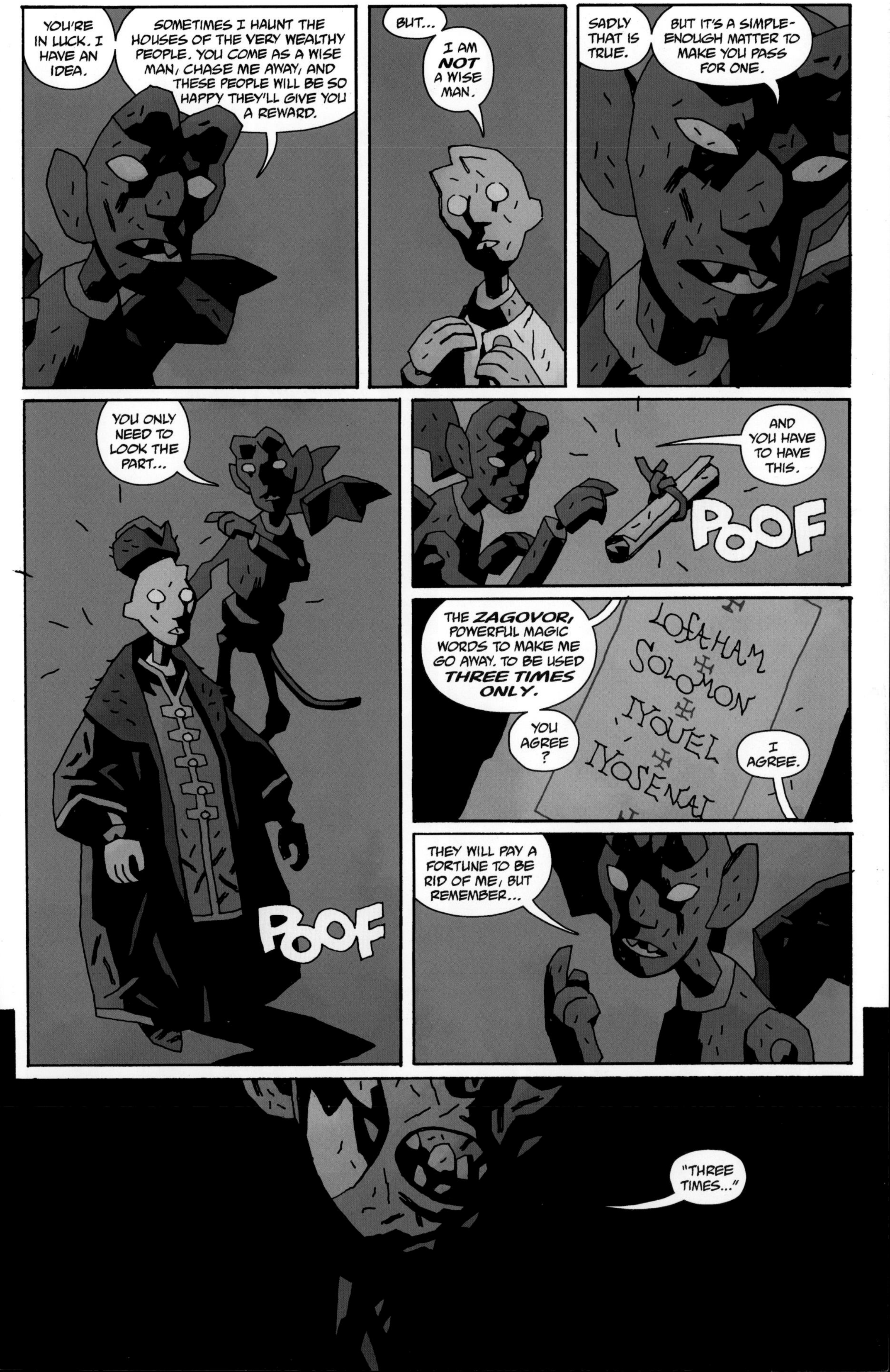

YOU'RE IN LUCK. I HAVE AN IDEA.
SOMETIMES I HAUNT THE HOUSES OF THE VERY WEALTHY PEOPLE. YOU COME AS A WISE MAN, CHASE ME AWAY, AND THESE PEOPLE WILL BE SO HAPPY THEY'LL GIVE YOU A REWARD.
BUT...
I AM **NOT** A WISE MAN.
SADLY THAT IS TRUE.
BUT IT'S A SIMPLE-ENOUGH MATTER TO MAKE YOU PASS FOR ONE.
YOU ONLY NEED TO LOOK THE PART...
POOF
AND YOU HAVE TO HAVE THIS.
POOF
THE ***ZAGOVOR,*** POWERFUL MAGIC WORDS TO MAKE ME GO AWAY. TO BE USED ***THREE TIMES ONLY.***
LOFAHAM
SOLOMON
IYOUEL
IYOSENAI
YOU AGREE?
I AGREE.
THEY WILL PAY A FORTUNE TO BE RID OF ME, BUT REMEMBER...
"THREE TIMES..."

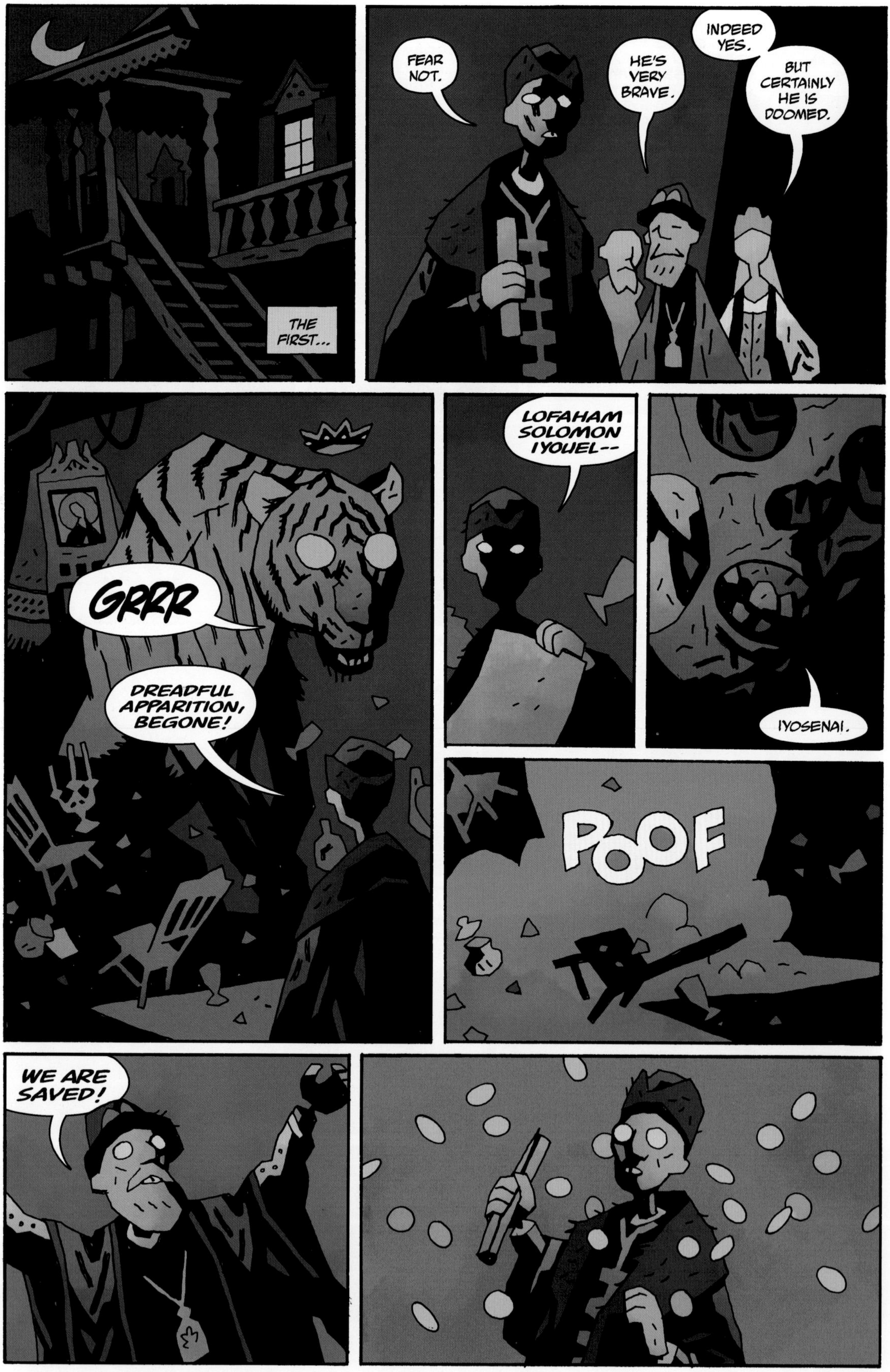
THE FIRST...
FEAR NOT.
HE'S VERY BRAVE.
INDEED YES.
BUT CERTAINLY HE IS DOOMED.
GRRR
DREADFUL APPARITION, BEGONE!
LOFAHAM SOLOMON IYOUEL--
IYOSENAI.
POOF
WE ARE SAVED!

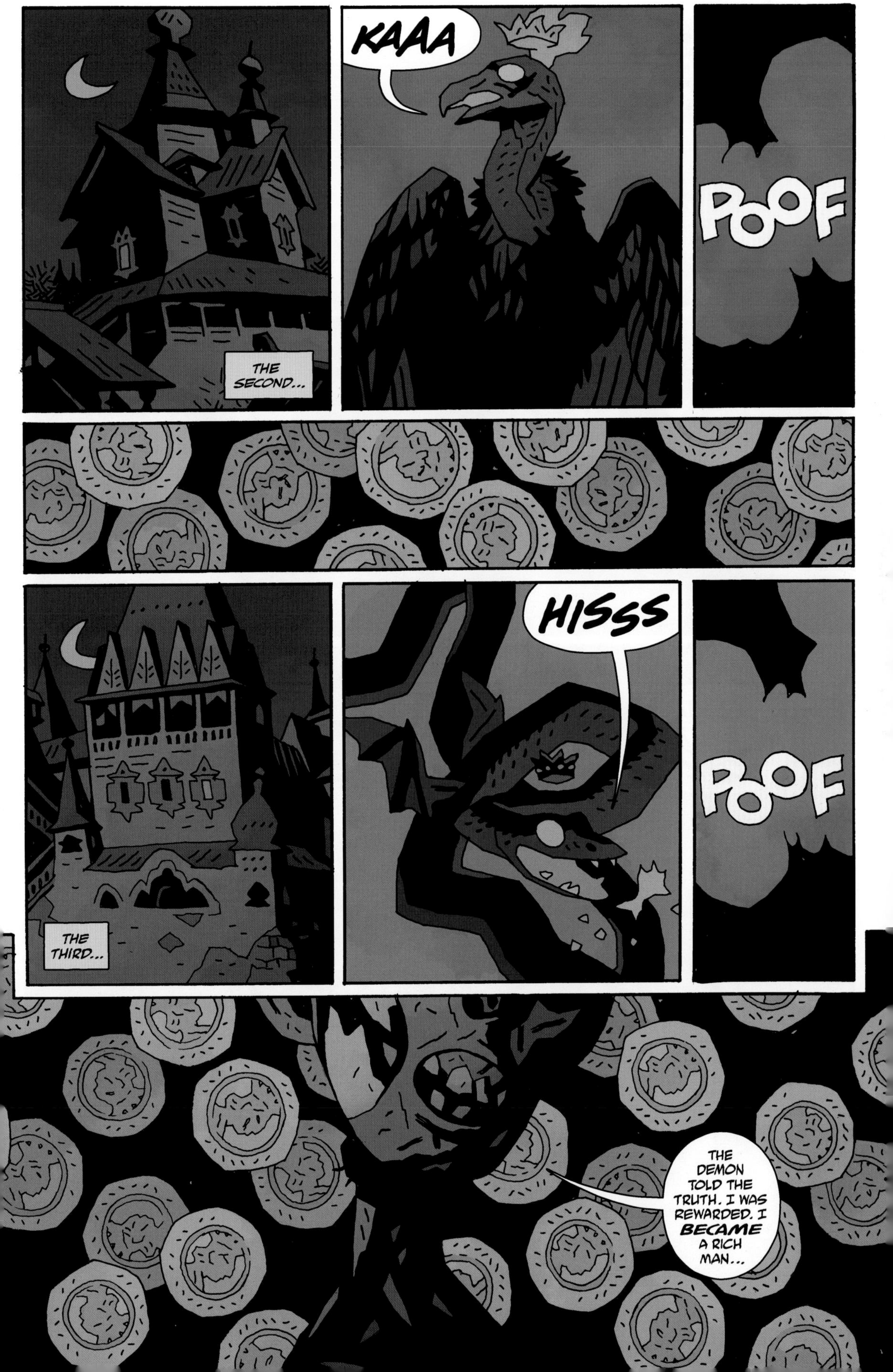
THE SECOND...
KAAA
POOF
THE THIRD...
HISSS
POOF
THE DEMON TOLD THE TRUTH. I WAS REWARDED. I **BECAME** A RICH MAN...

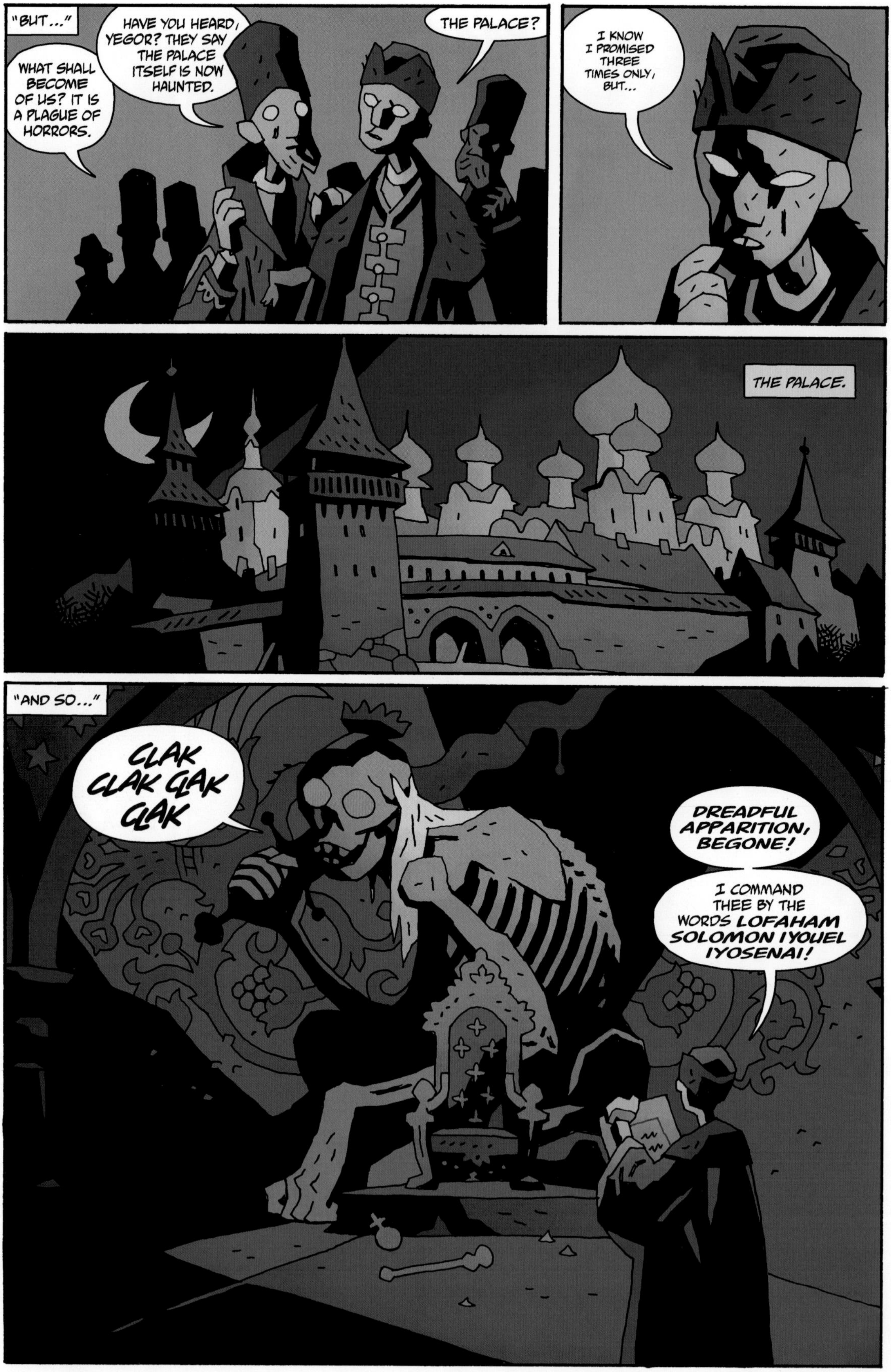
"BUT..."
WHAT SHALL BECOME OF US? IT IS A PLAGUE OF HORRORS.
HAVE YOU HEARD, YEGOR? THEY SAY THE PALACE ITSELF IS NOW HAUNTED.
THE PALACE?
I KNOW I PROMISED THREE TIMES ONLY, BUT...
THE PALACE.
"AND SO..."
CLAK CLAK CLAK CLAK
DREADFUL APPARITION, BEGONE!
I COMMAND THEE BY THE WORDS LOFAHAM SOLOMON IYOUEL IYOSENAI!

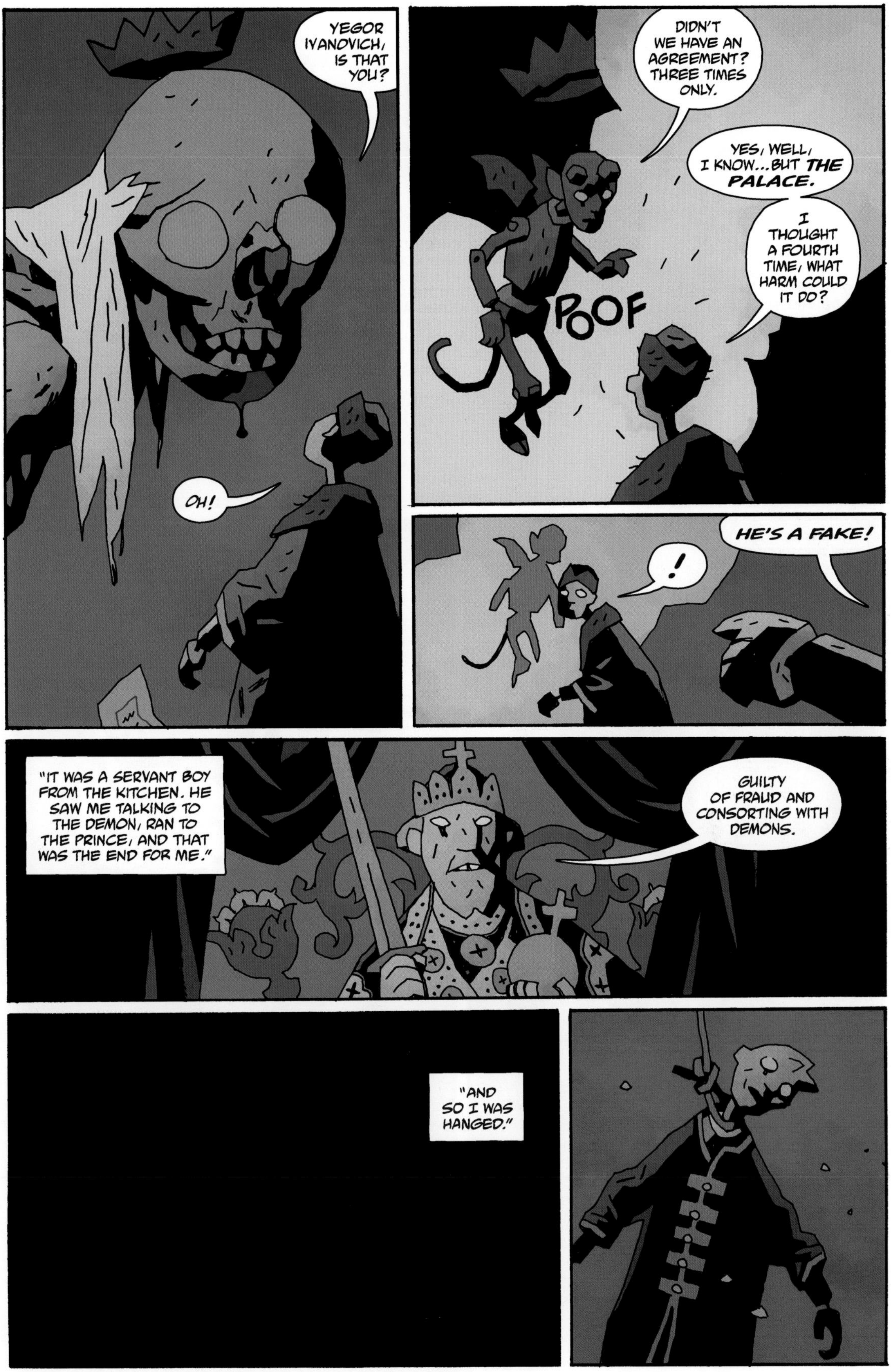
YEGOR IVANOVICH, IS THAT YOU?
OH!
DIDN'T WE HAVE AN AGREEMENT? THREE TIMES ONLY.
YES, WELL, I KNOW...BUT **THE PALACE.**
I THOUGHT A FOURTH TIME, WHAT HARM COULD IT DO?
POOF
!
HE'S A FAKE!
"IT WAS A SERVANT BOY FROM THE KITCHEN. HE SAW ME TALKING TO THE DEMON, RAN TO THE PRINCE, AND THAT WAS THE END FOR ME."
GUILTY OF FRAUD AND CONSORTING WITH DEMONS.
"AND SO I WAS HANGED."

POOR YEGOR IVANOVICH.

I WAS JUSTLY KILLED FOR MY FOOLISH BEHAVIOR. IF ONLY I HAD BEEN CONTENT.

YOU SHOULD KNOW YOUR WIFE IS HAPPY. SHE MARRIED THE DEMON AND NOW THEY LIVE IN A PALACE UNDERGROUND, AND SHE WEARS A COAT MADE OF JEWELS MINED FROM THE CENTER OF THE EARTH.

GROAN

WHAT ARE YOU, THE ADD-INSULT-TO-INJURY BIRD?

I AM THE VOICE OF TRUTH.

BUT FOR HIS GREED HE MIGHT HAVE BEEN A MAN. HE MIGHT HAVE USED HIS WEALTH TO DO GOOD, MIGHT HAVE BEEN A PILLAR OF HIS COMMUNITY WITH FRIENDS AND FAMILY, RATHER THAN AN UNHAPPY CORPSE HUNG FROM A TREE IN HELL.

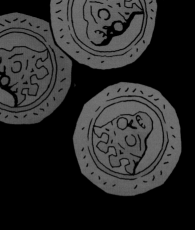

LEARN FROM HIS EXAMPLE AND SEE THAT YOU DO BETTER FOR YOURSELF.

THE END

HELLBOY™

SKETCHBOOK

Notes by Mike Mignola

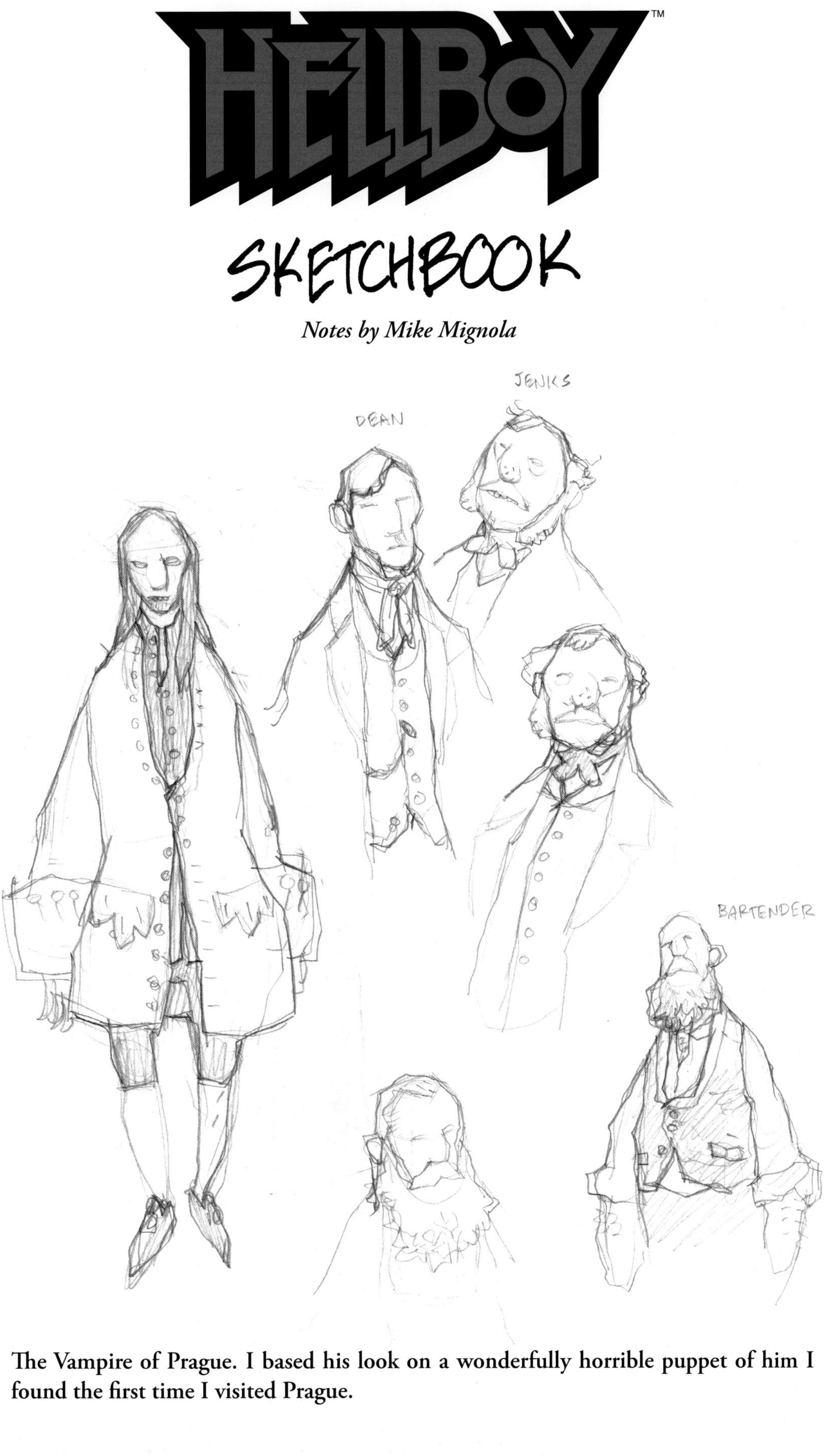
JENKS
DEAN
BARTENDER

The Vampire of Prague. I based his look on a wonderfully horrible puppet of him I found the first time I visited Prague.

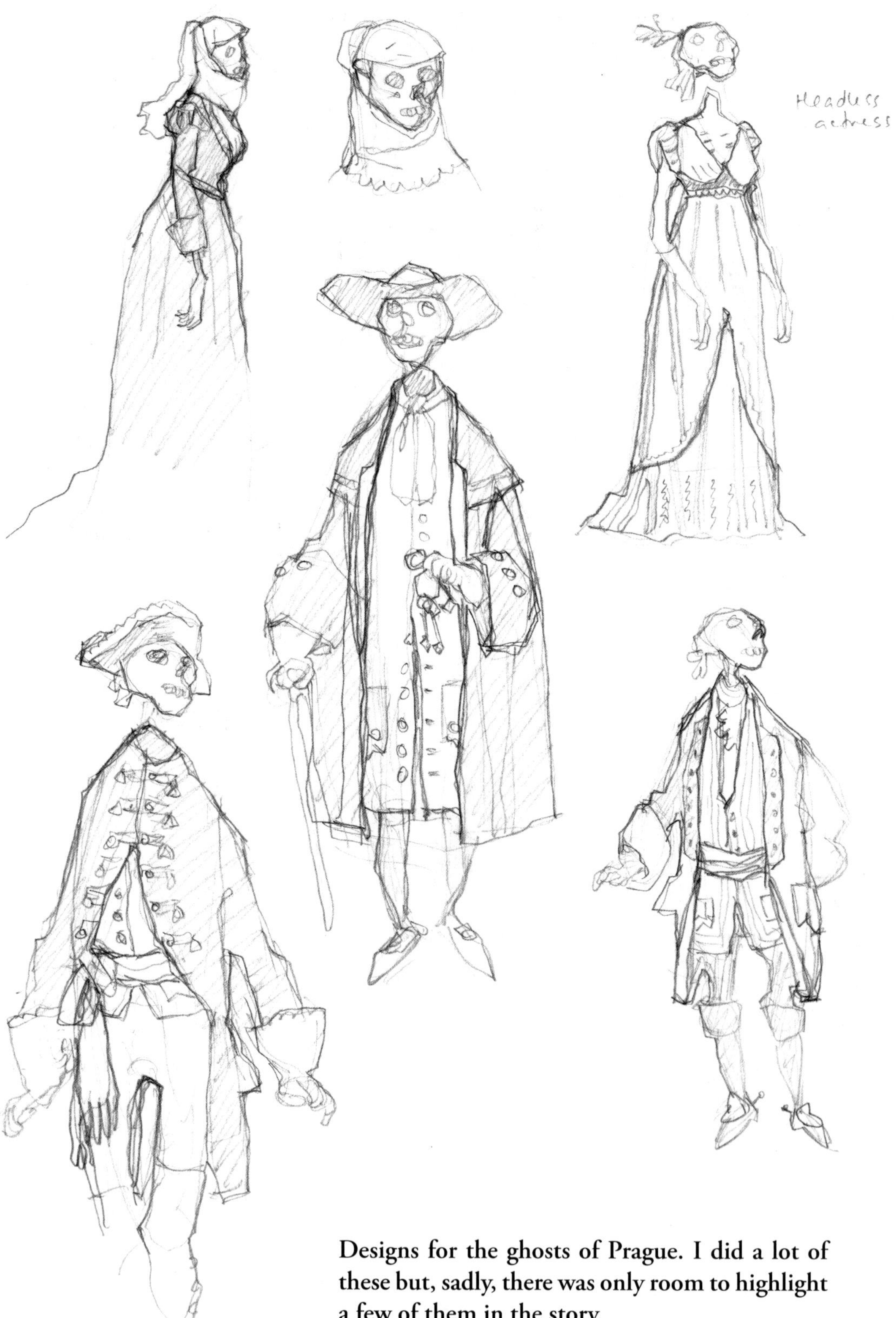
Headless actress

Designs for the ghosts of Prague. I did a lot of these but, sadly, there was only room to highlight a few of them in the story.

More ghosts. I spent a lot of time in Prague working on the first *Hellboy* film and saw a lot of weird stuff, but, sadly, no ghosts.

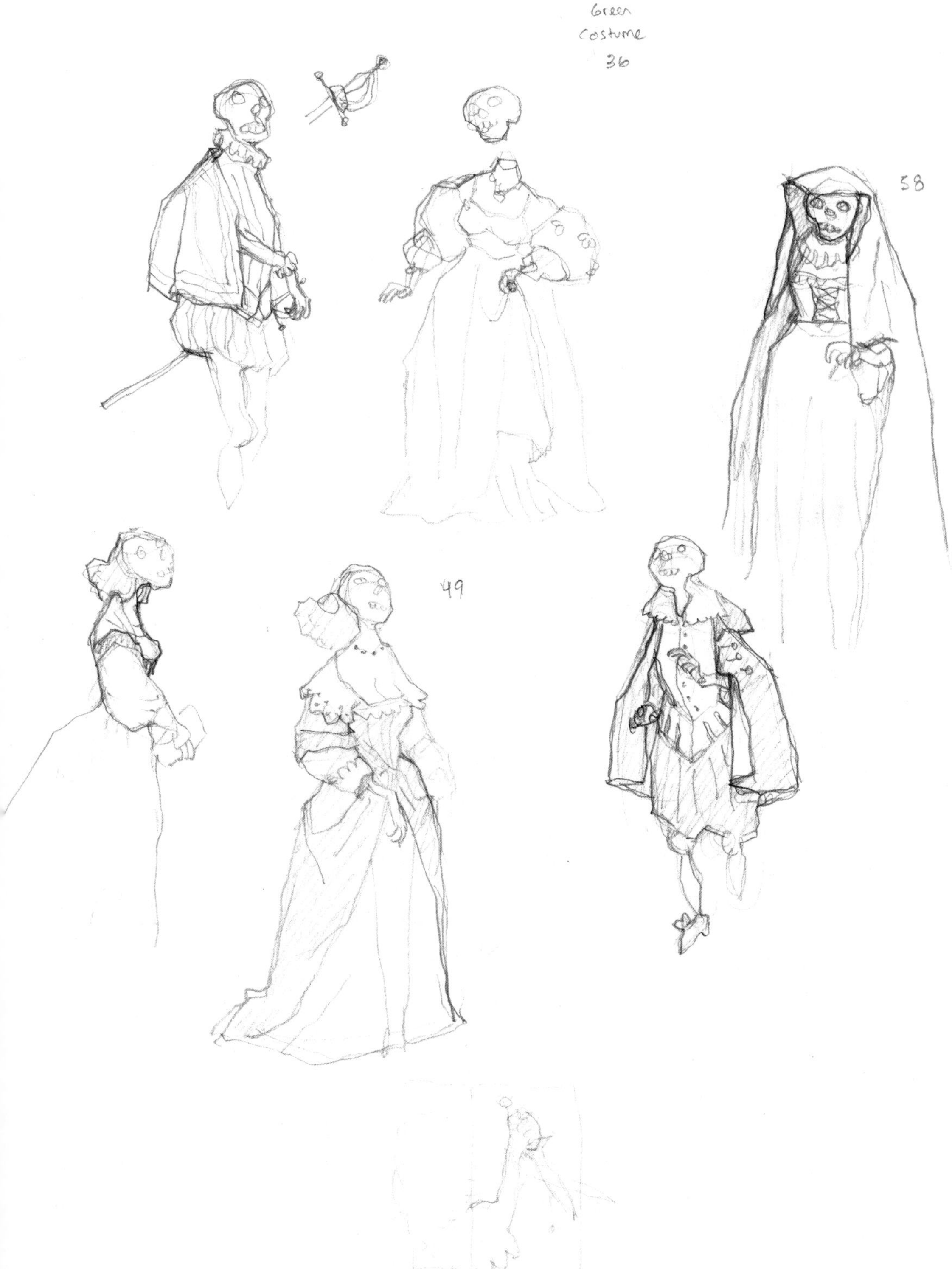
Green
costume
36
58
49

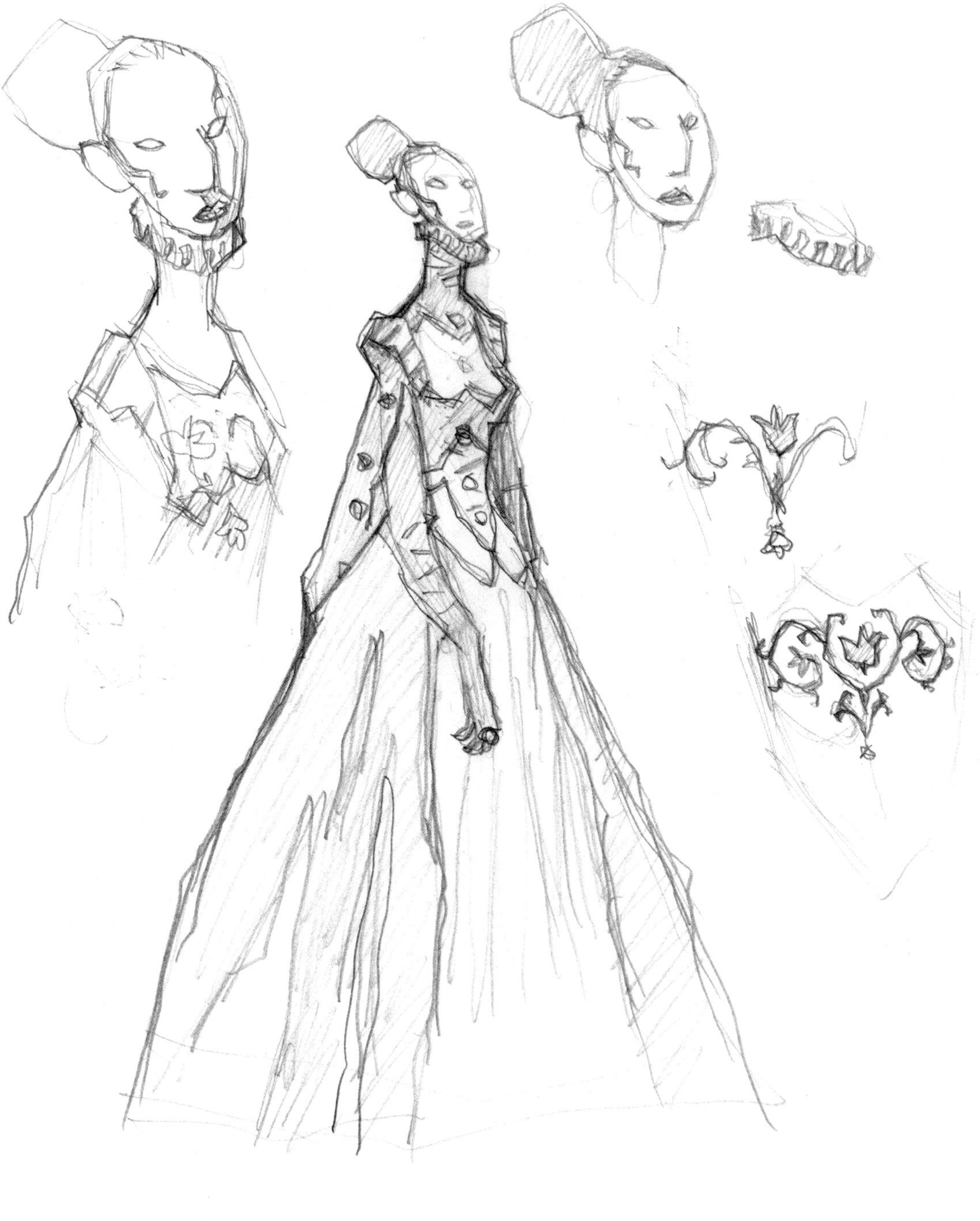

The Spanish Bride. The character was originally designed by Mick McMahon for the short story "Hellboy Gets Married." I'd intended to keep this look throughout my issue, but, honestly, just got a little bored drawing the big dress so (of course) I turned her into a monster.

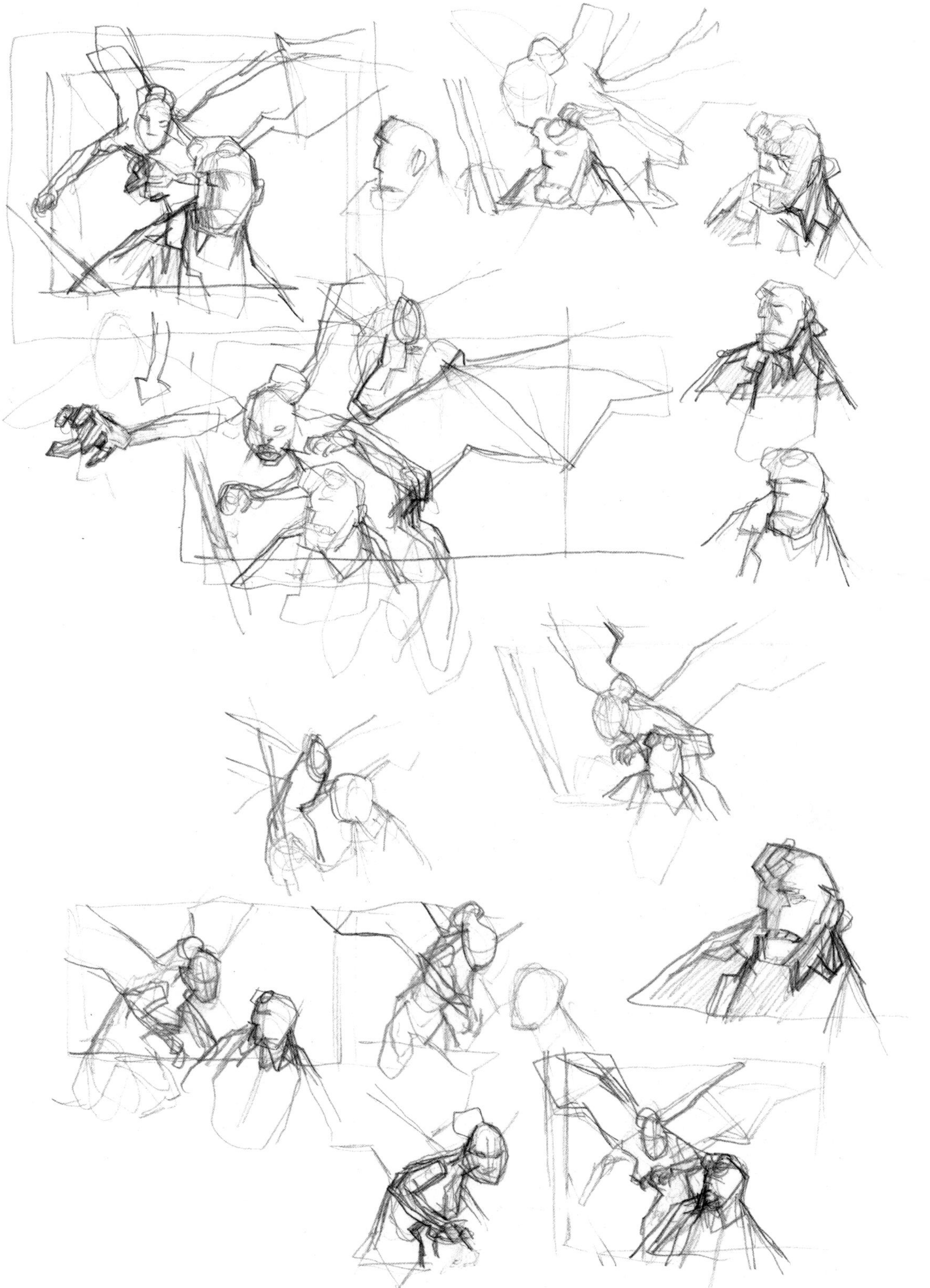

A flashback to Mick's original story, but I wanted to stage things a bit differently.

Demon designs. I actually sculpted their heads for reference and my wife named them—Donkey, Wonky, and Fizzer.

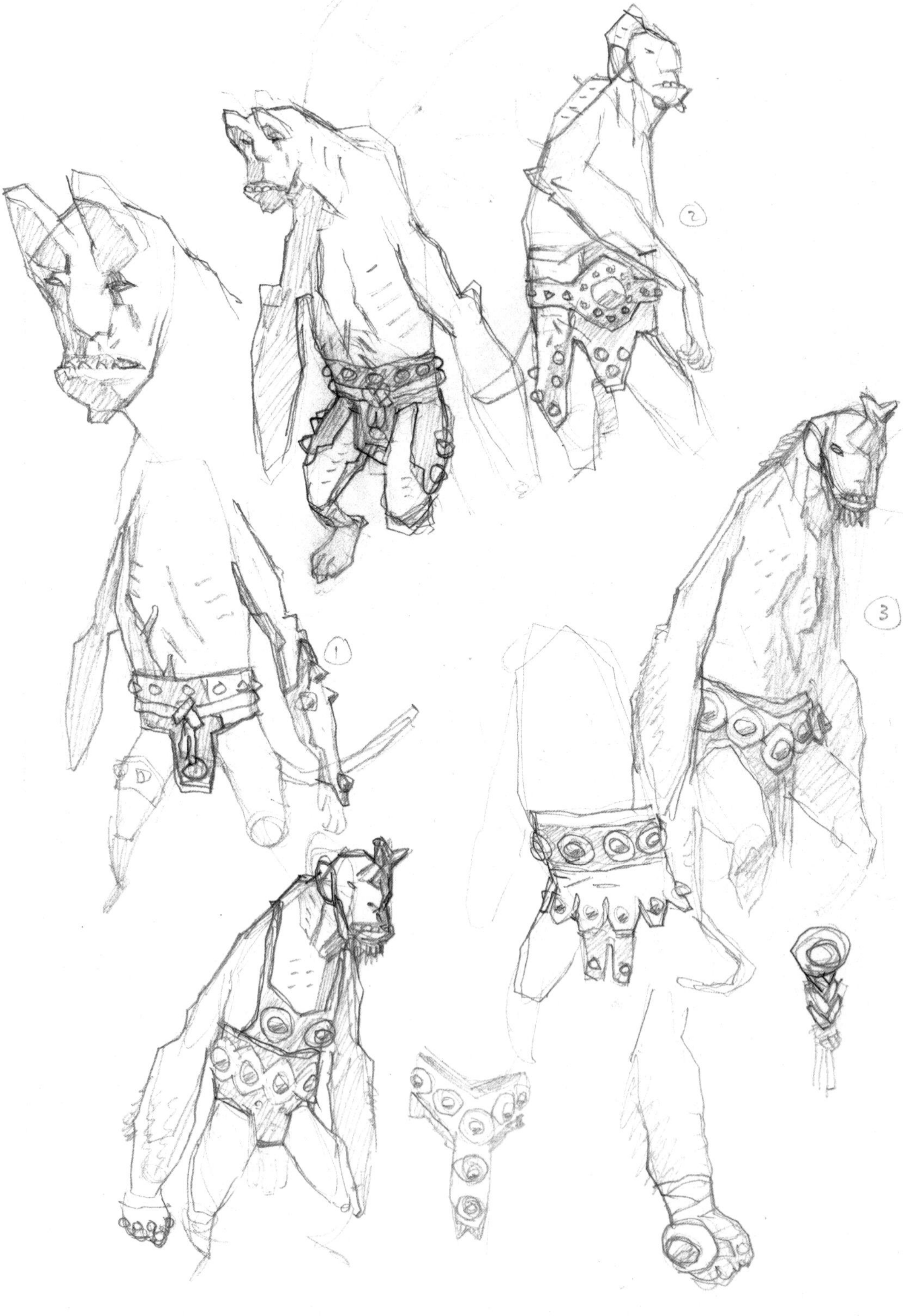
2
1
D
3

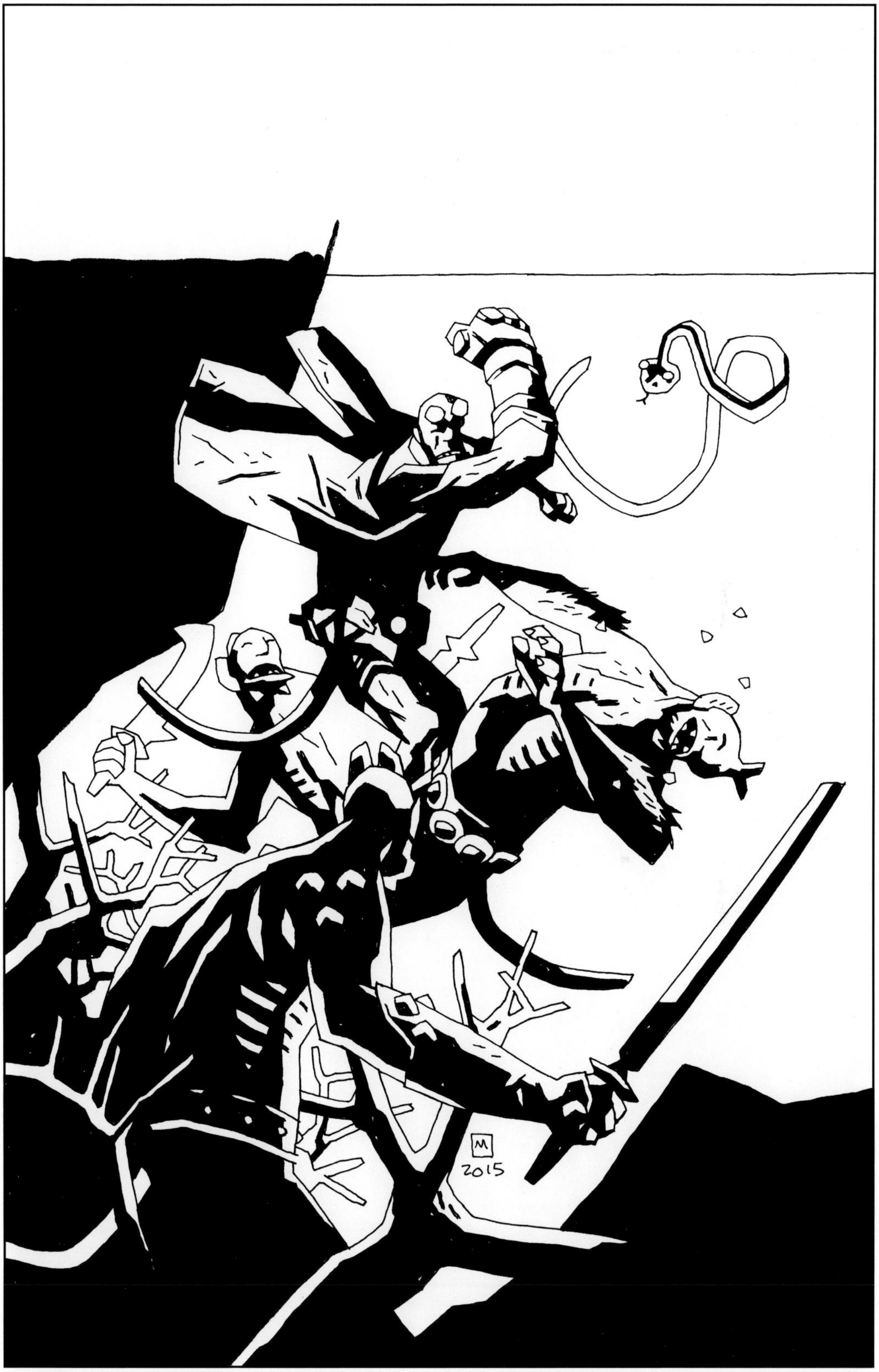
M
2015

My first attempt at the issue #9 cover. I liked it. I liked all the shapes going on, but, in the end, couldn't overlook the fact that one of the demons (Wonky) had no legs.

Following: The covers to *Hellboy in Hell* #7-10, and *Dark Horse Presents* #16.

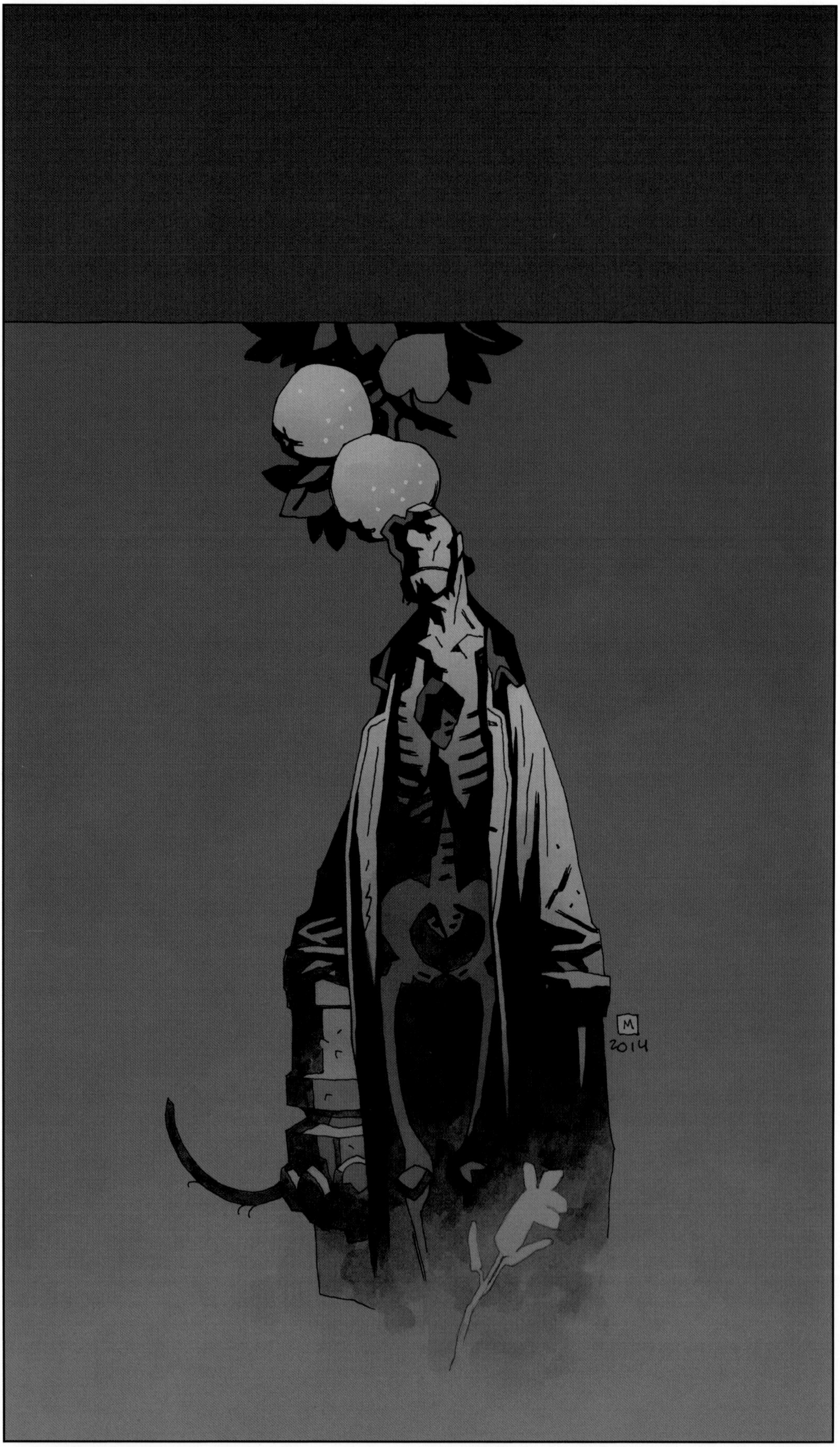
M
2014

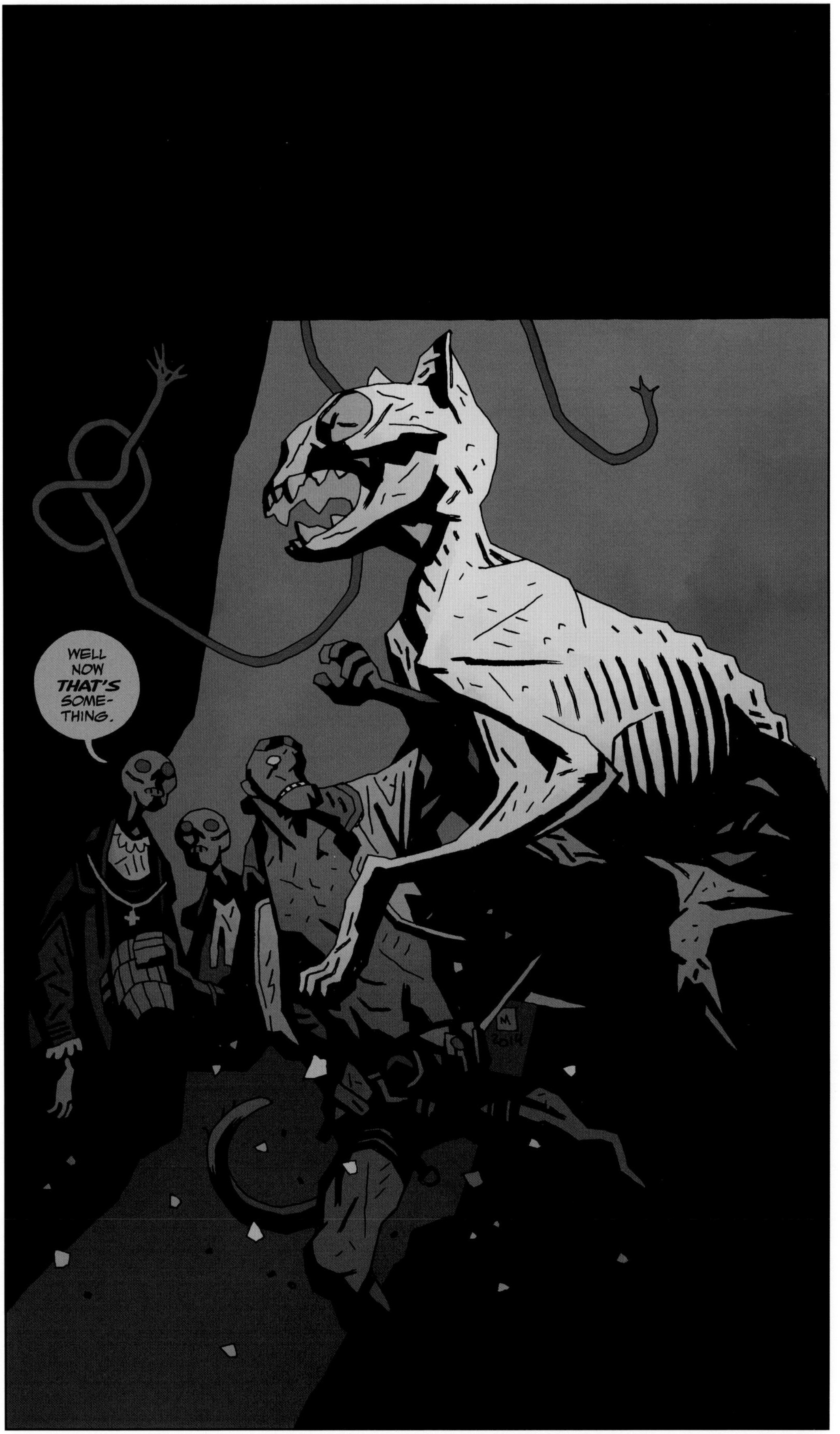
WELL NOW THAT'S SOME-THING.

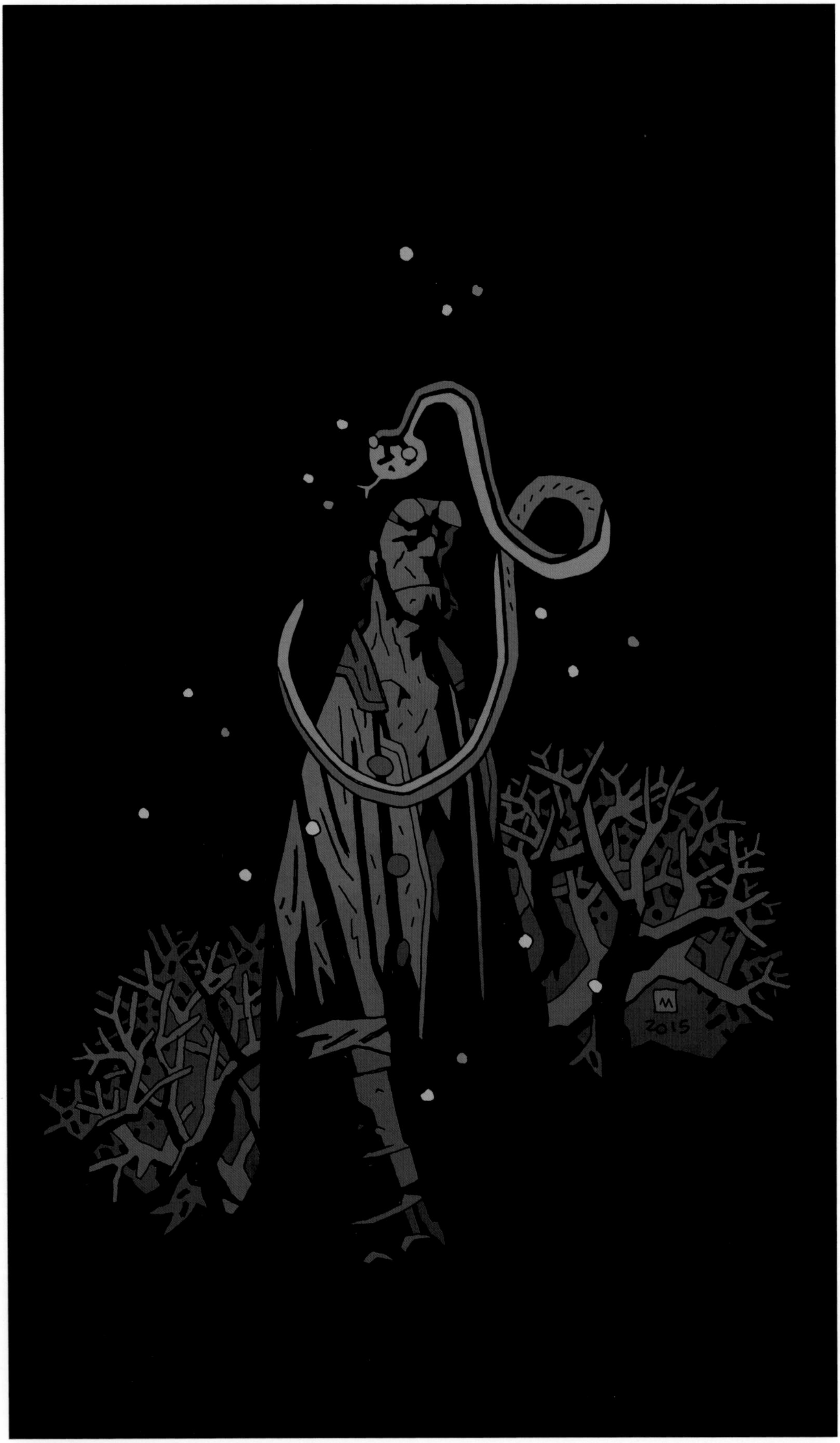
2015

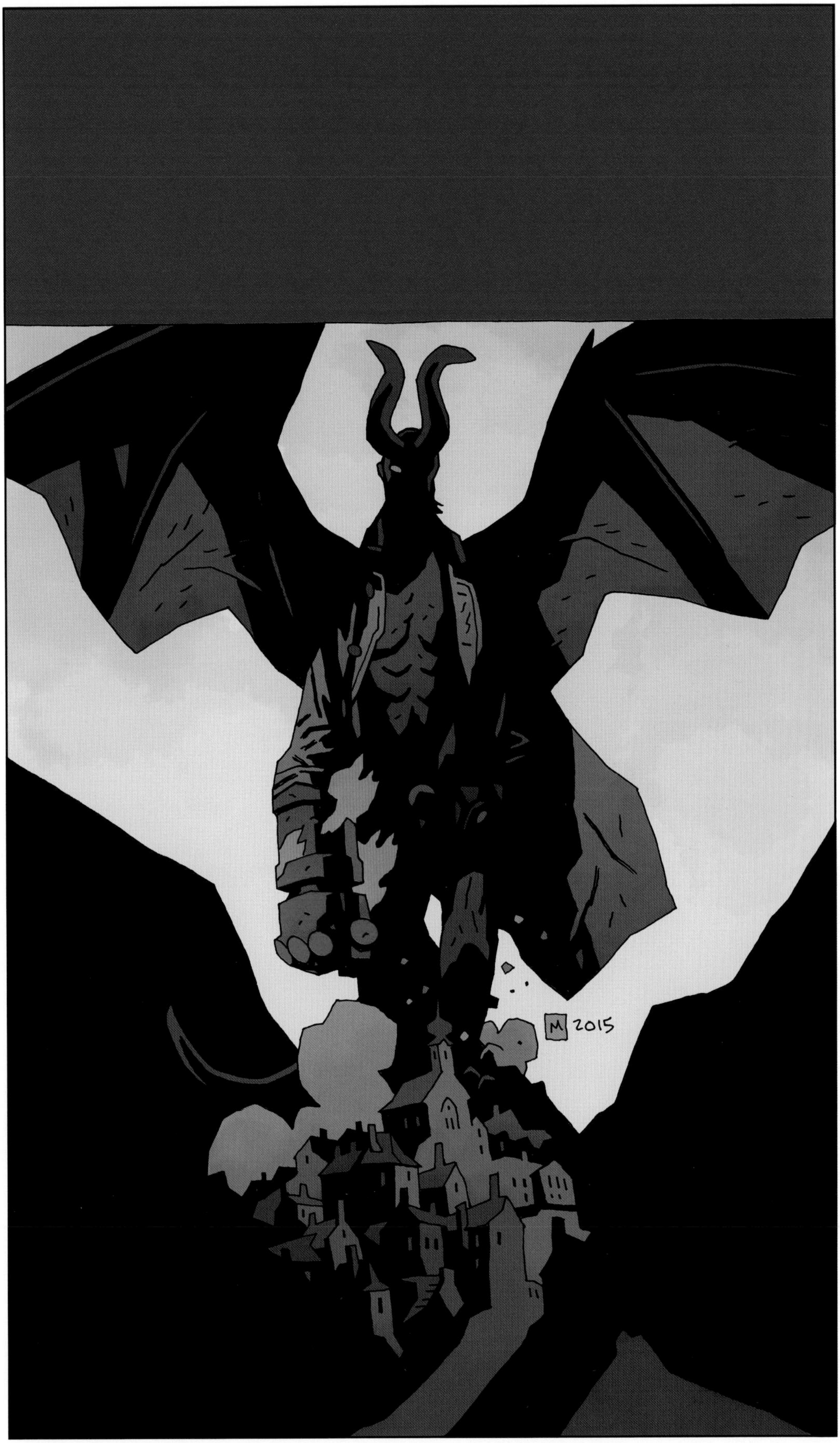
M 2015

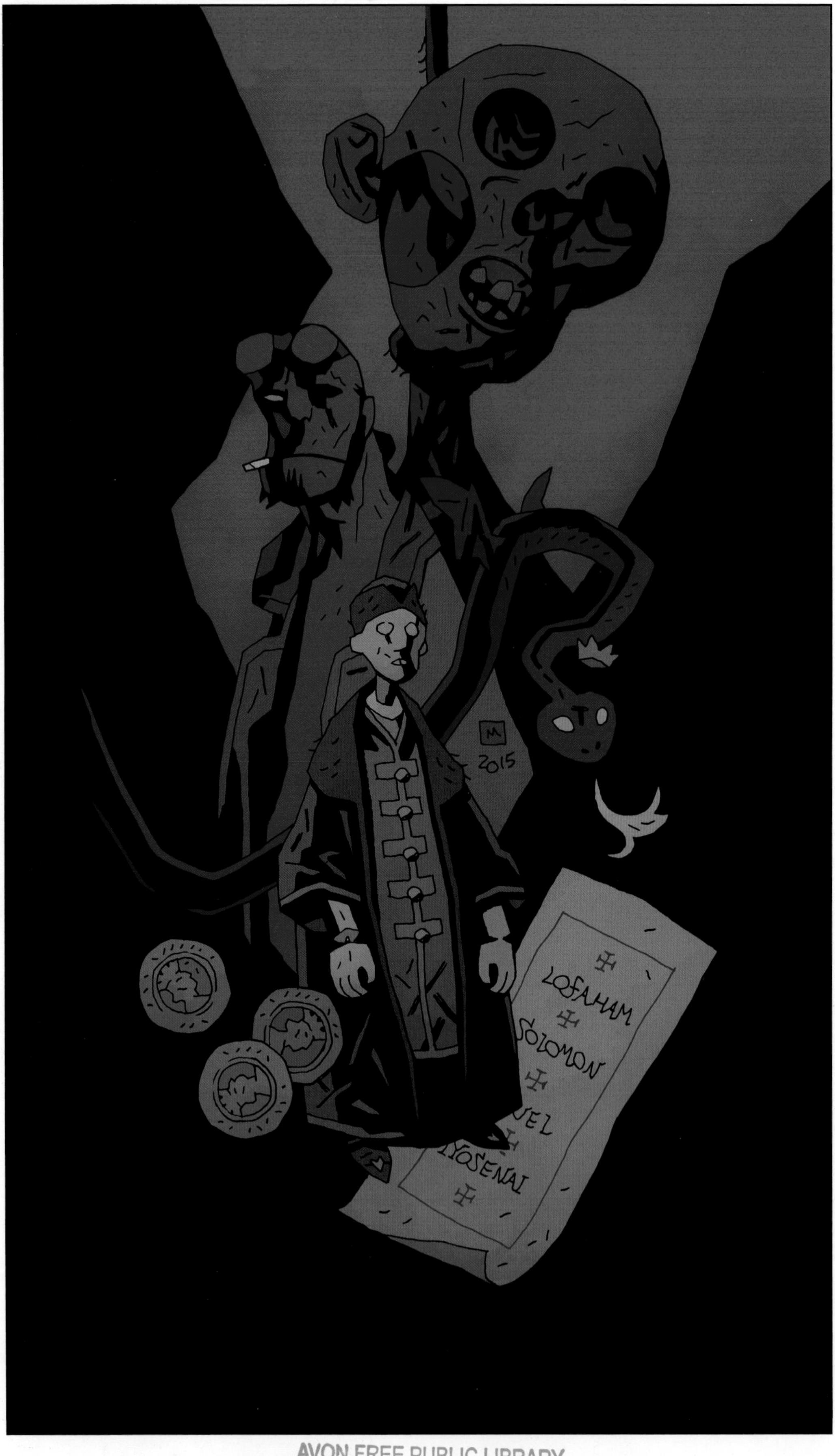
M
2015
LOSAHAM
SOLOMON
UEL
YOSENAI

Also by MIKE MIGNOLA

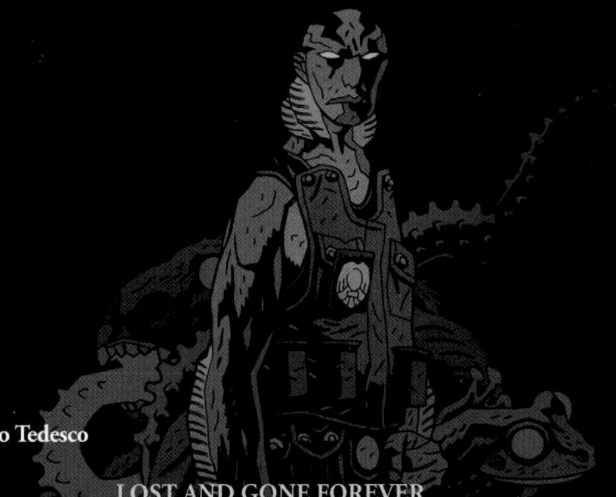

B.P.R.D.

PLAGUE OF FROGS
Volume 1
with Chris Golden, Guy Davis, and others
HC: ISBN 978-1-59582-609-1 | $34.99
TPB: ISBN 978-1-59582-675-6 | $19.99

Volume 2
with John Arcudi, Davis, and others
HC: ISBN 978-1-59582-672-5 | $34.99
TPB: ISBN 978-1-59582-676-3 | $24.99

Volume 3
with Arcudi and Davis
HC: ISBN 978-1-59582-860-6 | $34.99
TPB: ISBN 978-1-61655-622-8 | $24.99

Volume 4
with Arcudi and Davis
HC: ISBN 978-1-59582-974-0 | $34.99
TPB: ISBN 978-1-61655-641-9 | $24.99

1946–1948
with Joshua Dysart, Paul Azaceta, Fábio Moon, Gabriel Bá, Max Fiumara, and Arcudi
ISBN 978-1-61655-646-4 | $34.99

BEING HUMAN
with Scott Allie, Arcudi, Davis, and others
ISBN 978-1-59582-756-2 | $17.99

VAMPIRE
with Moon and Bá
ISBN 978-1-61655-196-4 | $19.99

B.P.R.D. HELL ON EARTH

NEW WORLD
with Arcudi and Davis
ISBN 978-1-59582-707-4 | $19.99

GODS AND MONSTERS
with Arcudi, Davis, and Tyler Crook
ISBN 978-1-59582-822-4 | $19.99

RUSSIA
with Arcudi, Crook, and Duncan Fegredo
ISBN 978-1-59582-946-7 | $19.99

THE DEVIL'S ENGINE AND THE LONG DEATH
with Arcudi, Crook, and James Harren
ISBN 978-1-59582-981-8 | $19.99

THE PICKENS COUNTY HORROR AND OTHERS
with Allie, Jason Latour, Harren, and Max Fiumara
ISBN 978-1-61655-140-7 | $19.99

THE RETURN OF THE MASTER
with Arcudi and Crook
ISBN 978-1-61655-193-3 | $19.99

A COLD DAY IN HELL
with Arcudi, Peter Snejbjerg, and Laurence Campbell
ISBN 978-1-61655-199-5 | $19.99

THE REIGN OF THE BLACK FLAME
with Arcudi and Harren
ISBN 978-1-61655-471-2 | $19.99

THE DEVIL'S WINGS
with Arcudi, Campbell, Joe Querio, and Crook
ISBN 978-1-61655-617-4 | $19.99

LAKE OF FIRE
with Arcudi and Crook
ISBN 978-1-61655-402-6 | $19.99

FLESH AND STONE
with Arcudi and Harren
ISBN 978-1-61655-762-1 | $19.99

METAMORPHOSIS
with Arcudi, Snejbjerg, and Julián Totino Tedesco
ISBN 978-1-61655-794-2 | $19.99

END OF DAYS
with Arcudi and Campbell
ISBN 978-1-61655-910-6 | $19.99

THE EXORCIST
with Cameron Stewart, Chris Roberson, and Mike Norton
ISBN 978-1-50670-011-3 | $19.99

ABE SAPIEN

THE DROWNING
with Jason Shawn Alexander
ISBN 978-1-59582-185-0 | $17.99

THE DEVIL DOES NOT JEST AND OTHER STORIES
with Arcudi, Harren, and others
ISBN 978-1-59582-925-2 | $17.99

DARK AND TERRIBLE AND THE NEW RACE OF MAN
with Allie, Arcudi, Sebastián Fiumara, and Max Fiumara
ISBN 978-1-61655-284-8 | $19.99

THE SHAPE OF THINGS TO COME
with Allie, S. Fiumara, and M. Fiumara
ISBN 978-1-61655-443-9 | $19.99

SACRED PLACES
with Allie, S. Fiumara, and M. Fiumara
ISBN 978-1-61655-515-3 | $19.99

A DARKNESS SO GREAT
with Allie, S. Fiumara, and M. Fiumara
ISBN 978-1-61655-656-3 | $19.99

THE SECRET FIRE
with Allie, S. Fiumara, and M. Fiumara
ISBN 978-1-61655-891-8 | $19.99

LOBSTER JOHNSON

THE IRON PROMETHEUS
with Jason Armstrong
ISBN 978-1-59307-975-8 | $17.99

THE BURNING HAND
with Arcudi and Tonci Zonjic
ISBN 978-1-61655-031-8 | $17.99

SATAN SMELLS A RAT
with Arcudi, Fiumara, Querio, Wilfredo Torres, and Kevin Nowlan
ISBN 978-1-61655-203-9 | $18.99

GET THE LOBSTER
with Arcudi and Zonjic
ISBN 978-1-61655-505-4 | $19.99

WITCHFINDER

IN THE SERVICE OF ANGELS
with Ben Stenbeck
ISBN 978-1-59582-483-7 | $17.99

LOST AND GONE FOREVER
with Arcudi and John Severin
ISBN 978-1-59582-794-4 | $17.99

THE MYSTERIES OF UNLAND
with Kim Newman, Maura McHugh, and Crook
ISBN 978-1-61655-630-3 | $19.99

FRANKENSTEIN UNDERGROUND

with Stenbeck
ISBN 978-1-61655-782-9 | $19.99

JOE GOLEM: OCCULT DETECTIVE—THE RAT CATCHER & THE SUNKEN DEAD

with Golden and Patric Reynolds
ISBN 978-1-61655-964-9 | $24.99

THE AMAZING SCREW-ON HEAD AND OTHER CURIOUS OBJECTS

ISBN 978-1-59582-501-8 | $17.99

BALTIMORE

THE PLAGUE SHIPS
with Golden and Stenbeck
ISBN 978-1-59582-677-0 | $24.99

THE CURSE BELLS
with Golden and Stenbeck
ISBN 978-1-59582-674-9 | $24.99

A PASSING STRANGER AND OTHER STORIES
with Golden and Stenbeck
ISBN 978-1-61655-182-7 | $24.99

CHAPEL OF BONES
with Golden and Stenbeck
ISBN 978-1-61655-328-9 | $24.99

THE APOSTLE AND THE WITCH OF HARJU
with Golden, Stenbeck, and Peter Bergting
ISBN 978-1-61655-618-1 | $24.99

THE CULT OF THE RED KING
with Golden and Bergting
ISBN 978-1-61655-821-5 | $24.99

NOVELS

LOBSTER JOHNSON: THE SATAN FACTORY
with Thomas E. Sniegoski
ISBN 978-1-59582-203-1 | $12.95

JOE GOLEM AND THE DROWNING CITY
with Golden
ISBN 978-1-59582-971-9 | $99.99

BALTIMORE; OR, THE STEADFAST TIN SOLDIER & THE VAMPIRE
with Golden
ISBN 978-1-61655-803-1 | $12.99

AVAILABLE AT YOUR LOCAL COMICS SHOP OR BOOKSTORE! • To find a comics shop in your area, call 1-888-266-4226.
For more information or to order direct visit DarkHorse.com or call 1-800-862-0052 Mon.–Fri. 9 AM to 5 PM Pacific Time.
Prices and availability subject to change without notice.

DarkHorse.com

HELLBOY™

by MIKE MIGNOLA

HELLBOY LIBRARY EDITION VOLUME 1:
Seed of Destruction and Wake the Devil
ISBN 978-1-59307-910-9 | $49.99

HELLBOY LIBRARY EDITION VOLUME 2:
The Chained Coffin and The Right Hand of Doom
ISBN 978-1-59307-989-5 | $49.99

HELLBOY LIBRARY EDITION VOLUME 3:
Conqueror Worm and Strange Places
ISBN 978-1-59582-352-6 | $49.99

HELLBOY LIBRARY EDITION VOLUME 4:
The Crooked Man and the Troll Witch
with Richard Corben and others
ISBN 978-1-59582-658-9 | $49.99

HELLBOY LIBRARY EDITION VOLUME 5:
Darkness Calls and the Wild Hunt
with Duncan Fegredo
ISBN 978-1-59582-886-6 | $49.99

HELLBOY LIBRARY EDITION VOLUME 6:
The Storm and the Fury and The Bride of Hell
with Duncan Fegredo, Richard Corben, Kevin Nowlan, and Scott Hampton
ISBN 978-1-61655-133-9 | $49.99

SEED OF DESTRUCTION
with John Byrne
ISBN 978-1-59307-094-6 | $17.99

WAKE THE DEVIL
ISBN 978-1-59307-095-3 | $17.99

THE CHAINED COFFIN AND OTHERS
ISBN 978-1-59307-091-5 | $17.99

THE RIGHT HAND OF DOOM
ISBN 978-1-59307-093-9 | $17.99

CONQUEROR WORM
ISBN 978-1-59307-092-2 | $17.99

STRANGE PLACES
ISBN 978-1-59307-475-3 | $17.99

THE TROLL WITCH AND OTHERS
with Richard Corben and others
ISBN 978-1-59307-860-7 | $17.99

DARKNESS CALLS
with Duncan Fegredo
ISBN 978-1-59307-896-6 | $19.99

THE WILD HUNT
with Duncan Fegredo
ISBN 978-1-59582-431-8 | $19.99

THE CROOKED MAN AND OTHERS
with Richard Corben
ISBN 978-1-59582-477-6 | $17.99

THE BRIDE OF HELL AND OTHERS
with Richard Corben, Kevin Nowlan, and Scott Hampton
ISBN 978-1-59582-740-1 | $19.99

THE STORM AND THE FURY
with Duncan Fegredo
ISBN 978-1-59582-827-9 | $19.99

HOUSE OF THE LIVING DEAD
with Richard Corben
ISBN 978-1-59582-757-9 | $14.99

THE MIDNIGHT CIRCUS
with Duncan Fegredo
ISBN 978-1-61655-238-1 | $14.99

HELLBOY IN MEXICO
with Richard Corben, Fábio Moon, Gabriel Bá, and others
ISBN 978-1-61655-897-0 | $19.99

HELLBOY IN HELL VOLUME 1: THE DESCENT
ISBN 978-1-61655-444-6 | $17.99

HELLBOY IN HELL VOLUME 2: THE DEATH CARD
ISBN 978-1-50670-113-4 | $17.99

HELLBOY: THE FIRST 20 YEARS
ISBN 978-1-61655-353-1 | $19.99

THE ART OF HELLBOY
ISBN 978-1-59307-089-2 | $29.99

HELLBOY II: THE ART OF THE MOVIE
ISBN 978-1-59307-964-2 | $24.99

HELLBOY: THE COMPANION
ISBN 978-1-59307-655-9 | $14.99

HELLBOY: WEIRD TALES
ISBN 978-1-61655-510-8 | $24.99

HELLBOY: MASKS AND MONSTERS
with James Robinson and Scott Benefiel
ISBN 978-1-59582-567-4 | $17.99

HELLBOY AND THE B.P.R.D: 1952
with John Arcudi and Alex Maleev
ISBN 978-1-61655-660-0 | $19.99

HELLBOY AND THE B.P.R.D: 1953
with Chris Roberson, Ben Stenbeck, Paolo Rivera, and Joe Rivera
ISBN 978-1-61655-967-0 | $19.99

THE HELLBOY 100 PROJECT
TPB: ISBN 978-1-61655-932-8 | $12.99
HC: ISBN 978-1-61655-933-5 | $24.99

NOVELS

HELLBOY: EMERALD HELL
By Tom Piccirilli
ISBN 978-1-59582-141-6 | $12.99

HELLBOY: THE ALL-SEEING EYE
By Mark Morris
ISBN 978-1-59582-142-3 | $12.99

HELLBOY: THE FIRE WOLVES
By Tim Lebbon
ISBN 978-1-59582-204-8 | $12.99

HELLBOY: THE ICE WOLVES
By Mark Chadbourn
ISBN 978-1-59582-205-5 | $12.99

SHORT STORIES

Illustrated by Mike Mignola

HELLBOY: ODDER JOBS
By Frank Darabont, Charles de Lint, Guillermo del Toro, and others
ISBN 978-1-59307-226-1 | $14.99

HELLBOY: ODDEST JOBS
By Joe R. Lansdale, China Miéville, and others
ISBN 978-1-59307-944-4 | $14.99

DARK HORSE BOOKS
DarkHorse.com